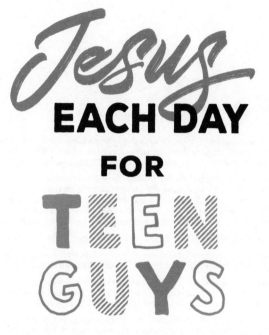

Jesus EACH DAY FOR TEEN GUYS

A 365-DAY DEVOTIONAL

BARBOUR
PUBLISHING

Published by Barbour Publishing, Inc., P.O. Box 719, Uhrichsville, Ohio 44683, www.barbourbooks.com

Our mission is to inspire the world with the life-changing message of the Bible.

Member of the
Evangelical Christian
Publishers Association

Printed in China.

THERE'S NO GREATER PERSONALITY THAN JESUS— SO WHY NOT MAKE TIME EACH DAY TO KNOW HIM BETTER?

This 365-day devotional highlights many aspects of Jesus' life and work, touching on His teaching, example, and ongoing impact on our lives. You'll find powerful insights for every day of the year.

These brief readings aren't heavily theological but inspirational. Each one will provide food for thought as you start or end your day—or take a devotional break somewhere in between!

Monthly themes tie the daily messages into the calendar:

- January: Beginnings
- February: Love
- March: Rebirth
- April: Blessings
- May: Growth
- June: Joy
- July: Freedom
- August: Perseverance
- September: Guidance
- October: Change
- November: Gratitude
- December: Nearness

The Creator, Sustainer, Savior, and Redeemer of humanity is worthy of every moment you devote to Him. . .*Jesus Each Day for Teen Guys* will help you do just that.

JANUARY 1

*If anyone is in Christ, the new creation has
come: The old has gone, the new is here!*
2 CORINTHIANS 5:17 NIV

How appropriate that New Year's Day arrives just a week after Christmas. January 1 is traditionally a time for new beginnings, though our resolutions (to exercise more, improve our grades, start looking for jobs, and so on) pale in comparison to the life change Jesus offers.

Christmas celebrates the Incarnation—that point in history when God became man, when Jesus "became flesh and made his dwelling among us." And because of this "one and only Son, who came from the Father, full of grace and truth" (John 1:14), we enjoy the unparalleled opportunity to be made new—no matter what traumas, failures, or personal bad behaviors darken our memory.

Christmas means Jesus, and Jesus means new beginnings. This year, let's spend just a few minutes each day pursuing the one who always pursues us. You'll soon find that Christmas is much bigger than December 25—it's a reality we live all year.

MY PRAYER STARTER:

Lord, thank You so much for the second chances You offer. Help me live every day of this new year for You.

JANUARY 2

The Word (Christ) was in the beginning. The Word was with God.
The Word was God. He was with God in the beginning.
He made all things. Nothing was made without Him making it.
JOHN 1:1–3 NLV

In order to have a new beginning, there must be an "old beginning." You can read all about that in the Bible's first book, Genesis.

This remarkable universe, filled with untold galaxies and planets and stars, sprang from the even more remarkable mind of God. This incredible earth, teeming with life from amoebas to human beings, reflects the even more incredible life of its Creator. And that Creator is Jesus.

The sweet little baby of Bethlehem, the helpless infant wrapped in cloths and lying in a manger, was actually the immense power behind everything we see, hear, feel, taste, and are. He can offer us a new beginning because He is the almighty God who commanded the old one.

Nothing exists beyond Jesus' creative decree, and nothing lies beyond His re-creative capability.

MY PRAYER STARTER:

Lord Jesus, I'm amazed at how impressive Your creation
is. Please use Your power to create in me something
even more awesome—a heart that's focused on You.

JANUARY 3

The LORD God said to the serpent... "I will put enmity between
you and the woman, and between your offspring and hers;
he will crush your head, and you will strike his heel."

GENESIS 3:14–15 NIV

In a perfect world, we wouldn't need new beginnings. But we don't live in a perfect world.

Blame Adam and Eve if you want, but we've all played a role in this life's conflicts, failures, and disappointments. Twice, as if to emphasize the point, the psalm writer David proclaimed, "There is no one who does good, not even one" (Psalm 14:3, 53:3). His message couldn't have been clearer.

Like Adam and Eve, we all make selfish choices. We all fail. We all need help. And that's why Jesus came to earth—not to make it perfect (not yet, at least) but to set us on the path of perfection. When we hear Jesus' voice and accept His invitation, we can stop listening to Satan's words and doing his bidding.

Listen carefully.

MY PRAYER STARTER:
Thank You for stepping in and setting me on
the right path, Lord. Grant me listening ears
and an open heart to hear Your voice.

JANUARY 4

For God so loved the world, that he gave his only
begotten Son, that whosoever believeth in him
should not perish, but have everlasting life.
JOHN 3:16 KJV

Only God knows the true number of souls on earth, but current estimates place the number between seven and eight billion. Around the globe, people's styles, beliefs, and experiences vary widely, but all human beings share two things: the commonality of birth and our need for rebirth.

That was Jesus' message to a man named Nicodemus: "Ye must be born again" (John 3:7). Within this conversation between the Lord and a highly regarded Jewish religious leader lies what is perhaps the best known scripture of all—and it earns this title for good reason. Verse 16 is a sublime summary of God's love, of Jesus' work, and of our opportunity for the ultimate new beginning.

How important you must be to God!

MY PRAYER STARTER:
God, when I think of all the billions of people on earth, it makes me a little lightheaded. But what's even more amazing is that You still care about me! Thank You.

JANUARY 5

*For [God] has rescued us from the dominion of darkness
and brought us into the kingdom of the Son he loves.*
COLOSSIANS 1:13 NIV

Knowing Jesus changes everything. As we've already seen, anyone who is "in Christ" is a "new creation" (2 Corinthians 5:17). Sure, we still live in a broken world in vulnerable bodies. But salvation through Jesus means this life—with all its dullness and disappointments—is only the beginning of a perfect life that will never end, a life without "death or mourning or crying or pain" (Revelation 21:4).

Jesus is the doorway to that life, and every one of us is welcome to enter. Every one of us can enjoy the new beginning that He bought for us by His death on the cross. Every one of us faces a question: *Will I accept that gift?*

Knowing Jesus changes everything. Forever.

MY PRAYER STARTER:
Lord, I'm so glad this life isn't all there is. Thank You for
dying for me so that I can have a perfect life forever.

JANUARY 6

*And he is the head of the body, the church: who is the
beginning, the firstborn from the dead;
that in all things he might have the preeminence.*
Colossians 1:18 kjv

Today's verse calls Jesus "the beginning." The beginning of what? The next few words provide the answer: as "the firstborn from the dead," He is the beginning of new life.

Jesus wasn't the first person to be raised from the dead. You can find Old Testament examples of resurrection in 1 Kings 17:17–24, 2 Kings 4:32–37, and 2 Kings 13:20–21. And before Jesus' own resurrection, He had brought His friend Lazarus back from the dead (John 11:39–44), as well as Jairus's daughter (Mark 5:25–43) and the widow of Nain's son (Luke 7:11–17).

But Jesus is the "firstborn" from the dead because His resurrection is *permanent*. Unlike these other Bible figures, He didn't come back to life only to die again. Jesus lives forever—and because of that, so will all of us who accept His gift of life.

MY PRAYER STARTER:
Thank You, Jesus, for rising from the dead so that I
can someday rise as well! Help me live my life right
now in preparation for that wonderful day.

For since the beginning of the world men have not heard,
nor perceived by the ear, neither hath the eye seen, O God,
beside thee, what he hath prepared for him that waiteth for him.

ISAIAH 64:4 KJV

Jesus' name doesn't appear in the Old Testament. But He's certainly all throughout it.

In fact, many call the book of Isaiah "the fifth Gospel" because Jesus is so prominent in it. It was Isaiah who prophesied of Jesus as "Immanuel" (or "God with us," 7:14) and, in chapter 53, as the Suffering Servant who would be rejected and beaten, bearing the sins of many for their salvation.

Isaiah 64, specifically a message to the sinful Israelites, includes a promise that the apostle Paul later applied to all sinful people whom Jesus forgives: "As it is written, Eye hath not seen, nor ear heard, neither have entered into the heart of man, the things which God hath prepared for them that love him" (1 Corinthians 2:9).

Through Jesus, all those incredible, yet-to-be-seen things are yours.

MY PRAYER STARTER:

Lord Jesus, it's sometimes hard to focus on things
I can't see yet. So thank You for telling me all I
need to know in the pages of Your Word.

JANUARY 8

*From the rising of the sun unto the going down of
the same the LORD's name is to be praised.*

PSALM 113:3 KJV

To get your blood pumping, do you begin your day with a workout? A dose of coffee? An ice-cold shower? Whatever your morning routine looks like, scheduling time for prayer and praise will improve your whole day.

King David, writer of many psalms, began his day in prayer. Psalm 5:3 says, "My voice shalt thou hear in the morning, O LORD; in the morning will I direct my prayer unto thee, and will look up."

Even Jesus started His day in prayer. "And in the morning, rising up a great while before day, he went out, and departed into a solitary place, and there prayed" (Mark 1:35).

Prayer is more than asking God for help—it's recognizing who's in charge. Praising God shifts your focus off your troubles and onto God's goodness. Be like Jesus—begin your day in God's presence. Then watch Him make something good out of the rest of your day.

MY PRAYER STARTER:
Between school, chores, and homework, it seems like I'm always busy, Lord. But let me never get so busy that I forget about You. Remind me of Your goodness each morning so that I can start each day with a smile and a prayer.

JANUARY 9

For no one can lay any foundation other than the
one already laid, which is Jesus Christ.
1 CORINTHIANS 3:11 NIV

Buildings must be constructed in a certain order. The roof goes on after the walls. Insulation happens before drywall. Plumbing is installed before the sink. But everything begins with a strong foundation.

Christianity is built on the foundation of Jesus Christ. As His disciples, we build on that foundation by practicing what we read in scripture and hear from faithful teachers. Jesus said, "Everyone who comes to me and hears my words and puts them into practice, I will show you what they are like. They are like a man building a house, who dug down deep and laid the foundation on rock. When a flood came, the torrent struck that house but could not shake it, because it was well built" (Luke 6:47–48).

Are you building your life on Jesus' foundation? If so, your "house" will protect you from the storms of life—and help shelter those you love.

MY PRAYER STARTER:
Lord, let my trust in You never be swayed
by peer pressure, disappointment, or sinful
distractions. Make my faith rock solid.

JANUARY 10

After his baptism, as Jesus came up out of the water, the heavens were opened and he saw the Spirit of God descending like a dove and settling on him. And a voice from heaven said, "This is my dearly loved Son, who brings me great joy."

MATTHEW 3:16–17 NLT

Jesus began His earthly ministry with a heavenly encounter. Although He had no sins to repent of, He chose to be baptized by John. This foreshadowed His death and resurrection—His payment for and victory over sin.

When you began your new life in Christ, the heavens probably didn't open. But the Holy Spirit showed up. And because of His presence, you can have strength in weakness (Romans 8:26), peace in troubled times (Romans 15:13), and the freedom to see God (2 Corinthians 3:17).

The Holy Spirit is the seal of our salvation (2 Corinthians 1:22), so we can have a hope and joy this world can't understand. What Jesus began at His baptism led to a new beginning for us. Praise God!

MY PRAYER STARTER:

Even though I can't see You physically, Lord, I know You're working behind the scenes to bring me home to You. Thank You for the reassurance that Your Holy Spirit brings.

JANUARY 11

*Then Jesus was led by the Spirit into the
wilderness to be tempted by the devil.*

MATTHEW 4:1 NIV

Trouble began for Jesus as soon as His baptism was over. Now empowered by the Holy Spirit after such a heavenly encounter, Jesus was immediately faced with Satan's temptation. Can you relate?

Temptations often feel strongest the moment we repent of sin and accept the Lord's forgiveness. Can't we have just a few minutes of peace? Well, yes. . .if we do what Jesus did. When tempted by the devil, Jesus answered, "It is written: 'Man shall not live on bread alone, but on every word that comes from the mouth of God' " (Matthew 4:4).

When you respond to temptation with God's truth, you put the devil in his place! He is no longer lord and master of your life. *Jesus* is. Jesus knows what temptation feels like, and He has proven that He's stronger than anything you'll ever face.

What verses will you quote next time you face temptation?

MY PRAYER STARTER:
Lord Jesus, I'd be foolish to think I could beat the devil on his home turf all by myself. That's why I need Your strength. Thank You for providing the power of Your Word.

JANUARY 12

Jesus was walking by the Sea of Galilee. He saw Simon and his
brother Andrew putting a net into the sea. They were fishermen.
Jesus said to them, "Follow Me. I will make you fish for men!"
MARK 1:16–17 NLV

In New Testament times, fishermen had a hard—and often unrewarding—job. Standing on the shore or in their boats, they threw nets into the sea. Then they would haul the nets up, see if they'd caught anything, and toss the nets again. It was monotonous and physically demanding. . .and there were no guarantees of success.

When Jesus called Simon, Andrew, James, and John to abandon their fishing career and become His disciples, He didn't promise an easier life. Jesus walked among sick, selfish, and sometimes violent people—and He was eventually murdered. However, after He rose again, Jesus told His disciples to keep fishing. . .for men.

How's your "fishing" coming along? Are you telling others about Jesus? Do your classmates or friends notice a difference in your life?

Fishing can be a monotonous business, and there aren't any guarantees of success. Fortunately, all you must do is simply keep casting your line—God's the one who will provide the catch.

MY PRAYER STARTER:
I have a lot of friends, Lord, who don't know You.
Enable me to keep casting the line of Your amazing
love out to them, no matter how weary I may get.

JANUARY 13

As he walked along, he saw Levi son of Alphaeus sitting at
the tax collector's booth. "Follow me,"
Jesus told him, and Levi got up and followed him.
MARK 2:14 NIV

The Jewish tax collectors of New Testament times were considered traitors. They collected money for the Roman government, and many used their position for extortion, threatening Roman retribution if the Jewish people didn't pay. Most of them were educated men, so they knew how to get what they wanted.

It must have come as a shock to everyone when Jesus called Levi the tax collector to become His disciple. But Levi got up and followed the Lord—then he used his training and skills to write the first Gospel. He communicated convincingly to his fellow Jews that Jesus was the Messiah.

Jesus offers us a similar new beginning, redeeming our skills for His service. What sort of talents do you have that can be used for His glory?

MY PRAYER STARTER:
Thank You, Lord, for giving me a unique set of talents.
Help me to never take them for granted; rather,
let me use them in a way that honors You.

JANUARY 14

Looking at his disciples, he said: "Blessed are you
who are poor, for yours is the kingdom of God."

LUKE 6:20 NIV

Jesus' teachings are often counterintuitive. Luke's account of
the Beatitudes—or "blessings"—lists groups of people who don't
sound very blessed at all. Blessed are those who are poor, hungry,
crying, and insulted? What a strange way to begin a sermon! Then
Luke includes a list of woes: Woe to those who are rich, well fed,
laughing, and spoken well of. Did Jesus get it wrong?

It may feel that way. . .until you realize that Jesus' perspective
is bigger than this world's. His perspective is eternal. Being poor
may not feel like a blessing, but when you willingly depend on God
for our care, you show Him (and the world around you) what it
means to belong to the heavenly kingdom. However, if you become
rich and popular on earth, you may learn nothing about your true
position before God. . .and miss out on the eternal blessings that
come with dependence.

What's your perspective?

MY PRAYER STARTER:

Lord, sometimes I long for more popularity, even
when I know I shouldn't. Constantly remind me of
the importance of Your eternal kingdom, causing
all other desires to vanish in comparison.

JANUARY 15

*"Come and see a man who told me everything
I ever did! Could he possibly be the Messiah?"*
JOHN 4:29 NLT

Emergency exit strategies make for some entertaining action films—but they aren't reserved only for life-or-death situations. Exit strategies are also important for people who get caught up in sin.

The Samaritan woman at the well was one such person (see John 4:1–42). Her exit strategy involved avoiding people by getting her water while the town's well wasn't busy. But she couldn't avoid Jesus.

Jesus offered the woman a new exit strategy. No longer did she have to avoid people in hopes of hiding her sin: after accepting forgiveness, she ran to bring others to Christ. She stepped out of the darkness of sin, letting the Light of the world expose and heal her.

Do you need an exit strategy from sinful choices? Just turn to Jesus, accept forgiveness, and enjoy a new beginning.

MY PRAYER STARTER:

Lord God, whenever the pressures of sin start closing in around me, give me the wisdom to choose Your exit strategy instead.

JANUARY 16

He came to His own town and taught them in
their places of worship. They were surprised and
wondered, saying, "Where did this Man get this
wisdom? How can He do these powerful works?"

MATTHEW 13:54 NLV

Imagine revisiting your hometown many years from now, only for nothing to seem familiar. Not only has the town changed, but few of its residents even recognize you.

That's what Jesus felt when He tried to show His old neighbors who He really was, only for them to reject Him. *Isn't this only Jesus, the carpenter's son?* His neighbors thought. Their preconceptions prevented them from experiencing Him as God's Son. Jesus knew that would happen, but He tried to reach them all the same.

When you experience a new beginning in your life, your friends may not recognize you—or they may not trust the new person you've become. Still, it's worth reaching out, as Jesus did, to help them see God's truth.

MY PRAYER STARTER:

Lord, don't let me be ashamed of who I've become now that I've found You. Help me wear my new identity with boldness, showing everyone what You've done in my heart.

JANUARY 17

As Jesus was walking along, he saw a man who had been blind from birth. "Rabbi," his disciples asked him, "why was this man born blind? Was it because of his own sins or his parents' sins?"
JOHN 9:1–2 NLT

Some beginnings are harder than others. Is God unfair? Are our disadvantages related to sin?

The Bible makes clear that everyone is born equally sinful before a holy God (see Romans 3:23, 1 John 1:8, and Psalm 51:5). So one person's earthly advantages over another cannot be because the first person is holier than the second.

"It was not because of his sins or his parents' sins," Jesus said of a man's lifelong blindness. "This happened so the power of God could be seen in him" (John 9:3).

We don't know why God allows some people to face more challenges. We do know, however, that He provides His strength in our weakness and that He calls us to trust Him at all times. Hard beginnings are not a reason to doubt but an opportunity to trust.

MY PRAYER STARTER:

God, help me not to compare my situation to others'—for better or for worse. Rather, let me use the circumstances You've given me as opportunities to grow closer to You.

JANUARY 18

As he neared Damascus on his journey, suddenly a light from heaven flashed around him. He fell to the ground and heard a voice say to him, "Saul, Saul, why do you persecute me?"

ACTS 9:3–4 NIV

Saul of Tarsus—later known as Paul the apostle, author of most of the New Testament—didn't begin his religious career as a Christian. Far from it! Saul, a zealous defender of the Jewish faith, was out to *kill off* Christianity by any means necessary. . .until he met Jesus.

Encounters with Christ will radically change the direction of a person's life. Saul went from "breathing out murderous threats against the Lord's disciples" (Acts 9:1) to saying, "To live is Christ and to die is gain" (Philippians 1:21).

At one time, Paul was zealous about keeping the Jewish faith pure. Then the Lord repurposed his passion to bring Gentiles and Israelites alike to Himself. Do you remember what you were passionate about before you encountered Jesus? If so, how has He repurposed your passions?

MY PRAYER STARTER:
Lord, thank You for giving me my passions and bending them to align with Your will. I refuse to let this gift go to waste. Help me make full use of it.

JANUARY 19

But the Comforter, which is the Holy Ghost,
whom the Father will send in my name, he shall
teach you all things, and bring all things to your
remembrance, whatsoever I have said unto you.

JOHN 14:26 KJV

God has set a pretty high standard for Christians: "As obedient children, not fashioning yourselves according to the former lusts in your ignorance: but as he which hath called you is holy, so be ye holy in all manner of conversation; because it is written, Be ye holy; for I am holy" (1 Peter 1:14–16).

Fortunately, you have help. Your holiness is not dependent on your own efforts but on Jesus' actions. As you mature—not just physically but spiritually as well—your decisions and thoughts will become increasingly guided by the Holy Spirit, whom Jesus sends to live within you.

In John 14:26, Jesus comforted His disciples by assuring them that even after His ascension, they wouldn't be on their own. God would send the Holy Spirit to help them, comfort them, advocate for them, and live inside them. And He's done the same for you.

MY PRAYER STARTER:
I know I could never measure up on my own, Lord, so thank You for offering a way to make me holy. Help me follow Your Spirit's leading as I grow into the man You want me to be.

JANUARY 20

The father instantly cried out, "I do believe,
but help me overcome my unbelief!"
MARK 9:24 NLT

Remember when the heavens opened at Jesus' baptism and God affirmed Him as His Son? The incident was repeated at Jesus' transfiguration on the mount. Mark 9:7 says, "Then a cloud overshadowed them, and a voice from the cloud said, 'This is my dearly loved Son. Listen to him.' "

You'd think this affirmation of Jesus' identity would make anyone a believer, but not everyone was there to hear it. After He came down from the mountain, Jesus encountered the desperate father of a demon-possessed boy who was caught in the center of an argument between the scribes and Jesus' disciples.

This father believed that God could help his son, but when the disciples proved unable to cast out the demon, the man appealed to Jesus. Jesus healed the boy, and the father's belief grew.

Whether your spiritual journey began with a mountaintop experience or a desperate cry for help, putting your faith in God's goodness will always result in growth.

MY PRAYER STARTER:
Thank You, God, for meeting me at exactly the right place and the right time for me to accept Jesus as my Savior. May my faith only grow upward from here.

The fear of the Lord is the beginning of wisdom.
To learn about the Holy One is understanding.

PROVERBS 9:10 NLV

Wisdom is the combination of knowledge, intuition, and resolve to achieve a specific goal. It is active, always striving toward something better. But where does it begin?

According to today's verse, wisdom begins with "the fear of the Lord." Properly understanding our relationship with God—contrasting His perfection with our imperfections—should do more than inspire us toward awe; it should frighten us. And yet Jesus has made us holy by His perfect sacrifice. Now we can simply ask God for the wisdom we lack (James 1:5).

When we ask, here's what we receive: "The wisdom that comes from heaven is first of all pure. Then it gives peace. It is gentle and willing to obey. It is full of loving-kindness and of doing good. It has no doubts and does not pretend to be something it is not" (James 3:17).

The wisdom of God is necessary for living well and bringing others to Jesus. It begins with fear, but it leads to peace.

MY PRAYER STARTER:
Lord, help me to fear You. But don't let it stop
there; help my fear grow into a loving appreciation
for Your awesome power and grace.

JANUARY 22

*And he said unto them, When ye pray, say, Our Father
which art in heaven, Hallowed be thy name. Thy
kingdom come. Thy will be done, as in heaven, so in earth.*
LUKE 11:2 KJV

Prayers from the Old Testament usually addressed God by His personal name, *YHWH*, which is rendered as *Jehovah* or LORD in our Bibles. This manner of addressing God honors His holy nature since God's personal name was considered too holy to even write down.

When Jesus taught His disciples to pray, He addressed God differently: "Our Father." This was no less respectful, as it still treats God's name as holy—or "hallowed"—but it was much more personal than the name Moses or the prophets typically used.

Jesus has reunited you with God by giving His holiness to you and making your adoption into God's family permanently possible. As such, God is still holy. . .but He's also Your personal, loving Father. So when you begin your prayers with "Our Father," thank Jesus for making it possible.

MY PRAYER STARTER:
Father, thank You for adopting me as Your son and
allowing me to approach You with confidence and love.
Let me never take such a privilege for granted.

JANUARY 23

Let us think of ways to motivate one another to acts of love and good works. And let us not neglect our meeting together, as some people do, but encourage one another, especially now that the day of his return is drawing near.

HEBREWS 10:24–25 NLT

How often do you attend church? Do you sometimes feel too busy with school, sports, or other activities to take some time off each Sunday?

Church is important, not because God cares whether you are warming a pew but because it requires sacrifice, draws you closer to Jesus, and puts you in touch with people who need your encouragement. It allows you to stop focusing on your own concerns and gives others an opportunity to show their concern for you.

Following Jesus means attending family gatherings. God doesn't *need* us in church, but He does *want* His children to be better family members. If it's been a while since you've been in church, it's time to head back. Begin your week with the family, motivating one another to love and good works.

MY PRAYER STARTER:

God, thank You for giving me a huge family that I can visit every week in church. Help me to never forget how blessed I am!

JANUARY 24

Your Word have I hid in my heart,
that I may not sin against You.
PSALM 119:11 NLV

Starting good habits takes intention and commitment. But left to our own devices, we can begin bad habits (which will then take commitment to break) without any effort at all.

Here's something worth intentionally pursuing: memorizing Bible verses. Knowing God's Word helps you keep His truth at the front of your mind so that you can live it out intentionally—the way Jesus did every day of His life on earth. Taking time to commit scripture to memory protects you from using that time selfishly. . .and when you come against specific temptations, you'll be equipped to fight them.

For biblical reasons to memorize scripture, take a look at 2 Timothy 3:16–17, Hebrews 4:12, Psalm 119:105, Mark 13:31, and Romans 15:4. Then search for some verses to "hide in your heart." You might even start by memorizing the powerful verses about Jesus found in this devotional.

MY PRAYER STARTER:
Thank You, Lord, for giving me a near-endless supply of encouragement and wisdom in Your Word. Help me to use my time wisely by reading and memorizing it each day.

JANUARY 25

Your heart should be holy and set apart for the Lord God.
Always be ready to tell everyone who asks you why you
believe as you do. Be gentle as you speak and show respect.
1 PETER 3:15 NLV

Beginning new practices like regular church attendance or memorizing scripture can be intimidating. But few things feel as monumentally nerve-racking as sharing your faith. Why?

Perhaps you think you're too young for such an important task. Maybe you're afraid you won't be able to answer a person's questions perfectly, thus doing more harm than good. And what if you offend others by suggesting their current belief system is wrong?

If sharing the gospel of Jesus Christ makes you uncomfortable, remember how uncomfortable it was for Jesus to provide for you. If you have been set apart for God, you must be ready to do what He asks. Besides, if you speak with gentleness and respect, most people will appreciate the fact that you care enough to share your life with them.

MY PRAYER STARTER:

Lord Jesus, I'm thankful that Your fear of the cross didn't prevent You from saving me. Give me the courage to share the gospel with others, no matter how awkward it feels.

JANUARY 26

Jesus said, "How can I describe the Kingdom of God?
What story should I use to illustrate it? It is like a mustard
seed planted in the ground. It is the smallest of all seeds,
but it becomes the largest of all garden plants; it grows
long branches, and birds can make nests in its shade."

MARK 4:30–32 NLT

Mustard seeds are tiny, but they can grow into plants up to ten feet tall. Mustard plants were considered weeds in Israel because they could quickly overtake a garden, and farmers would work hard to keep them out.

When Jesus compared God's kingdom to a weed, He meant it wasn't going to grow in orderly, controllable ways. Its hidden beginnings in a small Judean town were going to change the world.

When your life feels chaotic and unhinged, remember the mustard seed. God is still in control, and He may not want your garden to be orderly. He may be looking for ways to grow your faith from a tiny seed into a force of nature.

MY PRAYER STARTER:

I don't have anything under control, Lord, and that's just the way You've designed it. Thank You for letting me take a back seat and watch as You gloriously work out all the details.

JANUARY 27

The crowds that went ahead of him and those that followed shouted, "Hosanna to the Son of David!" "Blessed is he who comes in the name of the Lord!" "Hosanna in the highest heaven!"

MATTHEW 21:9 NIV

A week's beginning can look very different from its end. Crowds welcomed Jesus on Palm Sunday with shouts of "Blessed is he who comes in the name of the Lord!" Days later, crowds called for His crucifixion (Matthew 27:22).

Though the whims of a crowd can change dramatically, God never changes. His plans cannot be thwarted. For us to recognize God's perfect plan in our lives, it's our perspective that needs to change. After all, our redemption couldn't have happened without Jesus' crucifixion.

When it seems like your life is careening downhill, look up! You'll see that God's love is constant in every situation.

MY PRAYER STARTER:
Thank You, God, for being the one constant in my
life. I know that no matter what troubles I face,
You still love me—and that's all I'll ever need.

"Suppose one of you wants to build a tower.
Won't you first sit down and estimate the cost to see
if you have enough money to complete it?"

LUKE 14:28 NIV

The first step of any project? Figure out what you're getting yourself into. Action without forethought invariably leads to regret. Whether you're searching for a summer job, preparing a school presentation, or even planning a fun evening with your friends, it is wise to count the cost first.

But Jesus wasn't offering pocketbook advice. The context of this scripture is found in verse 26: "If anyone comes to me and does not hate father and mother, wife and children, brothers and sisters—yes, even their own life—such a person cannot be my disciple."

Following Jesus isn't just expensive—it is exclusive. To be a Christian means laying down everything—money, relationships, pride, goals—at the foot of the cross, knowing that what you'll get in return is worth incomparably more.

MY PRAYER STARTER:
Lord Jesus, following You takes a lot of courage and sacrifice, but I'm willing to do what it takes. Give me the guts and determination to stand strong when necessary.

JANUARY 29

*"Don't misunderstand why I have come. I did not
come to abolish the law of Moses or the writings of
the prophets. No, I came to accomplish their purpose."*

MATTHEW 5:17 NLT

When did Christianity begin? The early movement can be traced historically and archeologically to within a few years of Jesus' death and resurrection, but it didn't begin then. Not really.

Although the Lord's incarnation forever changed the way people interact with God, to say Christianity started with Jesus would disagree with what He said in today's scripture. Jesus wasn't looking to start a new religion but to finish what had been promised in the garden of Eden.

Christ's role in God's rescue plan is recorded in the serpent's curse: "And I [God] will cause hostility between you and the woman, and between your offspring and her offspring. He will strike your head, and you will strike his heel" (Genesis 3:15).

When the devil whispers half-truths to entice you to sin, remember that Jesus came to set you free—and He has already accomplished His purpose.

MY PRAYER STARTER:

Lord, I know that You've not only chosen me as Your child
but have been planning my salvation from the beginning
of time. Thank You for such unimaginable care.

JANUARY 30

Be very careful, then, how you live—not as unwise but as wise,
making the most of every opportunity, because the days are evil.
EPHESIANS 5:15–16 NIV

In 1923, a bank in Coshocton, Ohio, published an advertisement that said, "Half the game of getting ahead is getting started." Not only is that sound financial advice (the Bible echoes the statement in Proverbs 13:11), it applies to anything—even sharing zthe gospel of Jesus Christ.

It's time to begin. Investing in others now will one day yield heavenly rewards that are infinitely more valuable than money (Matthew 6:19–21). Plus, opportunities to bring others to Jesus are swiftly passing by—and no one knows when they will end completely.

How can you get started? By living wisely: confess your sins (1 John 1:9), care for those who are less fortunate than you (James 1:27), love God and your neighbor (Matthew 22:37–39), and dwell on godly things (Philippians 4:8).

You're halfway to success.

MY PRAYER STARTER:
Lord, I know there are hundreds of people in my
neighborhood who probably don't know You, and I want to
reach them with Your light. Show me how to get started.

JANUARY 31

Better is the end of a thing than the beginning thereof.
ECCLESIASTES 7:8 KJV

New beginnings are wonderful and essential. . .but they aren't everything.

As you close out the first month of this new year, think of the words of the preacher in Ecclesiastes: a successful conclusion excels the beginning of any endeavor.

Believers know that God the Father will finish what He started in their lives. As the apostle Paul wrote, "He which hath begun a good work in you will perform it until the day of Jesus Christ" (Philippians 1:6). And Jesus Himself guarantees our safety and security to the very end: "My sheep hear my voice, and I know them, and they follow me: and I give unto them eternal life; and they shall never perish, neither shall any man pluck them out of my hand" (John 10:27–28).

Beginning with Jesus ensures a perfect end.

MY PRAYER STARTER:
God, thank You for pulling me out of sin, placing me
on the path to heaven, and giving me the assurance of
a successful end as long as I keep following You.

FEBRUARY 1

*"There is no greater love than to lay down
one's life for one's friends."*
JOHN 15:13 NLT

Love takes center stage in February, with Valentine's Day at the midpoint of the month. The holiday is named for a third-century Roman Christian martyr. Though, like Christmas, Valentine's Day has become secular and commercialized, it can prompt us to ask good questions—like "What *is* love?"

Of course, there are plenty of lighter, less serious aspects to love: you might "love" pizza, puppies, and parades. You've experienced junior high crushes and thought you'd die when your "love" didn't reciprocate. You might even be in "love" right now.

However, if you marry and have children, you'll begin to plumb the deeper wells of love, drawing slowly closer to the dictionary definition of Jesus' type: "unselfish loyal and benevolent concern for the good of another."

What could've driven Jesus to leave the glory of heaven, live as a man on this sin-cursed earth, face the opposition of far lesser men, and ultimately die on a cross as payment for human sin? *Love.*

MY PRAYER STARTER:

Loving God, let me never confuse my passionate, fleeting feelings with Your love. Help me minimize the importance of the former while cultivating the latter in my heart.

FEBRUARY 2

Dear friends, let us continue to love one another, for love comes from God. Anyone who loves is a child of God and knows God. But anyone who does not love does not know God, for God is love.

1 JOHN 4:7–8 NLT

Humans need love. Babies who don't receive loving touches have higher mortality rates. Teenagers and even many adults are constantly searching for love, sometimes in unhealthy ways. Why is love so integral to the human experience?

Consider today's verse in light of Genesis 1:27: "So God created human beings in his own image. In the image of God he created them; male and female he created them."

We were made in the image of God, and God is love. We were created by, for, and in resemblance of love itself! When sin broke the world, we humans tried filling our love needs by ourselves. However, we were made to love and be loved by God—nothing else can satisfy this innate desire. Praise Jesus for making it possible for God's love to live in us.

MY PRAYER STARTER:
Lord, I realize that I'm in desperate need of meaning and love in my life. Thank You for putting an end to my search and offering such profound love freely.

FEBRUARY 3

We love him, because he first loved us.
1 JOHN 4:19 KJV

Jesus' love takes initiative. It doesn't wait for someone else to take the first step. It doesn't sit near the phone, waiting for the ring. Jesus' love reaches out first.

Jesus' love is bold. It isn't nervous about rejection, although rejection is a possibility. And only because we are able to reject Him does it mean anything when we choose to love Him in return. We may deny His love, but there's no denying that Jesus reached out first.

When we accept His love, we overflow, boldly initiating relationships with others. Jesus' love inspires action first. It opens us to the possibility of rejection but also to a chance for true connection.

When we love as Jesus loves, we forgive before the apology. We choose kindness while facing hostility. We turn the other cheek, give more than is requested, and go the extra mile. Though we realize our love for others may not change them, we do it anyway because Jesus' love has changed *us*.

MY PRAYER STARTER:
Jesus, if You had waited until I reached out to You first, I'd never have a hope for heaven. Thank You for taking the first step—and help me do the same with others.

FEBRUARY 4

Therefore, as God's chosen people, holy and dearly loved, clothe yourselves with compassion, kindness, humility, gentleness and patience. Bear with each other and forgive one another if any of you has a grievance against someone. Forgive as the Lord forgave you. And over all these virtues put on love, which binds them all together in perfect unity.

COLOSSIANS 3:12–14 NIV

What important step comes after washing up for the day but before going out in public? Getting dressed. We don't live in a pre-sin Eden anymore. Decent society expects us to be clothed.

In the same way, now that we've been made clean in Jesus, we need to get spiritually dressed before we interact with the world. But we're not talking socks and jeans—Christians are called to put on kindness, humility, gentleness, patience, and forgiveness. And on top of everything, we put on love. Love completes the holy ensemble.

When you're dressed for success, you'll be ready to focus on others more than yourself, and in doing so, you'll resemble Jesus Himself.

MY PRAYER STARTER:
Lord, just as I would never show up to class with nothing on, I don't want to go out in public without the shining armor of Your love. Remind me each morning to get spiritually dressed.

FEBRUARY 5

There is no fear in love. Perfect love puts fear out of our hearts.
People have fear when they are afraid of being
punished. The man who is afraid does not have perfect love.
1 JOHN 4:18 NLV

Why do you obey your parents? Is it because you love them, or is it because you fear the punishment for breaking their rules? If the rules are being obeyed, does it even matter why?

The same questions apply to your obedience to God. On one hand, your motivations matter to Him. On the other hand, you were born into disobedience, so you already deserve punishment: "For all have sinned, and come short of the glory of God" (Romans 3:23 KJV).

But thanks to Jesus, who has taken our punishment, we have been declared holy before a perfect God. We obey Jesus' commandments not for fear of punishment or even because the rules make sense—they sometimes will not—but because we love Him. And we know our obedience pleases Him.

MY PRAYER STARTER:

Lord, I love You because of who You are and what You've done for me. As a result, I want all my actions to align with Your will. Keep my deeds—and motivations—pure.

FEBRUARY 6

*But God showed his great love for us by sending
Christ to die for us while we were still sinners.*

ROMANS 5:8 NLT

Think of a sacrifice you've made for love. Maybe you went to a restaurant you don't like because your date wanted to eat there. Maybe you scrimped and saved to afford a really nice gift for someone. Maybe you did a household chore you hate because you know your parents were stressed at the time. It's easy to make these kinds of sacrifices for people you love, especially when they love you in return.

Now imagine making the ultimate sacrifice for someone who doesn't even know you—or worse, someone who *hates* you. That's the sacrifice Jesus made for us. While we were still His enemies, He laid down His life to make us right with God. That's the love we are called to show others.

If you ever find yourself near someone you don't like, pray for Jesus' love to fill your heart. Then make a sacrifice that reflects the "great love" of God.

MY PRAYER STARTER:

Lord, I'll never grasp the depths of love You showed while hanging on the cross for my sins. But help me understand just enough of it so that I can show it to others as well.

FEBRUARY 7

*Most important of all, continue to show deep love for
each other, for love covers a multitude of sins.*

1 PETER 4:8 NLT

It's good that Jesus doesn't hold grudges. We sin constantly, making mistakes and promising never to be trapped by sin again only to find ourselves sinning almost immediately. Jesus could be skeptical when we repent—He knows every sin we have committed and will commit in the future—but He isn't.

Being forgiven is wonderful, but if it doesn't produce forgiveness toward others, then you haven't truly understood Jesus' love. Jesus said, "If you forgive those who sin against you, your heavenly Father will forgive you. But if you refuse to forgive others, your Father will not forgive your sins" (Matthew 6:14–15).

When you truly experience Jesus' love, grudges melt away and forgiveness comes easily, covering "a multitude of sins" done against you. Ephesians 4:32 says it like this: "Be kind to each other, tenderhearted, forgiving one another, just as God through Christ has forgiven you."

MY PRAYER STARTER:

Father, may I never take Your infinite forgiveness for
granted. Help me constantly show my appreciation
by sharing it with others who have wronged me.

FEBRUARY 8

Husbands, love your wives. You must love them as
Christ loved the church. He gave His life for it.
EPHESIANS 5:25 NLV

The marriage relationship reflects Christ's union with His church. While marriage may seem like a distant prospect to you, the call to love self-sacrificially in today's scripture can apply to every Christian, married or not.

The purpose of marriage is given in Ephesians 5:26–27: "Christ did this so He could set the church apart for Himself. He made it clean by the washing of water with the Word. Christ did this so the church might stand before Him in shining-greatness. There is to be no sin of any kind in it. It is to be holy and without blame."

Marriage exists to make people holy, not happy—and the same is true with your own relationships, as other people often reveal the sin present in your own life. As you allow Jesus to make you holy, you are learning how to put the interests of others ahead of your own.

Strive to become more like our Lord, who gave Himself for us.

MY PRAYER STARTER:

Even if I'm not yet ready for marriage, God, help me use the relationships I have right now to prepare me for more important commitments—to my future wife and to You.

FEBRUARY 9

If ye love me, keep my commandments.
JOHN 14:15 KJV

God's laws were given to the nation of Israel as proof that they were His chosen people (Deuteronomy 7:9). When Israel obeyed these laws and loved God properly, they prospered. When they defied God, they suffered.

By the time of Jesus' arrival, Jewish leaders took God's laws very seriously—to the point of adding their own rules into the mix to make them seem like the holiest men around. But these new laws made life unnecessarily difficult for people.

In Matthew 11:29, Jesus had a better idea: "Take my yoke upon you, and learn of me; for I am meek and lowly in heart: and ye shall find rest unto your souls."

Jesus doesn't want to make your life harder. He's all about making peace between you and God, offering rest for your soul. The commandments He mentioned in John 14:15 are quite simple: love God above all else, and love your neighbor as yourself (Matthew 22:37–39).

MY PRAYER STARTER:
Lord, help me never to fall into the trap of only obeying Your rules out of a sense of obligation. Rather, let my obedience flow from my love and passion for Your holiness.

FEBRUARY 10

*If I could speak all the languages of earth and of angels,
but didn't love others, I would only be a noisy gong or
a clanging cymbal. If I had the gift of prophecy, and if
I understood all of God's secret plans and possessed all
knowledge, and if I had such faith that I could move
mountains, but didn't love others, I would be nothing.*

1 CORINTHIANS 13:1–2 NLT

First Corinthians 13 is sometimes called the "love chapter" of
the Bible. While the theme for this month of February is love,
we're going to look specifically at this passage from today until
Valentine's Day.

To put 1 Corinthians 13 in context, understand that chapter
12 is all about how people in the church—Jesus' beautiful bride—
have different gifts (like prophecy, hospitality, and wisdom), and
all of them are needed for the church to be complete. However,
today's scripture passage teaches that gifts alone are useless if
not carried out in love.

When our personal gifts are empowered by Jesus' love, the
world will be drawn to Christ.

MY PRAYER STARTER:
Lord, help me to remember the proper order of the
spiritual gifts You've given me. May I never misuse
any of them by employing them without love.

FEBRUARY 11

Love is patient, love is kind. It does not envy, it does not boast,
it is not proud. It does not dishonor others, it is not
self-seeking, it is not easily angered, it keeps no record of
wrongs. Love does not delight in evil but rejoices with the truth.
1 CORINTHIANS 13:4–6 NIV

You've probably heard today's scripture passage quoted in marriage ceremonies. But how can you apply it to your everyday life?

Read through these verses again and consider the focus of each of love's attributes. For love to be patient and kind, it must look beyond itself. For it not to be envious, boastful, or proud, it must look beyond itself. Love is not concerned with self; it is set on the good of others.

To this end, Jesus was the ultimate example of love. Humbling himself for our sakes (2 Corinthians 8:9), He forgave others freely (Luke 5:20) and remains the embodiment of truth and grace (John 1:14). To apply today's passage to your life, look to Jesus. . .then attend to the needs of those around you.

MY PRAYER STARTER:

I don't just want to say I love other people, Lord—I want
to show it through my empathy and compassion. Mold my
heart, making it resemble and reflect Your perfect love.

FEBRUARY 12

Love never gives up, never loses faith, is always
hopeful, and endures through every circumstance.
1 CORINTHIANS 13:7 NLT

True love cannot be shaken by changing circumstances, tragedy, or inconvenience. Love doesn't give up when the loving gets tough.

The love of Jesus is again the best example. For love, Jesus left the perfection of God's presence to come to our broken world (John 1:14). For love, He wandered from town to town without a place to rest His head (Matthew 8:20). For love, Jesus reached out to those society rejected (Luke 15:2). And for love, Jesus went to the cross to pay for your sins (John 3:16).

To love like Jesus, you have to be intentional and lay aside your comforts. Accept the outcast—that one, lonely person who may even hate you and all your friends—and keep loving that person, even when it costs you everything.

Real love is hard. It requires endurance. But when you endure, you prove that Jesus' love dwells within you.

MY PRAYER STARTER:
Lord Jesus, help me show Your love to the outcasts in
my life—whether they're in my class, down the street,
or even at church. Let them see You in my actions.

FEBRUARY 13

Love never fails. But where there are prophecies, they
will cease; where there are tongues, they will be stilled;
where there is knowledge, it will pass away.

1 CORINTHIANS 13:8 NIV

We live in a world of natural entropy and planned obsolescence. Cell phones are designed to fail over time so you need to buy another. Cars can be meticulously maintained, but their parts eventually wear down. Ultimately, everything breaks down. . .everything except love.

Jesus' love is as timeless as God Himself. Hebrews 1:3 says, "The Son is the radiance of God's glory and the exact representation of his being, sustaining all things by his powerful word. After he had provided purification for sins, he sat down at the right hand of the Majesty in heaven."

Jesus is waiting for the Father's "go" to bring us as His followers into our ultimate rest. . .and He never stops loving us. As this broken world continues to crumble, His love is as pure and whole as He is Himself. Jesus—and His love—will never fail.

MY PRAYER STARTER:
Lord, everything around me seems so transient and petty compared to Your grace. Thank You for Your reassuring love that will weather the storms of eternity itself.

FEBRUARY 14

And now we have these three: faith and hope
and love, but the greatest of these is love.
1 CORINTHIANS 13:13 NLV

Faith, hope, and love are all pretty great. The apostle Paul explained how they overlap in the Christian's life: "While praying to God our Father, we always remember your work of *faith* and your acts of *love* and your *hope* that never gives up in our Lord Jesus Christ" (1 Thessalonians 1:3, emphasis added).

But only in today's scripture does Paul recognize love as the greatest of the three. Why is love the greatest? Because if Jesus didn't love us through His obedient sacrifice, we would have no reason for faith. If His love had stayed in the tomb, we would have no reason for hope. But because Jesus' love took Him both to the cross and out of the grave, we have faith, hope, and love altogether.

On this Valentine's Day, don't forget Jesus, the one who made *love* the greatest thing of all.

MY PRAYER STARTER:
Thank You, Jesus, for offering a love that surpasses anything this world has to offer. Today, help me show this love to everyone I meet, even if they do not show it in return.

FEBRUARY 15

See what great love the Father has lavished on us,
that we should be called children of God!
And that is what we are! The reason the world
does not know us is that it did not know him.

1 JOHN 3:1 NIV

Adoption goes back to ancient times. In the Roman world of Jesus' day, it was fairly common, with both family adoptions (in which one family would legally become part of another) and individual adoptions (which is more commonly seen today). In either case, adoptees were legally considered part of the adoptive family, subject to the authority of the family head, and able to inherit that family's estate. In all cases, adopted people ceased to belong in any way to their original family.

Because of Jesus' love and sacrifice, we have become children of God (John 1:12–13). We no longer belong to the family of this world. Our love, then, shouldn't be for the world, but for our Father in heaven and our new family in Christ.

MY PRAYER STARTER:
Lord, I know that this world is fleeting, unkind, and
ultimately unsatisfying. Thank You for pulling me
out of its family and adopting me into Your own.

FEBRUARY 16

"Love your enemies! Do good to them. Lend to them without expecting to be repaid. Then your reward from heaven will be very great, and you will truly be acting as children of the Most High, for he is kind to those who are unthankful and wicked."

LUKE 6:35 NLT

Of course loving your enemies is hard—they're the last people on earth you would naturally feel like loving!

You may think, *But what if by loving them, I can change them and make them more lovable?* Unfortunately, that misses the point in two ways: First, your love cannot change anyone; only Jesus' love can. Second, loving your enemies isn't supposed to change *them*; it is supposed to change *you*.

When Jesus came to save the lost, He sought out tax collectors, prostitutes, and other enemies of society. He reached out with His pure love, and they were changed because of Him. You can only love your enemies when you stop thinking of them as enemies and love them with Jesus' love. . .just as He has loved you.

MY PRAYER STARTER:
Father, You know how hard it is to love those who don't return the favor. Give me the strength to keep loving them anyway—for their benefit and for mine.

FEBRUARY 17

Love each other as Christian brothers.
Show respect for each other.
ROMANS 12:10 NLV

If you have siblings, you know how easy it is to slip from brotherly love into rivalry. Just ask Cain and Abel. But it doesn't have to be that way. As followers of Christ, we are united by family bonds that are stronger than the blood in our veins. They are as strong as the blood of Jesus.

So what do brothers and sisters in Christ do when rivalries form between us? We don't ignore them—we must surrender them to God. When we find jealousy or anger within, the Bible tells us to go to God in prayer. If God won't honor our request, it may be because our desires are selfishly motivated. Only by giving up our selfish desires and respecting our siblings in Christ can we show the world that God's family means something special (James 4:1–3).

Jesus made us children of God so that we could love each other, not engage in conflicts.

MY PRAYER STARTER:
Lord Jesus, I know that people—even fellow Christians—can be annoying at times. I need Your help to put these differences aside and choose to embrace harmony instead.

FEBRUARY 18

No, in all these things we are more than conquerors through him who loved us. For I am convinced that neither death nor life, neither angels nor demons, neither the present nor the future, nor any powers, neither height nor depth, nor anything else in all creation, will be able to separate us from the love of God that is in Christ Jesus our Lord.
ROMANS 8:37–39 NIV

Jesus doesn't write break-up letters. He's in it for the long haul. Nothing can separate you from the love of Christ. Not your worries. Not your doubts. Not your fears. Not your mistakes. Not your sins. Not the size of your social media following. Not "trouble or hardship or persecution or famine or nakedness or danger or sword" (Romans 8:35). Not bears with chainsaws for arms or sharks with laser eyes or even a zombie apocalypse.

When Jesus says He loves you, He means He loves you *forever*. When you are "in Christ," you are in His love. . .no ifs, ands, or buts. Rest easy in such love.

MY PRAYER STARTER:
Thank You, Jesus, for Your grace that dwarfs every single one of my sins and fears. Thank You for letting me rest peacefully in Your promises. Thank You for Your love.

*But the Holy Spirit produces this kind of fruit
in our lives: love, joy, peace, patience, kindness,
goodness, faithfulness, gentleness, and self-
control. There is no law against these things!*
GALATIANS 5:22–23 NLT

Fruit is the naturally occurring, self-replicating, delicious evidence of God's love and provision for humanity. Yes, fruit farmers must cultivate and protect their crops, but they don't create the fruit. God does.

And just as physical fruit is a naturally occurring phenomenon, the fruit of the Spirit grows naturally when you allow Jesus to work in your life. In John 15:5, He said, "Yes, I am the vine; you are the branches. Those who remain in me, and I in them, will produce much fruit. For apart from me you can do nothing."

According to today's scripture, love is the primary evidence of the Spirit's work. It is a naturally occurring, self-replicating, delicious way that we show others what Jesus has done for us.

MY PRAYER STARTER:

Lord Jesus, when others look at me, may they not see the ugly, shriveled fruits of my own efforts; rather, let them see—and be nourished by—the vibrant fruit of Your love.

FEBRUARY 20

*But because of his great love for us, God, who is rich in
mercy, made us alive with Christ even when we were dead
in transgressions—it is by grace you have been saved.*

Ephesians 2:4–5 NIV

If you've ever taken a trip through a hard place—whether it was a minor life detour or the valley of the shadow of death—you know how life-giving a traveling companion's love can be. Perhaps a friend, a parent, or someone at church has offered a hug or a note of encouragement, fulfilling a need you didn't know you had. No matter the act, the love behind it breathed new life into you when you felt close to death.

When Jesus came to earth, He didn't simply give hugs or encouraging words. He came to give *life* to those who were truly dead in their sins. Because you live in a broken world, your new life in Christ may still take you through valleys, but you can always trust that the path will ultimately lead where He wants you to go. And you can be certain that He walks beside you every step of the way.

MY PRAYER STARTER:
Thank You, God, for walking beside me through my
darkest day—and for giving me the assurance that You
will never leave. Help me be faithful to You in return.

FEBRUARY 21

*Dear children, let's not merely say that we love each
other; let us show the truth by our actions.*

1 JOHN 3:18 NLT

An elderly couple was having dinner with some newlyweds when the young husband turned to his bride and said, "I love you." The elderly wife looked at her husband and said, "Why don't you tell me you love me like that?" The elderly husband responded, "I told you I love you years ago. I'll let you know if anything changes."

Saying "I love you" *is* important. It's good for others to be reassured, even if nothing has changed since they heard it last. But words alone are not enough. Jesus could have announced His love for humanity until He was blue in the face, but if He hadn't followed through with the crucifixion, His words would have been simply that—words.

But thanks to Jesus' fully enacted love—the love shown by both His words and His actions—we know without doubt where we stand with God. And now we have the ability to love others in word and in truth, following His example.

MY PRAYER STARTER:
Jesus, thank You for leaving no room for doubt when it comes to whether You love us. Help me demonstrate my love for You—and others—in both my word and deed.

FEBRUARY 22

Then Christ will make his home in your hearts as you trust in him. Your roots will grow down into God's love and keep you strong. And may you have the power to understand, as all God's people should, how wide, how long, how high, and how deep his love is. May you experience the love of Christ, though it is too great to understand fully. Then you will be made complete with all the fullness of life and power that comes from God.

EPHESIANS 3:17–19 NLT

If someone tried to teach you algebra when you were in preschool, they probably ended up frustrated. Without a basic understanding of math, you couldn't grasp the higher concepts. But once you learned simple addition, you built up to more complex functions over time.

When Jesus stepped into your life, you began a different kind of education. As you trust Him and live in His love, your understanding of God's nature and power will grow deeper and more complex. You'll begin to realize "how wide, how long, how high, and how deep his love is."

Of course, you'll never fully understand Jesus' love for you. But you were made to experience it all the same—and that's an education you can't get at school.

MY PRAYER STARTER:

Lord, I know I still have a lot to learn—mentally and spiritually. Give me the patience and perseverance to stay on track as You teach me more about Your love.

FEBRUARY 23

Live with love as Christ loved you. He gave Himself for us,
a gift on the altar to God which was as a sweet smell to God.
EPHESIANS 5:2 NLV

Think of baked apple pie, fresh-cut grass, peppermint, and pine. Now imagine an agitated skunk, a dirty locker room, and rotten eggs. The nose knows what it likes and what it doesn't. When you catch a whiff of something good, you take a deep breath and smile. When you smell a stench, you grimace, hoping the odor dissipates soon.

According to today's scripture, loving others with Jesus' unconditional love is "a sweet smell to God." Imagine Him breathing deeply and smiling as He watches you treat others with kindness, forgive their offenses, and give up your preferences so that they will feel loved. It's a much better image than that of Him holding His nose.

How can you improve the "scent" of your life? By living out the love of Jesus.

MY PRAYER STARTER:
God, clean out whatever pieces of scrap and spiritual junk that may lie moldy in my soul. Replace them with the sweet smell of Your Spirit and love.

FEBRUARY 24

*"I have loved you just as My Father
has loved Me. Stay in My love."*

JOHN 15:9 NLV

You are the house that God built. First Corinthians 6:19–20 says, "Do you not know that your body is a house of God where the Holy Spirit lives? God gave you His Holy Spirit. Now you belong to God. You do not belong to yourselves. God bought you with a great price. So honor God with your body. You belong to Him."

When you invited Jesus into your house, He didn't show up as a cleaning service. He came to set your affairs in order. He became a permanent roommate. He's even laid out some helpful house rules He wants you to follow: "The one who loves Me will obey My teaching. My Father will love him. We will come to him and live with him" (John 14:23).

Once Jesus moves in with His love, He's not going anywhere. Now, He's asking you to stay with Him.

MY PRAYER STARTER:
Thank You, Father, for allowing Your Spirit to dwell with
me inside my soul. Let me never be a disagreeable host;
rather, help me conform my behaviors to fit Your will.

FEBRUARY 25

*And thou shalt love the Lord thy God with all thy heart,
and with all thy soul, and with all thy mind, and with
all thy strength: this is the first commandment.*

MARK 12:30 KJV

In today's scripture, Jesus summed up the point of humankind's existence: we are meant to love God. Why? Because He loved us enough to sacrifice His only Son so we could be with Him again in perfection. Because Jesus went all in with His love for us, we should go all in with our love for Him.

But what does that mean? Think of a romantic relationship. If the guy isn't fully invested, it doesn't matter how faithful the girl is. When a guy chooses selfishness, heartbreak follows.

Jesus doesn't want that kind of heartbreak for you. He's already proven His love by dying for our sins. Now He wants the same level of commitment from you—not only for Himself but for your own good.

Are you all in?

MY PRAYER STARTER:
Lord, thank You for Your unimaginable devotion to
me. May the knowledge of this love strengthen my own
devotion to You. I never want to betray Your trust.

FEBRUARY 26

"The second is equally important: 'Love your neighbor as yourself.' No other commandment is greater than these."

MARK 12:31 NLT

When Jesus went all in with His love for you, He didn't half-fill your love tank. He filled it to overflowing. But what should you do with all that overflowing love? You pass it along to the people around you.

We were made to love God above all else, and one way to do that is to care for our neighbors, provide for the poor, take care of widows and orphans, and lend our voice to those whom society has refused to hear.

Jesus paid the ultimate price to give you His love. When He paid the cost of sin, your life obtained value in God's eyes. Now Jesus wants you to ascribe value to others in the same way.

Love your neighbor as yourself because Jesus' love overflows within you.

MY PRAYER STARTER:
God, I don't want to let my love grow half hearted and stale. You gave everything for me, so help me give what I have—for You and for others.

FEBRUARY 27

*By this shall all men know that ye are my
disciples, if ye have love one to another.*

JOHN 13:35 KJV

Uniforms make it easy to identify a person's livelihood. Firefighters wear turnout gear, chefs wear a white toque, and professional hockey players wear skates and lots of padding. But when it comes to identifying a person's faith, there is no physical uniform—no clothing embroidered with a cross or ichthys (the "Jesus fish").

But Jesus said the world would recognize that we follow Him when we love each other. That love should be visible, wholehearted, and markedly different from the love of the world. Christ's love enables us to see the needs of others, to meet them sacrificially, and to defer any praise we receive to the one who ultimately deserves it.

If your love for other believers is not as obvious as a firefighter's uniform, it isn't visible enough. Jesus doesn't want you to wear a Christian T-shirt; He wants you to *demonstrate* His love.

MY PRAYER STARTER:
Lord, let my life be a vibrant uniform, proclaiming
to everyone who sees me that I'm on Your team—
and giving them a reason to join as well.

FEBRUARY 28

Everything you do should be done in love.
1 CORINTHIANS 16:14 NLV

If love is the identifying trait of Christ-followers, then love should be evident in everything we do. Love isn't something we bring out for special occasions like birthdays and family reunions. Love should be present in every mundane task too.

Fold your laundry with love. Wash the dishes with love. Greet your neighbors—even the ones who don't clean up after their dogs—with love. Obey your parents with love. Do your homework with love. Go to church with love. Do everything with love.

Remember that love is defined as "unselfish loyal and benevolent concern for the good of another." Jesus lived, died, and rose again with love saturating His every action He took. Pray that *you* will be saturated with His overflowing love. Turn your heart and mind and soul and strength to God and to the people around you. And love like Jesus in everything you do.

MY PRAYER STARTER:

Having love as an attribute is nice, Lord, but I don't want to stop there. Help love be my primary motivator behind every action I perform—my sole purpose in living each day.

MARCH 1

Jesus Christ the same yesterday, and to day, and for ever.
HEBREWS 13:8 KJV

Rebirth. It's a spring thing—and it's beautiful. Not long ago, all the summer greenery turned orange, red, yellow, or brown. But when winter arrived, much of the old growth was dislodged from trees, gardens, and fields by the chill wind. Spring is that blank slate on which Jesus paints brilliant colors all around. He does it every year.

You can get used to this changing of seasons. When spring gives way to summer and summer's end is heralded by the coming of frost, "The grass withereth, the flower fadeth" (Isaiah 40:8). Then you wait again for the coming of spring.

Not all change is as predictable or pleasant. That's why Isaiah 40:8 continues with a beautiful promise: "The word of our God shall stand for ever."

Seasons change all the time. God's Word never does. So enjoy this spring as a time of physical rebirth, remembering that Jesus offers *spiritual* rebirth—one that forever begins and never ends.

MY PRAYER STARTER:
Lord, as the trees around me burst into full bloom,
let my spirit do the same. Rejuvenate my soul with
reminders of Your goodness and grace.

MARCH 2

. . .to be made new in the attitude of your minds;
and to put on the new self, created to be like
God in true righteousness and holiness.
EPHESIANS 4:23–24 NIV

Do you remember what your *old* life was like? It didn't require an education. *You* made the rules. You followed your heart. You didn't feel any obligation to obey anyone at any time for any reason. But as long as your decisions didn't match up with Jesus' plan for you, you never found freedom.

For Christians, the old life is a wardrobe we have to get rid of. Jesus planned it that way: "For we know that our old self was crucified with him" (as you give up your past way of living) "so that the body ruled by sin might be done away with, that we should no longer be slaves to sin" (Romans 6:6).

It's impossible to begin a new life when your old life hangs in the closet. Toss it out! Put on Jesus' new wardrobe.

MY PRAYER STARTER:

God, I never want to go back to the way things were before
I met You. If any remnant of my old life is still clinging
to me, help me find it and toss it out once and for all.

MARCH 3

*Put on your new nature, and be renewed as you learn
to know your Creator and become like him.*
Colossians 3:10 nlt

Jesus came so that you could be like Him—and you will never look more like Jesus than when you trust Him enough to obey. Even people who don't love Jesus still love people who show His compassion.

At some point, you will need to rethink your options. You can act like everyone else and blend in with all your friends—or you could change. Jesus called that rebirth, and He's ready to help. He explained, "Humans can reproduce only human life, but the Holy Spirit gives birth to spiritual life" (John 3:6).

Your mom gave you life, but Jesus gives you *abundant* life. You can live for the moment, or you can prepare for eternity. Stay the same or be different.

Sure, there's a process in rebirth, but change comes to those who ask. You won't be left alone to do the impossible. There will be all kinds of next steps, and Jesus takes each one with you. Keep walking with Him.

MY PRAYER STARTER:
Thank You, Lord, for offering me a chance to become more like You. Help me to use this privilege every chance I get, even if it means becoming unpopular. Your reward will be worth it all.

MARCH 4

*As Christ was raised from the dead by the great
power of God, so we will have new life also.*

ROMANS 6:4 NLV

God is especially wise, making sure that many of the things you read in the New Testament had a prequel in the Old Testament. For example, by bringing dead men back to life from a mass of dry bones before Ezekiel's eyes (Ezekiel 37), God foreshadowed Jesus' resurrection and gave Ezekiel a physical picture of what God would do spiritually.

New life implies the experience of a fresh beginning. Everyone starts physical life by dying spiritually, but Jesus made sure you have a second chance. He made it very clear how important His offer was when He said, "Unless a man is born again, he cannot see the holy nation of God" (John 3:3).

If you haven't accepted this new spiritual life, then you can't really look forward to a home in heaven. Look at it this way: God gave you a limited life on earth—Jesus gives the opportunity to enjoy a life that's new and eternal.

MY PRAYER STARTER:

Lord, help me to always see the significance of Your gift of salvation. May its awe-inspiring grandeur never be lost in the mundaneness of everyday life.

MARCH 5

For they that are after the flesh do mind the things of the flesh;
but they that are after the Spirit the things of the Spirit.

ROMANS 8:5 KJV

We live in a disposable world. None of your technology and clothing are meant to last, and no one even expects them to. Things that were once repaired are now simply replaced. Most of us think repair just isn't worth it.

But Jesus has a different, more radical idea. No one is left without the offer to be made new. This offer isn't self-help, a makeover, or upcycling—it's an exchange of spiritual components. What you have is faulty thinking and a deceptive heart. What you get is a new mind and the gift of God's Spirit, who leads you to truth. Jesus explained, "I will pray the Father, and he shall give you another Comforter, that he may abide with you for ever; even the Spirit of truth. . .for he dwelleth with you, and shall be in you" (John 14:16–17).

You did not have God's Spirit before you accepted Jesus' offer of rescue. Now? You have a Mentor, Teacher, and Guidance Counselor. You never have to be the same as you were before.

MY PRAYER STARTER:

Lord God, thank You for assuring me that, unlike all my
earthly hopes and possessions, Your new life is built to last.

MARCH 6

*Therefore, if anyone is in Christ, the new creation
has come: The old has gone, the new is here!*
2 CORINTHIANS 5:17 NIV

No one has ever been—or never will be—like Jesus. The most unusual thing about Him was that He never sinned. Not even once. Instead of demanding that others help Him, He *offered* help wherever He went. His life was not remembered for the many demands He made, but for the burdens He removed from the backs of sinners.

Those who met Jesus marveled at the mercy and power that followed Him. They said, "What is this? A new teaching—and with authority!" (Mark 1:27). His teaching on a new covenant led to new life, and forgiveness was delivered through the sacrifice of Himself—God's only Son. This is where grace made you part of God's family, where eternal life became standard.

Jesus had full authority on earth because He came with the full backing of the God who has always wanted a relationship with you. That relationship comes with new-life living.

MY PRAYER STARTER:
Lord Jesus, I know that I could never live up
to Your standard. Thank You for offering me
grace and eternal life despite my failures.

MARCH 7

All praise to God, the Father of our Lord Jesus Christ.
It is by his great mercy that we have been
born again, because God raised Jesus Christ from
the dead. Now we live with great expectation.

1 PETER 1:3 NLT

The idea of rebirth would never have been possible without Jesus. People had a date of birth and a date of death, but being right with God in between was impossible because every human has sinned (Romans 3:23). God accepts nothing less than perfection, so everyone is disqualified, early and often.

Satan used that fact to his own advantage. Jesus said, "The thief's purpose is to steal and kill and destroy." You've seen that in action. However, Jesus then explained why He came to live among humanity: "My purpose is to give them a rich and satisfying life" (John 10:10).

The life Jesus gives is now and forever. That's rebirth—and it can belong to you.

Rebirth is yours through three life-changing steps that Jesus exemplified—death-burial-resurrection. His sacrifice introduced rebirth to people who struggled to believe it was even possible.

MY PRAYER STARTER:

Thank You, Jesus, for coming to earth with a mission to offer us rebirth. May I always remember the price You paid— and how much better my life has become as a result.

MARCH 8

"This is what I tell you to do: Love each
other just as I have loved you."
JOHN 15:12 NLV

This book is called *Jesus Each Day*, and you'll meet Him right here—each day. There's plenty to talk about—even the Bible doesn't try to share every bit of His story. John 21:25 (NLV) says, "There are many other things which Jesus did also. If they were all written down, I do not think the world itself could hold the books that would be written."

You might hear the rest of His story someday, but the Bible provides everything you need to experience rebirth *today*. Here are the bare bones of the rebirth process: (1) you needed rescue, (2) you couldn't rescue yourself, (3) God sent Jesus as His rescue plan, and (4) you choose to accept His rescue.

You don't need to know everything Jesus did to know that He did more than enough. You don't need to know every word He said to know He spoke truth. You don't need to know His every example of compassion to know He loves you.

MY PRAYER STARTER:
Lord, thank You for making the rebirth process easy to understand. As I learn more about You, help me always remember and appreciate the gospel's beautiful simplicity.

MARCH 9

Jesus said, Suffer little children, and forbid them not,
to come unto me: for of such is the kingdom of heaven.
MATTHEW 19:14 KJV

New life can feel a bit like starting over as a small child. . .and that's okay. Children express wonder and delight. They throw themselves into the middle of adventure. They laugh and ask lots of questions. Everything is new and worth discovering. They don't always get things right, but that's to be expected. Jesus once said, "Except ye be converted, and become as little children, ye shall not enter into the kingdom of heaven" (Matthew 18:3).

Just as you are still maturing physically, you can't expect to be spiritually reborn as a fully grown adult. You'll have some growing to do. You won't pass every test. You might have selective hearing. You might even fall. But it's easier to trust when you're a child. New life is the starting line of a new race—with Jesus as your companion.

Don't be too sophisticated to embrace the faith of a child, too stubborn to let go of your past, or too smart to learn God's perspective.

MY PRAYER STARTER:
I realize, Lord, that I still have some spiritual growing
to do. Help me embrace the learning process as
You teach me more about Your truths.

MARCH 10

"If you love me, keep my commands."

JOHN 14:15 NIV

God's instructions for new life include obedience. You can't follow Jesus if you think the word *follow* is an option—something to take or leave based on your mood or preference.

Jesus wanted children to spend time with Him. They needed to learn. They needed to see love firsthand. It was easier for them to follow. God chose these words for the apostle Paul to write: "Children, obey your parents in the Lord, for this is right. 'Honor your father and mother'—which is the first commandment with a promise—'so that it may go well with you and that you may enjoy long life on the earth' " (Ephesians 6:1–3).

These verses can easily be applied to new Christians: "Children, obey the Lord, for this is right. Honor your Father so that it may go well with you and that you may enjoy eternal life." Obedience is what transforms your relationship with God.

Embrace this new life and take advantage of each opportunity to obey God. When you do, you'll find even greater satisfaction in this new-life adventure.

MY PRAYER STARTER:

Lord, help me not to see following You as a chore;
rather, help me love You so much that every
part of my soul desires to be obedient.

MARCH 11

*"I am the light of the world. If you follow
me, you won't have to walk in darkness,
because you will have the light that leads to life."*

JOHN 8:12 NLT

Jesus gave His life—perfect and pure. He paid the price for the sin of every human who has ever lived or ever will. When He rose, new life arrived—not just for Him but for you as well.

When you accept that new birth, you get to experience some of what His sacrifice was like. Jesus invites you to use the new life He gave you and sacrifice it for Him. As His great apostle, Paul, wrote: "Dear brothers and sisters, I plead with you to give your bodies to God because of all he has done for you." Just to clarify, God is not asking you to kill yourself. . .read on: "Let them be a *living* and holy sacrifice—the kind he will find acceptable" (Romans 12:1, emphasis added).

New life offers new opportunities to put your old ways to death. Old habits can be traded for new. Obedience is now preferred to rebellion. New life is abundant life, and it sacrifices everything that opposes God's efforts to make the changes you need.

MY PRAYER STARTER:

Lord God, I want to offer my whole life to You—
not just the parts I think I can afford giving up.
Give me the willingness to do so today.

MARCH 12

*Jesus said to them all, "If anyone wants to
follow Me, he must give up himself and his own desires.
He must take up his cross everyday and follow Me."*

LUKE 9:23 NLV

Before His death on the cross, Jesus invited His disciples to test-drive their new life. These men each had their own careers, and they had every reason to believe they would work their jobs for the rest of their lives. But then they heard Jesus say, "Follow Me. I will make you fish for men!" (Matthew 4:19).

The disciples would have a new job—to learn about the new life coming to humankind and then to share what they had learned. People would respond. It was impossible for anyone to know this fantastic news and keep quiet.

Sadly, some disciples hesitated, gave excuses, or refused. But Jesus offered those people the opportunity just like He does today.

If you have responded affirmatively, you have a new job: follow Jesus and fish for people! But if you're hesitating, giving excuses, or refusing to follow, consider this: the right choice results in an all-access pass to God's family—forever.

MY PRAYER STARTER:
God, help me be passionate about fishing for people.
Give me opportunities each day to share the good
news with everyone around me. Even if I only get
one "catch," it'll be worth a lifetime of effort.

MARCH 13

*Let us not be weary in well doing: for in due
season we shall reap, if we faint not.*

GALATIANS 6:9 KJV

Are you tired? Have you been waiting for summer break, the weekend, or even just a good night's sleep? If so, you know this process is neither fun nor productive. Fatigue demands a solution.

This weariness isn't a physical ailment but a weariness of the soul. It often shows up when we try to do everything on our own while silently rejecting Jesus' help. He understands more than we think. Maybe that's why He said, "Come unto me, all ye that labour and are heavy laden, and I will give you rest." This invitation sounds perfect, until Jesus says, "Take my yoke upon you, and learn of me." What? A "yoke" sounds like more work! But the promise continues: "And ye shall find rest unto your souls." Why? "My yoke is easy, and my burden is light" (Matthew 11:28–30).

This is more refreshing than ice cream on a hot day, rest after a long week, or an amazing vacation after a hard school year. New life knows where to find restoration. . .and that's with Jesus.

MY PRAYER STARTER:

Father, You know that I sometimes feel overly exhausted.
When this happens, teach me to lean fully on Your help
and understanding. Only then will I find true rest.

MARCH 14

Taste and see that the LORD is good;
blessed is the one who takes refuge in him.
PSALM 34:8 NIV

Rebirth requires a new diet. In our old lives, we feasted on a diet of anger, bitterness, and rage, but the benefits of new life are nourished by different "foods." Jesus said, "Man shall not live on bread alone, but on every word that comes from the mouth of God" (Matthew 4:4).

The Word of God offers every ingredient for a satisfying spiritual meal. Don't ever think scripture is just a nice snack if you have the time. This thinking yields weak and malnourished believers. A steady diet of anything less than God's Word leaves us sick and vulnerable to disease.

God created the physical food your body needs as well as the spiritual food that is essential to your soul. Even Jesus needed that bread, which is "every word that comes from the mouth of God." Follow His example, and eat well!

MY PRAYER STARTER:
Lord Jesus, just as food satisfies my body,
I know that Your Word satisfies my spiritual
hunger. Help me to never lose that craving.

MARCH 15

"I am giving you a new commandment: Love each other.
Just as I have loved you, you should love each other."

JOHN 13:34 NLT

It is human nature to treat others the way they treat you. But this reaction extends no forgiveness and offers no hope to the offender. It simply amplifies the problem, making it even bigger than it should be.

When we are angry over some offense or hurt, a canyon develops between us and other people. And our old, sinful selves devise punishments we believe fit the crime. Our world says, "If someone hurts you, return the favor." Jesus, though, has something else in mind: "Do to others whatever you would like them to do to you" (Matthew 7:12).

When we are reborn in Jesus, some things are turned upside down. We'll treat others with kindness when they are rude. We'll respond in love when hate shows up. We'll replace "I told you so" with compassion. New life means living a new way.

MY PRAYER STARTER:

Lord, help me react fairly to unfairness, kindly to rudeness, and lovingly to hatred. Help me treat others as You have treated me.

MARCH 16

There are many people who belong to Christ.
And yet, we are one body which is Christ's.
We are all different but we depend on each other.
ROMANS 12:5 NLV

Some people are good at speaking in public or giving a persuasive argument. Some are accomplished singers or painters. Have you wondered why not everyone can do these things with equal skill?

The church of Jesus Christ—what the Bible calls His "body"—would be ineffective if everyone were good at the same thing. You were given a unique gift, and Jesus wants you to use it to "go and make followers of all the nations." Take what you learn and "teach them to do all the things [Jesus has] told you." When that seems hard, remember Jesus' promise: "I am with you always, even to the end of the world" (Matthew 28:19–20).

A human body isn't a kneecap. It wouldn't do well if it were solely an earlobe, eyebrow, or philtrum (look it up). New life recognizes God's unique gifts, so instead of wanting to be what you're not, learn to be useful with who you are.

MY PRAYER STARTER:
Thank You, Lord, for giving me a unique gift. Grant me
the humility to work side-by-side with other Christians
as we use our gifts to draw nonbelievers to You.

MARCH 17

Jesus saith unto him, I am the way, the truth, and the
life: no man cometh unto the Father, but by me.
JOHN 14:6 KJV

When you began following Jesus, He gave you new life. But this life isn't based on your ability to do better in the future than you did in the past. It isn't a grading system. It isn't a competitive sport. It's trusting that Jesus' sacrifice was enough to make things right between you and God the Father. It's believing that second chances are for you. . .if you're willing to admit that God is right, you were wrong, and forgiveness is real.

Jesus didn't come into the world to make things hard for you. He's on your side! "God sent not his Son into the world to condemn the world; but that the world through him might be saved" (John 3:17).

The more you trust Jesus, the more you'll see that He's worth following. Since He's worth following, you might find yourself wanting to do for others what He's done for you. He brings truth, and that truth is that He loved you enough to save you forever.

MY PRAYER STARTER:
Thank You, Jesus, for making salvation easily available. After hearing such great news, how could I ever keep quiet about it? Give me courage to share the gospel with others.

MARCH 18

*"The kingdom of God has come near.
Repent and believe the good news!"*
MARK 1:15 NIV

Jesus once told a story about God's kingdom. He said it was like "yeast that a woman took and mixed into about sixty pounds of flour until it worked all through the dough" (Matthew 13:33).

Like yeast, your new life in Christ becomes larger in the waiting. Just as changes occur in the dough while the baker waits, changes happen within your own life (and the life of His entire family) as His kingdom grows.

There is wisdom in the waiting. Bread is ruined if the baker doesn't let the dough rise before putting it in the oven. Waiting is even important to God—it's a fundamental part of the mercy He shows toward His often-disobedient creation. And in God's perfect time, the kingdom will be filled with people who were rescued from their personal rebellion through Jesus' sacrifice.

While we wait, God's kingdom is growing.

MY PRAYER STARTER:
Lord, I realize that Your plan is much bigger
than I can grasp, so teach me how to be patient—
just as You have been patient with me.

MARCH 19

[Jesus] saved us, not because of the righteous things we had done, but because of his mercy. He washed away our sins, giving us a new birth and new life through the Holy Spirit.

TITUS 3:5 NLT

The jeweler knew that plenty of oysters meant plenty of pearls. For years, he searched (mostly in vain) for quality pearls, until one day, his trained eye spotted something he'd never seen in a pearl—perfection. Though he owned lots of things, selling them came easily. He traded quantity for quality. He purchased the perfect pearl.

This story summarizes a parable of Jesus that compares the worth of what we own with the value of what God offers. The jeweler was convinced that he was making a good deal: "When he discovered a pearl of great value, he sold everything he owned and bought it!" (Matthew 13:46).

Missionary Jim Elliot understood the value of trading what we know for everything God offers. He said, "He is no fool who gives what he cannot keep to gain that which he cannot lose." Like the pearl, this trade only increases in value.

What have you traded in exchange for God?

MY PRAYER STARTER:

Lord, Your gift of salvation is worth more than a million priceless pearls. May I never place so much value on the physical that I lose sight of Your spiritual reality.

MARCH 20

"I will never turn away anyone who comes to Me."
JOHN 6:37 NLV

A landowner needed help in his vineyard. He found workers, invited them to work for the day, and offered a full day's wage. Many accepted and went to work.

Because there was a lot of work to be done, the landowner went out three more times from morning to late afternoon to hire new help.

At the end of the day, he paid each worker a full day's wages. This angered those who had come to work early. After all, they reasoned, the others hadn't worked as long as they had, so they deserved less than those who came to work early should receive. Jesus spoke the words of the owner of the vineyard: "Do I not have the right to do what I want to do with my own money?" (Matthew 20:15).

This is the story of your rescue, your own change from law-breaker to Christ-follower. Given your age, you probably haven't been following Jesus as long as many of the adults in your church have. However, you—just like them—still receive *all* of God's love and forgiveness as well as His eternal kingdom.

MY PRAYER STARTER:
Lord, thank You for not discriminating based on
age or experience. Help me to keep working for You,
knowing Your rewards will be worth the labor.

MARCH 21

Draw nigh to God, and he will draw nigh
to you. Cleanse your hands, ye sinners;
and purify your hearts, ye double minded.
JAMES 4:8 KJV

Jesus once told His followers about a business owner who was going on a trip. The man gave his three managers some money, hoping they would get busy and make fruitful investments. When he returned, two of the managers had doubled their money. But the third man said, "I was afraid, and went and hid thy talent in the earth" (Matthew 25:25). This manager hadn't learned to invest wisely.

As Christians, the only things we truly own are the choices we make—everything else is a gift from God. New life in Jesus makes us managers of God's resources.

God has always wanted you to use your gifts to make Him famous, to help other people, and to do the things Jesus would do. You can play a role in advancing God's plans! Just be willing to use your new life to benefit those around you.

MY PRAYER STARTER:
Lord Jesus, may the gifts You've given me never lie
dormant on the shelf. Let me find new and creative
ways to use them to bring glory to You.

*Be kind and compassionate to one another,
forgiving each other, just as in Christ God forgave you.*
EPHESIANS 4:32 NIV

A banker lent money to two customers. After their time was up, one owed about eighteen month's salary, while the other owed about two month's worth. Neither could pay. After reviewing both files, the banker chose to forgive each man.

Jesus told this story and waited for His Pharisee host to respond. Which of the two men felt the most forgiven? Who would have a stronger emotional connection to the banker? Simon replied, "I suppose the one who had the bigger debt forgiven" (Luke 7:43).

This conversation was meant for the ears of those who were eating a meal with Jesus. The questioning started when a woman—who was a well-known sinner—came into Simon's house and wiped Jesus' feet with her tears, pouring expensive perfume on Him. And Jesus forgave her.

She heard Jesus' words too. This woman would remember this act of forgiveness more than most, and it would introduce her to new life. That is a picture of God's heart. And Jesus is our picture of God Himself.

MY PRAYER STARTER:
Father, Your forgiveness sometimes seems too good
to be true—and yet it's real. So when my friends and
enemies treat me poorly, help me remember this
forgiveness and reflect it toward others as well.

MARCH 23

"Be sure of this: I am with you always, even to the end of the age."
MATTHEW 28:20 NLT

Have you ever misplaced money? Perhaps you were saving up for a new video game, a new pair of shoes, or even a Christmas present for someone else. You looked for it, prayed about it, and wondered how you could ever replace it.

Jesus told a story like that. In this story, a woman lost a coin that she couldn't afford to lose. She made sure there was plenty of light for searching and a broom for reaching, and she kept straining her eyes for what was lost. She couldn't continue on without that coin. When she found it, she was so grateful she went door to door, sharing her joy with neighbors and friends.

The same Jesus who told this story looked for the lost *you*. He shined His light into darkness, reached into the place where you were, and kept His eyes focused on you. When He found you, all of heaven celebrated: "There is joy in the presence of God's angels when even one sinner repents" (Luke 15:10). This is rebirth. This is new life.

MY PRAYER STARTER:
Lord, thank You for searching for me before I even realized I needed to be found. Help me to always appreciate and revel in this magnificent grace.

MARCH 24

I am sure that God Who began the good work in you will keep
on working in you until the day Jesus Christ comes again.
PHILIPPIANS 1:6 NLV

Accepting Jesus is an invitation to lifelong learning. God knows
what you need to know more than you do—and no one can learn
it all in a single lecture.

So He offers ongoing education. You may want this learning
to be a crash course, or you might want to pick and choose the
classes you'll take. But God doesn't want you to minor in a subject
that interests you—He wants you to major in knowing *Him*.

When we find ourselves in the middle of new circumstances,
we struggle. We remember the past, wrestle with new choices,
and sometimes tell ourselves that class attendance is optional.

If you think you already know enough about God, resist the
urge to put your Bible aside. Pick it up and read, knowing that
Jesus said, "Everyone who listens to the Father and learns from
Him comes to Me" (John 6:45).

Learn from God—discover Jesus. Discover Jesus—find new
life. Find new life—enjoy fresh hope.

MY PRAYER STARTER:
Lord, thank You for being the perfect teacher. Help me not
to read Your Word like I'm in a stuffy classroom; rather, give
me a sense of awe that fuels my desire to learn even more.

MARCH 25

A new heart also will I give you, and a new spirit will I put within you: and I will take away the stony heart out of your flesh, and I will give you an heart of flesh.

EZEKIEL 36:26 KJV

New life. You can't enhance it, improve it, or even take credit for it. You might want to. You might even feel like you need to do something to earn it. But God owns grace and He created new life. They're His to give. He won't sell at any price. Ephesians 2:8 says, "By grace are ye saved through faith; and that not of yourselves: it is the gift of God."

New life is a gift of God, not a half-and-half deal in which God provides only a partial rescue. If it were something you could half do, you might think that was good enough. . .and miss out on the whole goodness of God. You'd be in a dangerous, half-rescued place, which is no rescue at all.

Broken, jaded, hardened people need full rescue. You can never manufacture new life on your own—that's why Jesus offers it all.

MY PRAYER STARTER:

Lord Jesus, since I am only human, I need continuous reminders of how helpless I am without Your mercy. Keep me humble and appreciative of this unthinkable gift.

MARCH 26

Everyone born of God overcomes the world. This is the
victory that has overcome the world, even our faith.

1 JOHN 5:4 NIV

Plenty of philosophies seek to convince us that we don't really need God's rescue. You might hear phrases like "Do what you want because this life is all you will ever have." Other voices say, "God is not real, so there's no reason to trust Him."

But in order to be rescued, you have to believe there is someone who rescues. If you don't believe, you won't accept. The apostle Paul knew people would need clarity on the subject, so he wrote, "For us there is but one God, the Father, from whom all things came and for whom we live; and there is but one Lord, Jesus Christ, through whom all things came and through whom we live" (1 Corinthians 8:6).

Your faith in God and His Son, Jesus, helps you overcome the obstacles that keep you from rebirth. Jesus overcame the philosophies men dreamed up—so when people say He can't save, just remember that He always has.

MY PRAYER STARTER:

Lord, all the different viewpoints that struggle for my attention can sometimes wear me down and confuse me. Help me to hear Your voice through the static.

MARCH 27

*We are citizens of heaven, where the Lord Jesus Christ
lives. And we are eagerly waiting for him to return as
our Savior. He will take our weak mortal bodies and
change them into glorious bodies like his own.*

PHILIPPIANS 3:20–21 NLT

Jesus healed some, fed others, and taught all who would listen. He had been doing all three when He was told that His friend Lazarus was dying. Jesus saw this HELP WANTED sign but delayed long enough that Lazarus died in the waiting.

When Jesus arrived, the dead man's sister Martha asked the Lord why He didn't come sooner. That's when Lazarus became an object lesson. Jesus told her, "I am the resurrection and the life. Anyone who believes in me will live, even after dying" (John 11:25). This must have confused Martha. She believed Jesus was the Messiah who could have healed her brother; however, she didn't anticipate Jesus' next move—to raise her brother from the dead!

Martha saw new life firsthand. Maybe she needed confirmation that the one who could rescue spiritually also had the power to rescue from death itself.

MY PRAYER STARTER:

Lord, I know death will come one day, even if I don't think of it often now. Help me never to view it with anxiety— because of Your victory over death, I have no reason to fear.

MARCH 28

Even when we were dead because of our sins, He made
us alive by what Christ did for us. You have been
saved from the punishment of sin by His loving-favor.
God raised us up from death when He raised up Christ
Jesus. He has given us a place with Christ in the heavens.
EPHESIANS 2:5–6 NLV

Jesus rose from the dead. He raised His friend Lazarus from the dead. And, if you believe in Him, Jesus will raise you from the dead too. "You get what is coming to you when you sin. It is death! But God's free gift is life that lasts forever. It is given to us by our Lord Jesus Christ" (Romans 6:23).

Rebirth brings new life, and that's just what you need—what you've *always* needed. You've tried everything you can to be perfect, but it's never happened. You've been dead spiritually, and there will come a time when you are dead physically. But that's not the end of the story.

Death is a part of the human experience. But because Jesus wanted you to spend eternity with Him, He offers life—abundant, free, eternal life.

MY PRAYER STARTER:
Even though I know I will die someday, Lord, I
know that You will be waiting for me on the other
side. Thank You for this glorious promise!

MARCH 29

*We are his workmanship, created in
Christ Jesus unto good works, which God hath
before ordained that we should walk in them.*

EPHESIANS 2:10 KJV

Have you ever started something new and immediately became an expert? No? Well, neither has anyone else. Even your most admired hero—whether he's a guitar player, athlete, actor, or scientist—has gone through an extensive, grueling learning process. He had to focus on learning, show perseverance, and allow his skills to develop.

In both the physical and spiritual realm, fruit doesn't start fully formed either. It begins as a seed then grows as it's nurtured and fed. In our Christian lives, Jesus does that through His Spirit. Here's how the apostle Paul described the end result: "The fruit of the Spirit is love, joy, peace, longsuffering, gentleness, goodness, faith, meekness, temperance: against such there is no law" (Galatians 5:22–23).

Whenever rebirth seems like a struggle, remember that Jesus is just getting started.

MY PRAYER STARTER:

Lord, my faith sometimes feels light-years behind where I want it to be. Thank You for giving me a lifetime of second chances. Help me not to squander even one of them.

MARCH 30

*I am not ashamed of the gospel, because it is the power
of God that brings salvation to everyone who believes.*
ROMANS 1:16 NIV

If you have new life in Jesus and are living in that new life, why would you even want to hide it? Perhaps you remember times when you've acted in front of your friends like Jesus was no big deal to you. Maybe you've been a bit like Peter, denying that you know Him in order to stave off ridicule. This is why Jesus said, "Let your light shine before others, that they may see your good deeds and glorify your Father in heaven" (Matthew 5:16).

Jesus is light and He brings you light. He is life and He brings you life. He is love and He brings you love. This is the best news of the day, and it's made for sharing. That's what people with new life do. What can you do today to share the good news?

MY PRAYER STARTER:
Lord, my friends sometimes don't understand what You've done in my life, but that doesn't mean I have to hide it. Give me courage to shine Your light—even when it's unpopular.

MARCH 31

Those who belong to Christ Jesus have nailed the passions and desires of their sinful nature to his cross and crucified them there.
GALATIANS 5:24 NLT

Today you get one more look at rebirth. The apostle Paul spoke personally when he wrote, "My old self has been crucified with Christ. It is no longer I who live, but Christ lives in me. So I live in this earthly body by trusting in the Son of God, who loved me and gave himself for me" (Galatians 2:20).

Maybe you connect with Paul's words. Maybe you can say, "Every part of who I was has to be set aside daily so that I can make the choices God created me to make. Jesus died for me, and I put my past to death so that I can live in a broken body with an immortal heart. I will trust that Jesus is the only one who can help me live this new life."

You've been given new life. It's important. It has value. Others need to know about it. Acknowledge your imperfections and then introduce your friends and neighbors to a perfect Savior. You can't save others, but you know who can. Make *Him* known.

MY PRAYER STARTER:
Lord, may my every word and action point beyond myself and toward Your Spirit who is working within. Help me replace pride with praise. Let others see You in me.

APRIL 1

*God is able to do much more than we ask or
think through His power working in us.*

EPHESIANS 3:20 NLV

Today we begin a month dedicated to blessings. It's not about the shape or size of the blessing—it's about the appreciation of God's generosity and abundance.

Jesus never shortchanges when it comes to blessings. His good friend John spoke of Jesus' blessings when he wrote, "From Him Who has so much we have all received loving-favor, one loving-favor after another" (John 1:16).

One blessing after another! Benefits that never end! Care that commits to the long haul! This is Jesus. This is a summary of His blessings. They arrive when you least expect them, subtly nudging you into the center of His path.

April is a month dedicated to blessings. One month is not nearly enough, but it's a start. These next few weeks will prove that Jesus loves you. He always has.

MY PRAYER STARTER:

Lord, I'd never be able to thank You enough for all the undeserved benefits You've given me. When life gets rough, help me count my blessings and turn my attention to You.

APRIL 2

In lowliness of mind let each esteem other better than themselves.
PHILIPPIANS 2:3 KJV

Walking toward Jericho, a Jewish man was ambushed, beaten, robbed, and left injured and alone. The traveler needed help. It didn't seem like he was in line for a blessing.

Two men who could (and should) have helped simply walked past without stopping. But a man from Samaria—a rival culture that didn't get along with the Jews—chose to reach out and help the injured traveler. The Samaritan then "set him on his own beast, and brought him to an inn, and took care of him" (Luke 10:34).

This parable of Jesus tells a story of blessings from unexpected places. The Jewish religious leaders didn't want to hear that God would help anyone other than the Jews. Many were surprised that Jesus would speak kindly of people who were considered outcasts.

Maybe you know some people at your school or church who simply don't fit in—who are rejected by the "popular" crowd. Just as God cared about the Samaritans, He cares about those people too—and so should you.

MY PRAYER STARTER:
Lord, open my eyes to the "Samaritans" in my life.
Help me not to be afraid to reach out to them and tell them about You—they might be some of the only ones who will listen.

APRIL 3

*"Seek first his kingdom and his righteousness,
and all these things will be given to you as well."*

MATTHEW 6:33 NIV

Worry inhibits our blessing vision. The more you worry, the less attention you'll pay to the non-stop stream of blessings. If you don't believe that, it may be beneficial to remember that you're still alive, breathing, and aware of your surroundings. Countless people no longer share that luxury—but you do. God has taken care of you in the past, and He is strong enough to keep providing. If He took a break, nothing would survive.

But God never takes breaks. That's why Jesus said, "Do not worry, saying, 'What shall we eat?' or 'What shall we drink?' or 'What shall we wear?' . . . Your heavenly Father knows that you need them" (Matthew 6:31–32).

You can't use worry as a prayer. Worry doesn't request—it wonders. It asks questions that become billboards of doubt for others to read. Worry admits you aren't sure God's blessings are real.

Count your most visible blessings and keep counting. Your blessing vision will improve.

MY PRAYER STARTER:

Lord God, replace my worry with gratitude. May the memory of Your blessings in the past guide my thoughts about the future.

APRIL 4

[God] has given me a new song to sing, a hymn of praise to our God. Many will see what he has done and be amazed. They will put their trust in the LORD.

PSALM 40:3 NLT

Psalm 139 indicates God knew you before you were born. Nothing about you is unknown to Him. John 3 indicates He loved you enough to rescue you. Ephesians 1:3 says God has "blessed us with every spiritual blessing in the heavenly realms because we are united with Christ." Your blessing plate is full.

God made you, knows you, loves you, and keeps blessing you. This combination should lead to praise. Praise is more than being grateful. It includes honor and glory. God is all that you need and more than you could expect. He gives you more than you can ever give Him, yet what He wants most is a place in your life that influences decisions, changes thinking, and offers the best kind of adventures.

If God blesses you and you find it amazing, then tell your friends. When you receive more than you know you deserve, praise Him. By taking time to remember His goodness, you can make His name famous.

MY PRAYER STARTER:
Father, may I never grow complacent with the blessings You've given me. May open praise always be my natural response so that others can know what You've done.

APRIL 5

Christ was tempted in every way we
are tempted, but He did not sin.
HEBREWS 4:15 NLV

It might be easy to tell God, "But you just don't understand!" But He does understand. In fact, "Christ became human flesh and lived among us." Jesus knew the pain involved in maturing into adulthood. He knew how it felt to be tempted, ridiculed, and overlooked. He knew the difficulties of being human. But instead of becoming jaded and frustrated, Jesus "was full of loving-favor and truth" (John 1:14).

It would be hard to interact comfortably with a God who doesn't understand you. Therein lies the blessing. God wanted you to understand Him, but you couldn't. His Son became like you so that there would be no misunderstanding about the struggles you face. Consequently, the God who understands you can now help you understand Him. That's relationship. That's blessing.

You may have never realized what a blessing it was that God took such lengths to help you understand Him. Think about it now, and let this truth sink deep into your soul: you'll never face anything that Jesus can't understand.

MY PRAYER STARTER:
Thank You, Jesus, for leaving the perfection
of heaven in order to find common ground
between us. Thank You for being so relatable.

APRIL 6

Let your conversation be without covetousness;
and be content with such things as ye have: for he hath
said, I will never leave thee, nor forsake thee.
HEBREWS 13:5 KJV

Some say that God wants you to choose poverty. Others argue that God wants you to seek wealth. Jesus did say, "Blessed be ye poor: for yours is the kingdom of God" (Luke 6:20). But this verse describes a spiritual condition, not a socioeconomic status.

You can be physically poor yet rich in spirit. You can be rich in the world's eyes yet poor in spirit. But you can also be poor (or rich) in both ways. If that seems confusing, then know this: the biggest tests you face are less about money and more about contentment.

Imagine yourself in ten years. Would you still seek God if you had a perfect, high-income job? Would you despise Him for lack of a raise?

When you realize how little your bank account means compared to what you have in Jesus, you can begin to understand Luke 6:20.

Both being rich and being poor can be a blessing—but being content puts those blessings in perspective.

MY PRAYER STARTER:
I don't know where I'll end up in life, Lord. But no matter if I become the richest man alive or find myself unemployed with nowhere to go, help me keep my focus on You.

APRIL 7

Jesus declared, "I am the bread of life.
Whoever comes to me will never go hungry,
and whoever believes in me will never be thirsty."

JOHN 6:35 NIV

It's never fun to do without something you really want. It's worse when you can't see the sacrifice as simply seasonal or view the deprivation as a blessing. Jesus said, "Blessed are you who hunger now, for you will be satisfied" (Luke 6:21).

This hunger can be more than physical. It could be hunger for a relationship, better friends, good grades, more money, increased popularity, or even a healthier family life. Just remember that a blessing often arrives as something that seems less than ideal. God's timing may differ—a lot—from your own. But as long as you "hunger and thirst for righteousness" and your longing for purpose remains strong, God promises that you "will be filled" (Matthew 5:6).

When you hunger for the things God wants, you'll find ultimate satisfaction—and your blessing will be supersized.

MY PRAYER STARTER:

Lord Jesus, help my hungers to align with Your plan for
my life. That way, I can enjoy the double benefit of finding
satisfaction while also knowing that my life pleases You.

APRIL 8

All praise to God, the Father of our Lord Jesus Christ.
God is our merciful Father and the source of all
comfort. He comforts us in all our troubles so that we
can comfort others. When they are troubled, we will be
able to give them the same comfort God has given us.

2 Corinthians 1:3–4 nlt

Everyone has moments of profound grief and loss—you may even be experiencing that right now. If so, it's okay to mourn because it hurts, to shed a tear for the loss you've endured. But remember: this painful, splintered path can lead to blessings. Jesus said, "God blesses those who mourn, for they will be comforted" (Matthew 5:4).

The losses you suffer reassign your limited, personal comfort sources to the God of all knowledge and power, the God who knows how to care for the brokenhearted.

He is not in the business of making you sad. But God can take your sadness and use it to help you know Him even better.

MY PRAYER STARTER:

God, You know that on my darkest days, I sometimes
feel like I'm all alone. Thank You for proving me
wrong each time. Thank You for Your comfort.

APRIL 9

*"Those who show loving-kindness are happy,
because they will have loving-kindness shown to them."*

MATTHEW 5:7 NLV

A kind and compassionate response looks like Jesus, who is always our example. He said, "Give, and it will be given to you. You will have more than enough." Then He discussed the measuring cup of kindness: "The way you give to others is the way you will receive in return" (Luke 6:38).

You'll notice that Jesus left the giving column wide open. He didn't say, "Give money"; He just said, "Give." You can give your time to a noble cause, your resources to an organization you believe in, or your helping hand to someone in need.

You are blessed both when you give your kindness and when someone receives it. And if you wonder whether your giving will really result in a blessing, don't worry. Jesus will ultimately say, "Well done," even when no one else seems grateful for your help. No matter what anyone else thinks, God is the ultimate judge—the one who blesses those who are kind.

MY PRAYER STARTER:

Thank You, God, for planting Your compassionate love in my heart. Help me never to grow tired of doing good, even when no one seems to notice. Your approval is all I need.

*Follow righteousness, faith, charity, peace,
with them that call on the Lord out of a pure heart.*
2 TIMOTHY 2:22 KJV

If you want to be as close to God as you possibly can, you need to learn the value of obedience. If a pure heart follows righteousness, it is free from blemishes and imperfections. And while it's impossible for you to be both *perfect* and *human*, it is possible to make obedience your best response. If you wonder why a pure heart is so important, Jesus gave this blessing: "Blessed are the pure in heart: for they shall see God" (Matthew 5:8).

The goal of following is not to see how far away from God you can get and still detect Him. It's to get as *close* as you can. It's recognizing Jesus' footprints in your affairs. This approach to your Christian life is a blessing because obedience doesn't require correction or time-outs. It makes you faithful now so that you can be faithful again. It doesn't require the attention of other humans. It doesn't ask for a competition. It's a blessing because Jesus said it is.

How close are *you* willing to get to God?

MY PRAYER STARTER:
Lord Jesus, help me to follow You with an attitude of eagerness and joy, not fearful obligation. Make my life a constant upward trajectory—aiming straight toward You.

APRIL 11

*"Take my yoke upon you and learn from me, for I am gentle
and humble in heart, and you will find rest for your souls."*
MATTHEW 11:29 NIV

You probably want to appear strong in front of your friends. That's understandable. Being strong seems to give you an advantage, and power seems practical. Being weak can be inconvenient and discouraging. But *weak* isn't the word Jesus used when He said, "Blessed are the *meek*, for they will inherit the earth" (Matthew 5:5, emphasis added).

Let's try this description for meekness: people who are meek are disciples first. They choose to follow Jesus' example and use the strength God gives through the power of His Spirit. They have a controlled strength—they aren't bullies. Instead, they become wise without wanting people to notice their intelligence. These are the people in line for the inheritance Jesus spoke of.

Be strong in the power of God's Spirit. Then be meek in the presence of Jesus, the servant leader who blesses in ways we can't even imagine.

MY PRAYER STARTER:
*God, I know that the only way to earn true respect is by
restraining what power I have and choosing to offer kindness
instead. Help me to show meekness, not weakness.*

APRIL 12

Do all that you can to live in peace with everyone.
ROMANS 12:18 NLT

Many people are just hard to get along with—you've probably met quite a few of them yourself. Their constant tendency to retaliate over even the most minor offenses can make you tense up when you meet them in the hall. That's why the people who help resolve arguments—some Bible translations call them "peacemakers"—have a high status in God's eyes. Jesus said, "God blesses those who work for peace, for they will be called the children of God" (Matthew 5:9).

God's family members are defined as people who are willing to seek peace. That can mean loving another person enough not to fight about trivial things. It may mean realizing that fighting places a wedge between people. It may mean stopping an argument before it causes long-term damage.

Jesus said things that needed to be said, and because He was God's Son, those things were always correct. We don't have all the answers ourselves, but we know the one who does. So when people want to argue, let them argue with God. He will always win. And when He wins, so does everyone else.

MY PRAYER STARTER:

Lord, help me look past people's surface anger and see into their soul. Then give me the wisdom to connect with them so that they can connect with others—and with You.

APRIL 13

"If the world hates you, you know it hated Me before it hated you."
JOHN 15:18 NLV

In a perfect world, people would be celebrated for doing the right thing. But we don't live in a perfect world. Many times, people gain bragging rights through what they (supposedly) get away with. This can be disheartening when *you* make it a priority to please God by doing the right thing. But no matter what the world thinks, you should never be ashamed for doing what's right.

Jesus calls the desire to do good a blessing. He knew there would be times when it would be tough to do the right thing: "Those who have it very hard for doing right are happy, because the holy nation of heaven is theirs" (Matthew 5:10).

You might have experienced ridicule for choosing to follow Jesus. If so, you're not alone—some people have even died for their faith. Yet Jesus still calls them blessed. Why? The right thing is still right no matter what argument someone might use. And for every moment of injustice that Christians endure, an eternity of moments without pain, tears, or injustice awaits.

MY PRAYER STARTER:
Lord, help me not to feel discouraged when others mock my faith. Rather, let the experience serve as an encouraging reminder of the rewards that await me in heaven.

APRIL 14

Whether it's being grounded, getting a time-out, or receiving a verbal lashing from a teacher or parent, being corrected is no fun. It wasn't fun when you were little and it's even less fun now. When you aren't allowed to do the things you want to do, it can seem unfair.

True correction, though, is less about punishment and more about course readjustment. God's Word recognizes both the struggle and the blessing of correction: "No chastening for the present seemeth to be joyous, but grievous: nevertheless afterward it yieldeth the peaceable fruit of righteousness unto them which are exercised thereby" (Hebrews 12:11).

You weren't born knowing everything, and you might end your life feeling like you didn't learn all the stuff you should have. Between those mile markers, however, Jesus can teach, guide, and correct you when you get off track. Accept the blessing of training, retraining, and exchanging your thinking for His instruction. Doing anything less wastes time and short-circuits the positive impact you could have on those around you.

MY PRAYER STARTER:

Help me never to see Your discipline as unfair, Lord. Whenever You correct me, give me the discernment to see my error and change course, knowing it's for my own good.

APRIL 15

I urge, then, first of all, that petitions, prayers,
intercession and thanksgiving be made for all people—
for kings and all those in authority, that we may live
peaceful and quiet lives in all godliness and holiness.

1 TIMOTHY 2:1–2 NIV

Tax Day has come to the United States. No adult you've ever met has probably thought of this as a day of celebration—but it can be. When the day comes that you start paying taxes (it won't be as long as you think), consider the blessing behind these words from Jesus: "Give back to Caesar what is Caesar's, and to God what is God's" (Matthew 22:21).

Perhaps that sounds like you'll *have* to pay taxes and that you *owe* God things you might prefer to keep. But Jesus' words become a blessing when you consider that God gives you the skills and strength to do things that will one day be taxable by the government (and helpful to you). On the other hand, you may have been given so much from God that you want to give back in gratitude. You could grumble about the impending taxes, or you could just tell God, "Thanks."

You aren't blessed by obeying some compulsory duty. You're already blessed by God. . .and acknowledging that only adds to the blessing.

MY PRAYER STARTER:

God, thank You for me providing the opportunity to give.
Help me be cheerful in my giving, no matter the occasion.

APRIL 16

Those who trust in the LORD will find new strength.
They will soar high on wings like eagles. They will run
and not grow weary. They will walk and not faint.

ISAIAH 40:31 NLT

The disciples were confused. And who could blame them? Jesus had said how difficult it would be for some people to see their need for rescue. Some wouldn't accept that truth at all. So Jesus' followers asked if *anyone* could be saved. Jesus told them, "Humanly speaking, it is impossible. But with God everything is possible" (Matthew 19:26).

Salvation is a blessing because it's a free gift. You can't aid in your own rescue. If you could rescue yourself, you would have already done that. But you can't. Jesus can.

His gift of rescue is not possibility or probability—it's certainty. Your trust invites the strength of Jesus, the adventure of God, and the endurance of God's Spirit. Each contributes value-adding benefits that are yours when you trust Jesus. He made this impossibility possible.

What a blessing!

MY PRAYER STARTER:

Thank You, Jesus, for making salvation free. May I never take advantage of this gift; rather, may I embrace it as my identity and spread the good news to others.

*Try to understand other people. Forgive each
other. If you have something against someone,
forgive him. That is the way the Lord forgave you.*

COLOSSIANS 3:13 NLV

It is a blessing to be a blessing. Don't think so? Well, Jesus said, "Love those who work against you. Do good to those who hate you." *Whoa, hold on a minute. . .*this sounds like the Golden Rule at maximum difficulty, right? You understand that God wants you to treat people with the same kindness you want for yourself, but isn't this too much? Jesus continued, "Respect and give thanks for those who try to bring bad to you. Pray for those who make it very hard for you" (Luke 6:27–28).

Blessing others who don't deserve it can be very hard. But it can become an incredible personal blessing. You might get a front-row seat to a life change. You might see stubborn walls topple over. You might even find your own attitude changing in the process.

Bless others—and discover blessings in return.

MY PRAYER STARTER:

Lord, help me overcome my natural tendency to
withhold blessings from my enemies. May I treat all
people with equal kindness as I show them Your love.

APRIL 18

Every good gift and every perfect gift is from above,
and cometh down from the Father of lights, with whom
is no variableness, neither shadow of turning.

JAMES 1:17 KJV

John called himself the "disciple Jesus loved." He felt the encouragement and blessings of the only one who could rescue his soul, and he learned the value of blessing others because Jesus had blessed him. You can read about this blessing for yourself: "I wish above all things that thou mayest prosper and be in health, even as thy soul prospereth" (3 John 2). Short, sweet, and to the point, this blessing is proof that John wanted for others what Jesus wanted for him.

If you think the blessing was primarily about health and money, read the verse again. Your greatest material needs always come after (or alongside) a God-enriched soul. Jesus knew that whenever your soul is rich and you seek Him most, whatever you receive from Him will be plenty.

The blessing you can pass on to others reflects the recognition that you have been abundantly blessed.

MY PRAYER STARTER:

God, thank You for the material blessings You've given me. May I always put them in perspective, however, and use them to bless others—which is the biggest blessing of all.

APRIL 19

*Let us consider how we may spur one
another on toward love and good deeds.*
HEBREWS 10:24 NIV

You'd probably be okay with a little honor, right? Maybe when you do your chores or help that one kid pick up his textbooks, you start hoping the press release looks good, the photo op is well timed and complimentary, and the celebration to name that street after you won't be too over the top. Okay, so maybe that's a slight exaggeration, but some recognition for your good deeds would be nice.

Jesus said, "When you give to the needy, do not let your left hand know what your right hand is doing." The idea is, *don't make a big deal out of it to be noticed by others*. Why? Because "your Father, who sees what is done in secret, will reward you" (Matthew 6:3–4). The one who counts most notices what you do.

Remember, you were made to bless others by being a blessing, not the grand marshal of a personal parade. When you try to bless, who are you really seeking to honor?

MY PRAYER STARTER:
Lord Jesus, help me follow Your example of
humility by refusing to take credit for the good
works that You're working through me.

APRIL 20

The Holy Spirit produces this kind of fruit in our lives:
love, joy, peace, patience, kindness, goodness,
faithfulness, gentleness, and self-control.
There is no law against these things!

GALATIANS 5:22–23 NLT

Set your sights on something and you might find it running away from you faster than you can chase it. If you can't catch it one way, you might try coming at it from another angle. But some things refuse to be caught.

Of course, the Bible has some guidance on such issues. Jesus taught the apostle Paul, who later taught a young minister named Timothy. Here is Paul's advice to help his protégé know what to chase: "Pursue righteousness and a godly life, along with faith, love, perseverance, and gentleness" (1 Timothy 6:11). Chase these things in your youth, and you'll find that God will help you catch them for the rest of your life. This is how He blesses your pursuits and then helps you use them to bless others.

Imagine how much you can bless others when you are full of love, joy, peace, patience, kindness, goodness, faithfulness, gentleness, and self-control. Let the chase begin!

MY PRAYER STARTER:
Lord God, may I never pursue anything other than You.
Use my obedience to draw others closer to Your truth.

APRIL 21

"You have done well. You are a good and faithful servant."
MATTHEW 25:23 NLV

Jesus is faithful, right? He keeps His promises, right? Yes and yes. This too is a blessing. First Thessalonians 5:24 says, "The One Who called you is faithful and will do what He promised."

Promises kept are blessings. You don't feel blessed when friends let you down, especially if they keep doing it. But by keeping His promises, Jesus assures you that He can be trusted.

Don't take your cues from people who break promises—take them from Jesus. Don't follow those who disappoint you—follow the one who will never let you down.

It's easy to look at other people's lives and think their promise-breaking gives you permission to do the same. God's blessing, through the example of Jesus Christ, should dismiss that thought immediately. Don't you want to hear Him acknowledge *you* for being a faithful blessing to others?

MY PRAYER STARTER:
Lord, I've been disappointed by many people,
even those whom I trusted deeply. Thank You for
assuring me that You'll never disappoint.

APRIL 22

My God shall supply all your need
according to his riches in glory by Christ Jesus.
PHILIPPIANS 4:19 KJV

You follow Jesus, say you love Him, and try to do what He says. But if you expect God to bless you but withhold blessings from unbelievers, you might be disappointed. Jesus said, "[God] maketh his sun to rise on the evil and on the good, and sendeth rain on the just and on the unjust" (Matthew 5:45).

Everyone experiences something they call a blessing, and God doesn't discriminate when choosing who gets those blessings. But blessings like sunshine and rain are different from the specific, tangible blessings reserved for God's children. Things like faith, hope, and love take on fresh meaning for the rescued.

Those who don't follow Jesus don't have faith in God, so their hope is misplaced. Their perception of love is something with strings attached. Does that sound like a blessing to you?

Jesus said that some blessings are for everyone. But the Bible makes it clear that other blessings—the really important ones—are only for God's family.

MY PRAYER STARTER:

Lord, help me not to become envious when nonbelievers receive some of the good things of life; rather, help me pray that those blessings open their eyes to Your goodness.

APRIL 23

"Peace I leave with you; my peace I give you. I do not give to you as the world gives. Do not let your hearts be troubled and do not be afraid."

JOHN 14:27 NIV

Blessings are not one-time events. Jesus continually blesses you, so don't think that blessing others is something you check off your to-do list, never to return to it again. You wouldn't expect that from Jesus, so you shouldn't allow it of yourself.

First Thessalonians 5:11 says, "Encourage one another and build each other up, just as in fact you are doing." The people of Thessalonica *were* blessing each other and speaking life into those around them. And they were encouraged to never stop.

One of the most profound observations about blessing is that God the Father and Jesus the Son always bless first before They ask you to go against human nature and bless others.

You need reminders that God is good, that His peace is perfect, and that He will provide everything you need to live here and love forever.

Re-read Jesus' words above. Don't be afraid to keep on blessing.

MY PRAYER STARTER:

I know You've blessed me beyond comprehension, Lord, and I'm thankful that You still haven't stopped. Help me show the same degree of generosity when I bless others.

"May the LORD bless you and protect you.
May the LORD smile on you and be gracious to you.
May the LORD show you his favor and give you his peace."
NUMBERS 6:24–26 NLT

You have been blessed, and you can bless others through prayer. When Jesus prayed, He was able to focus on the blessings His disciples would receive. He said, "I have revealed you to them, and I will continue to do so. Then your love for me will be in them, and I will be in them" (John 17:26). You can use these words in your own prayers, asking God to use you to bless others by revealing Him. Pray that God's love would fill others and change their lives.

There are many passages that can be transformed into prayers for God to bless others. You could use them to pray for your friends, your enemies, your siblings, your parents or guardians, your teachers, your neighbors, and even total strangers.

When you ask God to bless others by using His own words, don't be surprised if something changes within you. Go ahead—use the blessing prayer above to kick off a whole chain of them!

MY PRAYER STARTER:
Lord, may Your blessings fall on everyone I
know—and even those I don't know. Let them see
Your goodness and honor You as a result.

APRIL 25

I pray that because of the riches of His
shining-greatness, He will make you strong with
power in your hearts through the Holy Spirit.
EPHESIANS 3:16 NLV

Can you imagine what a blessing it was for the disciples to walk with Jesus in the flesh and by His side? They could've shared all kinds of things about their time with Him—and they did. But Jesus continued to prove that He came to bless. He spoke to many people after He rose from the dead. He prayed with His disciples, "and while He was praying that good would come to them, He went from them (and was taken up to heaven and they worshiped Him). Then they went back to Jerusalem with great joy" (Luke 24:51–52).

Jesus' grace was sufficient and His mercy was personal. Furthermore, His blessings didn't end with His sacrifice on the cross. He continues to bring good to those who love Him, and His blessings bring great joy.

MY PRAYER STARTER:

Thank You, Jesus, not just for Your ultimate blessing of salvation but for the little blessings that You give me each day. Help me never to lose my sense of gratitude!

APRIL 26

God commendeth his love toward us, in that, while
we were yet sinners, Christ died for us.
ROMANS 5:8 KJV

The life of Jesus is worth reading about again and again. His healings were blessings. His miracles were blessings. His teaching and compassion were blessings. He came for sinners and blessed them by offering new life. Many seemed willing to follow Him for such generous blessings, but then He gave instructions few wanted to hear: "Love your enemies, bless them that curse you." That seemed hard, but Jesus took it a step further: "Do good to them that hate you, and pray for them which despitefully use you, and persecute you" (Matthew 5:44).

Bless the persecutor? Pray for those who use you? Love those who never prove to be a friend? Love and help those who hate you? *Yes!*

We might think it's no problem to follow Jesus—but what He's asking in this verse is just too much. *He doesn't understand how hard this is*, you might think. *He's asking the impossible.* But it's not impossible. It's exactly what He's done—for you. He can help you do what you can't do on your own. *That's* a blessing!

MY PRAYER STARTER:
Lord Jesus, may I never think that Your command to love my enemies is simply too hard to follow. With Your Spirit living inside me, I know all things are possible.

APRIL 27

Do your best to present yourself to God as one
approved, a worker who does not need to be ashamed
and who correctly handles the word of truth.

2 TIMOTHY 2:15 NIV

Jesus was on a mission to save humankind. And in the rescue process, He experienced everything humankind experiences every day. In His sacrifice, He experienced the physical and mental pain of people's sin. But despite all He went through, He never wavered on the idea of blessing. He would ask all His followers to bless others in the way He blessed them.

Jesus lived the life He was meant to live, and He died the death that saved mankind. Then He rose to new life, defeating the stronghold of death and bringing new life to unlikely people. The vicious persecutor Saul, for instance, would one day follow Jesus' love, even when no one believed he had really changed. As the apostle Paul, he would say, "Brothers and sisters, stand firm. Let nothing move you. Always give yourselves fully to the work of the Lord, because you know that your labor in the Lord is not in vain" (1 Corinthians 15:58).

Be blessed, be a blessing, and keep blessing.

MY PRAYER STARTER:

God, give me a fiery determination to bless others.
Just as Jesus maintained His love to the death, so may I.

APRIL 28

The LORD is my strength and shield. I trust him with
all my heart. He helps me, and my heart is filled
with joy. I burst out in songs of thanksgiving.
PSALM 28:7 NLT

Every human who has ever lived has a lot in common with sheep—both are confused, misguided, anxious, fearful, and weak. You can glance over a crowd and think you're better or worse off than the people you see, but in reality, in most ways you're very much like the others.

You may see needs in other people but for various reasons feel unable or unwilling to help. However, when Jesus saw a crowd, "he had compassion on them because they were confused and helpless, like sheep without a shepherd" (Matthew 9:36).

The greatest need humankind will ever have is knowing Jesus. When you follow His example of blessing others, others will start to see the truth behind this statement. You believe Jesus can be trusted, that He is who He says He is, and that He has the power to help. Now *that's* a message worth saying.

MY PRAYER STARTER:
Lord, give me the same sense of compassion that
You felt toward the crowds who were hungry for
Your Word. Help me reach out to those around me
with the message they need to hear today.

APRIL 29

God kept us from what looked like sure death and He is keeping us. As we trust Him, He will keep us in the future.

2 CORINTHIANS 1:10 NLV

A full array of blessing is seen in the Bible. The source of this blessing is God. The one who delivered God's eternal blessing was Jesus. Understanding blessings means understanding God, and understanding God means accepting His Son. God doesn't short-change anyone when it comes to understanding how and why He blesses: "Everything that was written in the Holy Writings long ago was written to teach us. By not giving up, God's Word gives us strength and hope" (Romans 15:4).

You've learned by now that God blesses certain attitudes and behaviors. What you do matters. What God does is a promise fulfilled.

The rescue Jesus offers comes with the promise of eternal life. This isn't just the ability to live forever but to live eternally *with God*. It means face-to-face encounters, heart-to-heart conversations, and old-to-new life transformations. And Jesus will be with you until His eternity becomes your reality.

MY PRAYER STARTER:
God, may I take full advantage of all the blessings
You've given me, using them to grow into a
deeper and more fulfilling walk with You.

APRIL 30

*God is able to make all grace abound toward
you; that ye, always having all sufficiency in all
things, may abound to every good work.*

2 CORINTHIANS 9:8 KJV

Many of the Old Testament prophecies about Jesus—from His arrival on earth to His death—are found in the Psalms. Mixed in between are blessings extending beyond this month's readings. Spend some final moments this month marveling at the depth of the blessings in store for followers of Jesus:

The blessing of trust: "Blessed are all they that put their trust in him" (Psalm 2:12).

The blessing of faithfulness: "Blessed are they that dwell in thy house: they will be still praising thee" (Psalm 84:4).

The blessing of God's strength: "Blessed is the man whose strength is in thee" (Psalm 84:5).

The blessing of righteous living: "Blessed are they that keep judgment, and he that doeth righteousness at all times" (Psalm 106:3).

The blessing of continually following: "Blessed are the undefiled in the way, who walk in the law of the LORD" (Psalm 119:1).

The blessing of the seeker: "Blessed are they that keep his testimonies, and that seek him with the whole heart" (Psalm 119:2).

MY PRAYER STARTER:

Lord, thank You for the instructions in Your Word on how
to receive Your blessings. Help me follow them to the best
of my ability—I don't want to miss out on a single one.

MAY 1

*Don't be misled—you cannot mock the justice of
God. You will always harvest what you plant.*
GALATIANS 6:7 NLT

Have you ever tried growing a garden? Maybe your thumb is more gray than green, but that doesn't mean you can't cultivate something magnificent. . .with the help of the one who makes everything grow.

Jesus used many gardening illustrations to help people understand His teaching. And the law of "sowing and reaping," which the apostle Paul referenced in Galatians, was something the Lord's audience understood well. You harvest what you plant. That's true in the natural world, and it's true in the spiritual world. If you plant and tend peas, you'll harvest peas. If you plant doubt and worry in your heart, that's exactly what you'll reap.

Jesus wants to plant good things in the soil of your heart. If you allow Him to work, you'll harvest in ways you could never have imagined. As Paul wrote, "The Holy Spirit produces this kind of fruit in our lives: love, joy, peace, patience, kindness, goodness, faithfulness, gentleness, and self-control" (Galatians 5:22–23).

Let's dig into growth this month.

MY PRAYER STARTER:
*Lord, help me plant the seeds of Your Word in my heart today—
only then can I harvest the perfect fruits of Your Spirit.*

MAY 2

"I am the Vine and you are the branches. Get your life from Me. Then I will live in you and you will give much fruit. You can do nothing without Me."

JOHN 15:5 NLV

You don't need to be a professional gardener to know that different plants tend to grow better in particular climates and soils—settings where other plants won't thrive. For example, pineapple does great in the warm, wet climate of Hawaii, but it wilts and dies in cooler, drier places—where a crop like wheat produces a big yield.

Thankfully, Jesus knows exactly what we need to grow in our relationship with Him—no matter where He's "planted" us. There is no guesswork involved. He doesn't have to bring in a specialist to decipher growing problems or send samples away to a lab. That's because Jesus Himself is our strong and healthy vine. We are the branches that grow from Him. His very life inside us is all we need. Invite Him in and ask Him to grow His spiritual fruit in your life.

MY PRAYER STARTER:

Lord Jesus, thank You for making it clear to me how I can grow in You. Help me be receptive to the work of Your Spirit so that I can thrive as a branch on Your vine.

MAY 3

"Every tree that does not have good fruit is cut down and thrown into the fire. So you will know them by their fruit."

MATTHEW 7:19–20 NLV

The Bible talks a lot about fruit—*spiritual* fruit. When Jesus is Lord over our lives, His presence within starts to transform us, enabling us to produce fresh spiritual fruit as we grow ever more like Him.

In Matthew 7:20, Jesus said we can recognize people by the fruit their lives produce—that is, we can tell which people are letting Jesus live out His life through them by seeing the good fruit in their lives. Selfish people produce bad fruit, but those who live in and for Jesus produce the best stuff.

What kind of fruit are you producing? Do parts of your life need more pruning? Is there an area that requires tending? A place that isn't growing at all? Allow Jesus to be your personal fruit inspector. Give yourself entirely to Him, and He will gladly grow good fruit in your life.

MY PRAYER STARTER:
Lord God, I need You to inspect my soul. If You
find any bad branches or rotten fruit inside,
please remove them immediately—I want my
life to look as much like Yours as possible.

MAY 4

But anyone who does not love does not know God, for God is love.
1 JOHN 4:8 NLT

In the famous and beloved "Fruit of the Spirit" passage (Galatians 5:22–23), the first quality mentioned is love. You might think of love as a feeling, but true biblical love is more than simple emotion. This kind of love is a choice, meaning you can *decide* to love another person even when you don't feel like it. That's the kind of love God calls His followers to demonstrate.

The apostle Paul told us more about true love: "Love is patient and kind. Love is not jealous or boastful or proud or rude. It does not demand its own way. It is not irritable, and it keeps no record of being wronged. It does not rejoice about injustice but rejoices whenever the truth wins out. Love never gives up, never loses faith, is always hopeful, and endures through every circumstance" (1 Corinthians 13:4–7).

Love like that isn't possible apart from Jesus living and working inside you. It's the kind of love that will fill your heart as you faithfully follow Him.

MY PRAYER STARTER:
Father, may my love be based on far more than
a feeling—may it be founded on my firm resolve
to treat others as Your Word teaches.

MAY 5

For the Kingdom of God is not a matter
of what we eat or drink, but of living a life of
goodness and peace and joy in the Holy Spirit.
ROMANS 14:17 NLT

How can we be blessed and feel God's joy inside? Blessing and joy are by-products of being with Jesus. Joy is a fruit of the Spirit who lives in every follower of Christ, and it remains in both the good and bad times of life. Even in the midst of chaos, we can have joy. Why? Because of this promise: "We know that God causes everything to work together for the good of those who love God and are called according to his purpose for them" (Romans 8:28).

Just as an apple or a pear or an orange must develop over time, so does your spiritual fruit. Joy grows as you realize that God is with you, working everything out for your good. Considering He sent Jesus to die for our sins (Romans 5:8), how could it be otherwise?

MY PRAYER STARTER:
Sometimes, Lord, life just doesn't feel that joyful. Thank You for providing a far deeper joy—one that runs underneath my superficial feelings and pervades my very soul.

MAY 6

The peace of God is much greater than the human mind can understand. This peace will keep your hearts and minds through Christ Jesus.
PHILIPPIANS 4:7 NLV

It's been said that "peace isn't the absence of trouble, but the presence of God in the midst of the trouble." Indeed, the peace of God gives you a supernatural ability to remain calm in the midst of anything. Peace is a deep assurance that God always has His eye on you and that He's at work behind the scenes. Divine peace is beyond your ability to fully understand. You don't create it yourself—only God can grow this spiritual fruit in your heart.

Our heavenly Father wants you to take your worries to Him in prayer. . .read the rest of Philippians 4. When you tell Him what's on your mind, thanking Him for what He has already done for you, you'll sense a growing confidence in what He *will* do. And this peace comes through our Lord Jesus Christ.

MY PRAYER STARTER:
Father, whether I'm facing stress at school, relationship problems, or even family issues, I know You're the one source of true peace I can always rely on. Thank You.

*Since God chose you to be the holy people he loves,
you must clothe yourselves with tenderhearted mercy,
kindness, humility, gentleness, and patience.*

COLOSSIANS 3:12 NLT

Patience can be a tricky fruit to grow, but it's one God wants us to have. Check out these verses:

- "And not only so, but we glory in tribulations also: knowing that tribulation worketh patience" (Romans 5:3 KJV).

- "Always be humble and gentle. Be patient with each other, making allowance for each other's faults because of your love" (Ephesians 4:2 NLT).

- "Brothers and sisters, we urge you to warn those who are lazy. Encourage those who are timid. Take tender care of those who are weak. Be patient with everyone" (1 Thessalonians 5:14 NLT).

If you've had trouble growing the fruit of patience, go to God in the name of Jesus—the only perfect person in human history will be glad to help.

MY PRAYER STARTER:

Lord, I know You've been incredibly patient with me before, so help me follow in Your footsteps by becoming patient myself. Teach me how to wait on Your perfect timing.

MAY 8

The Lord came to us from far away, saying, "I have
loved you with a love that lasts forever. So I have
helped you come to Me with loving-kindness."

JEREMIAH 31:3 NLV

God is kind, and so are all His ways. The Bible is filled with examples of His loving-kindness. Scripture tells us that's how He draws us to Himself (Romans 2:3–4).

God showed His great kindness by offering salvation to all through Jesus. When you know Jesus, you must allow Him to grow that spiritual fruit of kindness in your life. So many people—whether they're in your family, school, or even church—misunderstand God, so it's your job as a Christian to show them who He really is.

Jesus said He came to provide an abundant life (John 10:10). Part of that abundance is the true kindness that God's Spirit grows in you. As you allow that fruit to develop, others will see Jesus—the kindest man who ever lived—in you. And hopefully, they will be drawn to salvation through Him.

MY PRAYER STARTER:

Jesus, help me reflect Your kindness to everyone I meet,
even if I don't think they deserve it. I might be the only
representative of You they'll ever meet, so help me do it well.

MAY 9

*Trust in the LORD and do good. Then you will
live safely in the land and prosper.*
PSALM 37:3 NLT

It's hard to do the right thing all the time, especially when people around you do not. That's why you need God's help in growing the spiritual fruit of goodness.

First John 5:18 says: "We know that God's children do not make a practice of sinning, for God's Son holds them securely, and the evil one cannot touch them." Because Jesus protects us, we can stay away from sin and make right choices. His Spirit will grow goodness in our lives when we ask Him to guide our choices.

We all make mistakes. We all sin. But when we do, God wants us to run *to* Him, not *from* Him. You can always go to God with confidence because you are covered in the righteousness of Jesus.

Just trust Him. . .and do good.

MY PRAYER STARTER:

God, I know my own goodness is not nearly enough.
I need Your own goodness to live inside me and guide
my actions. Only then can I look more like You.

MAY 10

"His owner said to him, 'You have done well. You are a good and faithful servant. You have been faithful over a few things. I will put many things in your care. Come and share my joy.' "

MATTHEW 25:21 NLV

As you draw closer to Jesus, faithfulness is another fruit the Holy Spirit will grow in your life. God has given us all work to do as we wait for Jesus to return. Each of us has gifts and talents to use as we serve God and share the good news of Jesus with others. The Spirit provides the desire, energy, and ability to pour out these gifts in productive ways.

In His parable of the talents, Jesus taught that human faithfulness begins with God (He gives responsibility to His children), continues with us (we use the ability He's given), and circles back to God again (He gives us even more ability and responsibility). We work with God to grow the fruit of faithfulness in our lives.

Are you being faithful in your current responsibilities?

MY PRAYER STARTER:

Lord, I know that as I grow older, my responsibilities will grow more serious. May Your Spirit guide me into becoming the mature, responsible adult You want me to be.

MAY 11

Let your gentleness be evident to all. The Lord is near.
<small>PHILIPPIANS 4:5 NIV</small>

Are you gentle with the people around you? What about with yourself?

When life becomes busy and stressful, it's easy to forget about gentleness. Sometimes you might say whatever's on your mind, not giving a thought to anyone else's feelings. And you might be hard on yourself too, internalizing negative thoughts that drag you down even further.

But our gentle Lord doesn't want us to live this way. Jesus—who welcomed little children, the sick, the lame, the blind, and the outcasts of society—wants us to allow His Spirit to grow the fruit of gentleness within us. According to the apostle Paul, we should be gentle because "the Lord is near."

Jesus is coming soon. When He comes, may He find a healthy, fully developed crop of gentleness within His people.

MY PRAYER STARTER:

Lord God, I know that harsh words and attitudes do nothing but drive me farther from You. Help me to show gentleness—both toward others and toward myself.

MAY 12

*For this very reason, make every effort to add to your
faith goodness; and to goodness, knowledge; and
to knowledge, self-control; and to self-control,
perseverance; and to perseverance, godliness; and to
godliness, mutual affection; and to mutual affection, love.*

2 PETER 1:5–7 NIV

Today's scripture passage is quite a list! How in the world can we manage all of that?

The apostle Peter gave the answer just a few verses earlier: "[God's] divine power has given us everything we need for a godly life through our knowledge of him who called us by his own glory and goodness" (2 Peter 1:3).

You don't have to grow these godly characteristics in your own power! It is "divine power" at work inside of you that makes all good things happen. As the fruit of God's Spirit grows inside of you (Galatians 5:22–23), the virtues listed above will come along too. As you die to yourself every day, allowing God's power to work inside you, you'll have more and more of the qualities of 2 Peter 1:5–7. You'll look more and more like Jesus.

MY PRAYER STARTER:

I know I can never master all the qualities in today's verse
on my own, Lord. That's why I need Your Spirit to take me
over and work through my mouth, hands, and feet.

MAY 13

And this is my prayer: I pray that your love will grow more and more. I pray that you will have better understanding and be wise in all things.... And I pray that you will be filled with the fruits of right living. These come from Jesus Christ, with honor and thanks to God.

PHILIPPIANS 1:9, 11 NLV

Is the Spirit of God working in your heart? If so, you should notice a number of spiritual fruits beginning to grow. Take a quick inventory: love, joy, peace, patience, kindness, goodness, faithfulness, gentleness, self-control. Are these taking root and developing in your heart?

If you recognize that some of these qualities aren't growing inside you, take your concern to Jesus. Ask Him to clear the weeds out of your heart, making room for the good things He wants to grow there.

We're all sinful human beings, so there's no shame in asking—the real problem would be to pretend you're okay! The "fruits of right living" come from Jesus Himself. He is your source of growth, and He wants to prepare your heart to bear real fruit.

MY PRAYER STARTER:
Lord, don't ever allow me to become complacent about my spiritual progress. Help me evaluate my soul frequently so that I don't stray from Your will for my life.

MAY 14

Let us not become weary in doing good, for at the proper time we will reap a harvest if we do not give up.

Ever beaten yourself up for a mistake? For struggling with the same sin over and over? If so, may this passage encourage you: "Let us run with perseverance the race marked out for us, fixing our eyes on Jesus, the pioneer and perfecter of faith. For the joy set before him he endured the cross, scorning its shame, and sat down at the right hand of the throne of God" (Hebrews 12:1–2). When you try to grow your own spiritual fruit in your own strength, catastrophe inevitably results.

As "pioneer and perfecter," Jesus starts and finishes our faith. It was His endurance of the shame of the cross that led to our salvation, so all we must now do is accept His work. Jesus' goodness covers our badness!

He gives us all His strength to rise again and keep on going—and growing. Jesus is with you, and He is at work in you. Don't give up!

MY PRAYER STARTER:
Whenever I stumble, Lord, You pick me back up with assurances of Your mercy. Thank You for never leaving me. Help me never to leave You.

MAY 15

For God is the one who provides seed for the farmer
and then bread to eat. In the same way, he will
provide and increase your resources and then
produce a great harvest of generosity in you.
2 CORINTHIANS 9:10 NLT

Gardening is an eloquent—and accurate—illustration of the spiritual life. The seed comes from the hand of God. It's planted in the ground, and as the gardener tends to it, it sprouts and grows, eventually producing an abundant harvest that's more than enough to feed the gardener and his family.

When we follow Jesus, we become part of God's garden. He plants His "seed" of kindness and compassion within us and then guarantees "a great harvest of generosity."

Just as God loved the world so much that He gave Jesus (John 3:16), we as followers of Christ should overflow in our giving. Everything starts with God anyway, so why not be open-handed? Always remember that Jesus laid down His life for His friends (John 15:13).

MY PRAYER STARTER:
Lord, I know many people who need to see Your love and
generosity in action. Plant these seeds in my heart, and
let them produce fruit that nourishes everyone I meet.

MAY 16

*We can rejoice, too, when we run into problems
and trials, for we know that they help us develop
endurance. And endurance develops strength of
character, and character strengthens our confident
hope of salvation. And this hope will not lead to
disappointment. For we know how dearly God loves us, because
he has given us the Holy Spirit to fill our hearts with his love.*

ROMANS 5:3–5 NLT

Life on earth is like a pendulum: happiness and disappointment,
wonder and heartache, breathtaking highs and overwhelming
lows. But these tensions help us grow.

Can you imagine watching a movie in which nothing bad
happens—where there's no struggles and nothing to overcome?
That sounds boring. You'd probably move on to a story with a little
more excitement.

The best adventures have highs and lows. And the adventure
of the Christian life will too. But with Jesus always at our side and
His Holy Spirit filling our hearts with love, we can rejoice in all
things. Through Jesus, we have the hope of eternal salvation. . .and
we will not be disappointed.

MY PRAYER STARTER:
Lord Jesus, thank You for promising a perfect end to
my life's story. While I'm on earth, teach me to embrace
the highs and lows and praise You through it all.

*But grow in the grace and knowledge of our Lord and Savior
Jesus Christ. To him be glory both now and forever! Amen.*

2 PETER 3:18 NIV

Jesus was "full of grace and truth" (John 1:14). As His followers, we
are to "grow in the grace and knowledge of our Lord and Savior." If
truth is the seed, then grace is the rich soil that allows it to bloom
into a garden of love. You know how important love is: "Now these
three remain: faith, hope and love. But the greatest of these is
love" (1 Corinthians 13:13).

You can grow in truth, obtaining more and more knowledge. . .but if it isn't seasoned with love, the apostle Paul says
it means nothing (1 Corinthians 13:2). Love is the most important thing.

If you're growing in the knowledge of Jesus but not in grace
and love, you'll accomplish nothing for the kingdom of God. Ask
Jesus to align your heart with His.

MY PRAYER STARTER:

Father, I don't want to grow only in knowledge. When
others hear me speak about You, may they hear not just a
collection of facts but an outpouring of Your grace and love.

MAY 18

*And now, just as you accepted Christ Jesus as your
Lord, you must continue to follow him. Let your roots
grow down into him, and let your lives be built on him.
Then your faith will grow strong in the truth you were
taught, and you will overflow with thankfulness.*

COLOSSIANS 2:6–7 NLT

A tree with deep roots is strongly attached to the earth and can
easily find the water it needs to stay healthy. Therefore, it's far
less likely to topple when storms come.

The Bible tells us to let our roots grow down deep into Jesus
Himself. We are to build our lives on Him. So, how are your roots?
Are you firmly planted in the Word? Is your faith strong enough to
keep you upright during life's storms? Healthy in times of drought?

You can grow deep roots fast by spending lots of quality time
with Jesus. Be present with Him in every moment, and you'll
grow stronger for the challenges of life. You'll even find yourself
overflowing with thankfulness.

MY PRAYER STARTER:

Without Your help, Lord, my faith is like a desert shrub,
easily uprooted by the slightest breeze. Help me become
a sturdy tree that grows by the river of Your Word.

MAY 19

"And the seeds that fell on the good soil represent honest, good-hearted people who hear God's word, cling to it, and patiently produce a huge harvest."

Jesus' parable in Luke 8 describes a farmer who scattered seeds. Some fell on the pathway, some on the rocks, and some in the thorns. But the only seeds that produced a crop were those that fell on the good soil.

Jesus later explained the parable: the seed that produced the good crop stands for people who hear God's Word and follow through—they make a decision for Jesus and continue following Him no matter what. They patiently trust God for all things. . .and He blesses them for it.

Read the rest of Luke 8 to understand the other kinds of soil. Which one describes you? If you have a poor soil type, ask Jesus to break up the hard surface, carry away the rocks, or root out the weeds. He'll be happy to clear out the land so that His fruit can grow.

MY PRAYER STARTER:

Lord, please cultivate the soil of my heart, making it receptive to Your Word and to Your Spirit's leading.

MAY 20

So we have not stopped praying for you since we
first heard about you. We ask God to give you complete
knowledge of his will and to give you spiritual
wisdom and understanding. Then the way you live
will always honor and please the Lord, and your lives will
produce every kind of good fruit. All the while, you will
grow as you learn to know God better and better.
COLOSSIANS 1:9–10 NLT

Can you work for God. . .without God? Yes, you can. Maybe you've spent years gaining biblical knowledge, going to church camp, and even pursuing ministry endeavors. But doing "Christian" things doesn't mean you are growing in Christ. Many times, less is more—less doing means more real listening to God.

Jesus is the source of all knowledge and wisdom and understanding. You grow in your faith and produce good fruit for Him when you ask Him to lead and guide you.

MY PRAYER STARTER:
God, may my walk with You be less about doing and more about listening. Only after You've given me the green light will any of my plans ever succeed.

MAY 21

*The man who is right and good will grow like the
palm tree. He will grow like a tall tree in Lebanon.
Planted in the house of the Lord, they will grow well
in the home of our God. They will still give fruit when
they are old. They will be full of life and strength.*

PSALM 92:12–14 NLV

An apple tree can live up to eighty years, producing an abundance of fruit throughout its lifetime. Blueberry plants can produce fruit for up to fifty years. And citrus trees can live and produce fruit for more than fifty years. Notice the word *can*: all of these plants depend on careful tending for their health and longevity. It's much the same with people.

Today's scripture says that "the man who is right and good will grow." Other versions say "the godly" or "the righteous" will flourish. As a Christian, you know that you're only righteous—considered clean in God's sight—because of Jesus (Philippians 3:9). As you allow Him to tend to you, you continue to grow. As you root yourself deeply in Him, you'll produce fruit all the days of your life. . .whether that's fifty or eighty years, or even longer.

MY PRAYER STARTER:

Lord, I still have a long life ahead of me, so I want to make
every second of it count. Help my spiritual life flourish
more and more as I'm nourished by Your righteousness.

MAY 22

Oh, the joys of those who do not follow the advice
of the wicked, or stand around with sinners,
or join in with mockers. But they delight in the law
of the LORD, meditating on it day and night.
They are like trees planted along the
riverbank, bearing fruit each season. Their leaves
never wither, and they prosper in all they do.
PSALM 1:1–3 NLT

Have you ever been canoeing? If so, you might have noticed that
the trees growing along the riverbank are usually big and healthy.
That's because they are planted beside a source of life. In John
7:38, Jesus said, "Anyone who believes in me may come and drink!
For the Scriptures declare, 'Rivers of living water will flow from
his heart.' "

When we are firmly planted and rooted in Christ, we have the
living water—the very source of life itself—alive and at work in
us! So stop striving to make things work out on your own. Simply
rest in the fact that the source of life Himself will help you grow
like a tree on a riverbank.

MY PRAYER STARTER:
Thank You, Jesus, for being the water that gives
me true life. Help me never seek satisfaction
or nourishment in any other source.

*Don't copy the behavior and customs of this world,
but let God transform you into a new person by
changing the way you think. Then you will learn to know
God's will for you, which is good and pleasing and perfect.*

ROMANS 12:2 NLT

The life of Jesus within you is bringing about transformation. But transformation isn't always easy.

Think of a butterfly. Before that beautiful creature appears, a caterpillar has to stop eating, hang itself upside down, and spin a cocoon where the transformation will take place. This "metamorphosis" changes the lowly crawler into a colorful flyer—which is akin to your growth when you come to Jesus. His life changes you into all that He wants you to be, polishing and perfecting your own personal gifts, abilities, and desires.

When you change the way you think—when you consciously turn your thoughts to Jesus—you will grow. You will understand God's pleasing and perfect will. And you'll help to change the world for good.

MY PRAYER STARTER:
God, change can be frightening and even unpleasant.
That's why I thank You for assuring me that, as
long as I have You in my life, each change
I face is directing me down a better path.

MAY 24

"Oh, that we might know the LORD! Let us press on to know him. He will respond to us as surely as the arrival of dawn or the coming of rains in early spring."

HOSEA 6:3 NLT

The Lord wants you to know Him personally. Isn't that amazing? He's not playing hide-and-seek. He's not leading you down some path to ultimate disappointment. No—God is good, and He has your best interest at heart.

Don't forget that Jesus came looking for you first: "For the Son of Man came to seek and save those who are lost" (Luke 19:10). *He* was looking, but He wanted *you* to find Him.

Are you "pressing on" to know Jesus? The apostle Paul used those words to describe the work he did to know and grow: "I have not achieved it, but I focus on this one thing: Forgetting the past and looking forward to what lies ahead, I press on to reach the end of the race and receive the heavenly prize for which God, through Christ Jesus, is calling us" (Philippians 3:13–14).

MY PRAYER STARTER:

Thank You, Lord, for searching for me and allowing me to be found. Help me respond by seeking You all the days of my life.

MAY 25

Jesus said to her, "I am the resurrection and the life. The one who believes in me will live, even though they die; and whoever lives by believing in me will never die. Do you believe this?"

JOHN 11:25–26 NIV

New life begins the moment we begin our walk with Jesus, but the rate at which we grow and change is different for each person. Christians experience Jesus in many different ways. Some have a "come to Jesus" moment and are instantly and miraculously transformed from their former way of life. Many others begin the walk of faith and then grow gradually as the Holy Spirit trains them in the ways of Jesus.

It's important to have grace for yourself—and for others—as you journey through this life with Jesus. We humans will never get everything right, and every journey is different. Enjoy the growth process with great hope for the future. When you believe in Jesus, you will live and never die!

MY PRAYER STARTER:

Lord, thank You for guiding me with Your Spirit. Help me to never fall behind or attempt to outpace Your efforts—give me the patience and endurance I need to stay the course.

Now you are the body of Christ, and each one of you is a part of it.
1 CORINTHIANS 12:27 NIV

Once you know Jesus, believe what He has said about Himself, and understand who you are because of Him, everything changes. Jesus is alive, and He's helping you grow in your relationship with Him. Now you are free to live the life God created you to live, no matter what anyone else thinks.

As a believer, you are part of Jesus' body here on earth. You belong because God says you belong. Nothing and no one can change that. You can love and be loved no matter what. As you grow and mature in Christ, you grasp this truth ever more firmly.

There's no need for insecurity or any feeling that you don't belong. You are where you are for a reason, and you can now partner with Jesus on His mission of extending the Father's kingdom. And as you grow individually, you build up the body of Christ.

MY PRAYER STARTER:

Thank You for making me a part of Your rapidly growing body—the church. May I also find ways to help others grow by showing them encouragement and love.

MAY 27

*When I was a child, I talked like a child, I thought
like a child, I reasoned like a child. When I became
a man, I put the ways of childhood behind me.*

1 CORINTHIANS 13:11 NIV

When you were small, did you ever throw temper tantrums? If so, the memory is probably uncomfortable, even though you know why it happened: you were just a child, and children are naturally immature. But do you know what's even more uncomfortable? Watching an *adult* throwing a temper tantrum. Why? Because we expect grown-ups to act like grown-ups.

Today's scripture is smack-dab in the middle of 1 Corinthians 13, also known as "the Love Chapter." Why would a verse about childishness be included there? Because growing up in Jesus means putting away our youthful ideas and desires and learning to love our fellow Christians. The way we love is actually the measure of our maturity in Christ. Jesus Himself said, "By this everyone will know that you are my disciples, if you love one another" (John 13:35).

MY PRAYER STARTER:

Lord, as I grow physically, help me also to grow spiritually,
learning how to love others unselfishly. Help me to leave behind
my "childish" ways and step into a more mature walk with You.

Then we will no longer be immature like children.
We won't be tossed and blown about by every wind of new
teaching. We will not be influenced when people try to trick
us with lies so clever they sound like the truth. Instead, we
will speak the truth in love, growing in every way more and
more like Christ, who is the head of his body, the church.

EPHESIANS 4:14–15 NLT

Though the devil is often portrayed in horns and a red cape, he doesn't really show up that way. He would be too easily noticed! No, Satan typically masquerades as something good—maybe even as something you've always wanted. The devil is so tricky that Jesus called him the father of lies (John 8:44).

When we're young, we're more easily tricked. But as we get older, we're not as easily fooled. . .or at least that's how it should be. In the spiritual realm, are you spending time in God's Word? Are you praying in the Spirit? Are you patterning your life after the perfect life of your Lord, Jesus Christ? May this always be true of you, so that you won't be tossed by every wind of new teaching.

MY PRAYER STARTER:
Father, as I grow in Your Word, give me wiser eyes.
Give me the ability to spot the devil's lies from a mile away.
And most importantly, give me the strength to avoid them.

MAY 29

Be sure to use the gift God gave you. The leaders saw
this in you when they laid their hands on you and said
what you should do. Think about all this. Work at it so
everyone may see you are growing as a Christian.
1 TIMOTHY 4:14–15 NLV

In Matthew 5:16, Jesus said, "Let your light shine in front of men. Then they will see the good things you do and will honor your Father Who is in heaven." He wanted His followers to consistently model kindness, forgiveness, and good behavior. The apostle Paul, in today's scripture, urged his protégé Timothy to "think about" and "work at" his Christian life. Then everyone would see that he was "growing as a Christian."

God has given each of us particular spiritual gifts. Our faithful development and use of these gifts will both bring honor to the Father and Son and draw unbelievers into God's family. Our growth in grace is for God's glory and the benefit of others. So as Paul said, "Work at it."

MY PRAYER STARTER:
Thank You, God, for my spiritual gifts. Help me use them wisely—to glorify You and to point others to Your love.

MAY 30

*Remember this: Whoever sows sparingly will
also reap sparingly, and whoever sows
generously will also reap generously.*
2 CORINTHIANS 9:6 NIV

Serious gardeners take notes, tracking their progress and their harvest throughout the season. They want to learn from both their mistakes and their successes. Of course, depending on their climate and locale, what works for one gardener may not work for another. In many ways, that's true of our spiritual lives too. Don't compare your own spiritual growth with someone else's. You have your own garden. . .and a good and loving God helping you tend it.

Use this moment to take inventory of your growth. Is the fruit of the Spirit sprouting and growing in your life? How are you doing with love? Joy? Peace? Patience? Ask Jesus to help you build on the successes and correct the mistakes. He is all about your ultimate success—not in terms of wealth and popularity but your growth in grace and likeness to Him.

MY PRAYER STARTER:
Heavenly Father, pull out whatever weeds of pride,
hatred, and discontent that might be growing within
me, and replace them with the fruits of your Spirit.
Make the garden of my soul pleasing in Your eyes.

MAY 31

*And I am certain that God, who began the good work
within you, will continue his work until it is finally
finished on the day when Christ Jesus returns.*

PHILIPPIANS 1:6 NLT

Imagine a gardener spending countless hours planning and preparing a garden—working hard all season, cultivating the soil, pulling weeds, tending each plant carefully, and anticipating a great return. Then, as the autumn arrives, he walks away without his harvest.

Who would do that? Certainly not God, who has a vested interest in growing His spiritual fruit in you. He sent Jesus to earth to provide the salvation you needed, and He will absolutely not leave you on your own. The responsibility to grow and prosper is not all on your shoulders.

Your part is to stay faithful. In the meantime, Jesus will be praying for you (Hebrews 7:25). He will nourish you with His living water. He will finish the job He started in your life the day you were born again.

MY PRAYER STARTER:

Thank You, Lord, for not just walking away after planting Your seeds in my life. Thank You for the constant guidance and nourishment You provide as I grow to be like You.

JUNE 1

The angel said to them, "Do not be afraid. I bring you good news that will cause great joy for all the people. Today in the town of David a Savior has been born to you; he is the Messiah, the Lord."
LUKE 2:10–11 NIV

For most teens, the beginning of summer is a highly anticipated time. School is almost out, and a general attitude of joy fills the air. But today, let's take a quick look at the Christmas season.

Before that angel appeared and announced the birth of the Messiah, joy probably wasn't an emotion the shepherds around Bethlehem felt. They were up late, as always, keeping a sharp eye out for trouble among their smelly, silly charges.

But God chose this particular group of shepherds to hear the best news humankind has ever heard: God had come in the flesh to save people from their sin. No wonder the angel said the news would "cause great joy for all the people."

Here, on June 1, is a special reminder of the incredible, miraculous, life-changing birth of Jesus in Bethlehem. A Savior has been born to you. Does the news make *your* heart leap for joy?

MY PRAYER STARTER:
Lord God, thank You for the miraculous gift of
Your Son. Help me find joy in Your goodness
no matter what time of year it is.

JUNE 2

The seventy-two returned with joy and said,
"Lord, even the demons submit to us in your name."

LUKE 10:17 NIV

When you think of spiritual warfare, *joy* is probably not the first word that comes to mind. But after Jesus sent out seventy-two followers to tell others of the coming kingdom of God, they returned with great joy because demons were submitting to His name. Notice that these disciples didn't rejoice in their own power but in the power of their Lord.

That was a good perspective on their part, but Jesus took things a step further. "I have given you authority to trample on snakes and scorpions and to overcome all the power of the enemy," He told them. "Nothing will harm you." But even better than that, He said, "Rejoice that your names are written in heaven" (Luke 10:19–20).

What could be more joyous than that?

MY PRAYER STARTER:

Lord, thank You for giving me the power with which I
can fight off the enemy's attacks. But even more, thank
You for promising me the ultimate victory in the end.

JUNE 3

*While he was blessing them, he left them and was
taken up to heaven. So they worshiped him and then
returned to Jerusalem filled with great joy.*

LUKE 24:51–52 NLT

Jesus' disciples—the twelve He specifically selected and the other men and women who followed Him regularly—got to experience some amazing things. They saw Him heal the sick, raise the dead, calm a storm, walk on water, appear again after His death, and even ascend into heaven! After all the emotion of the previous weeks, no wonder they were "filled with great joy"!

We have not seen Jesus, heard Him, or touched Him. But we do have the written Word of God—the unchanging, powerful scriptures—that tell us everything we need to know about Him.

One thing we know is that He promised to return to heaven and "prepare a place for you" (John 14:2). Just thinking of that ought to fill your heart with joy.

MY PRAYER STARTER:

Lord Jesus, I may not be able to see You physically, but I can feel You in the form of the joy You bring to my heart. Help this joy grow as I continue walking with You.

JUNE 4

*Go, eat your food with gladness, and drink your wine with a
joyful heart, for God has already approved what you do.*
ECCLESIASTES 9:7 NIV

Do you realize that God intends for His children to enjoy the
simple pleasures of this life? Ecclesiastes 9 mentions things like
food, drink, clothing, and so on. We don't have to wonder whether
these are good—God tells us to partake of them with a joyful heart.

Jesus said that He came to bring His followers life "to the full"
(John 10:10). That doesn't necessarily mean physical abundance,
but it certainly indicates spiritual growth, blessings, and ultimately
eternal life. What could be better?

When you consider today's scripture and John 10:10 together,
you'll see that Jesus intends for you to enjoy your life on this earth
while continuing to grow in grace, knowing that heaven draws
nearer each day. With the proper perspective, you'll find that
your heart is full of joy over what you have now *and* what you'll
experience in the future.

MY PRAYER STARTER:
God, help me not to see Your physical blessings as things
that should be avoided. Rather, help me enjoy them,
knowing that my ultimate home will be infinitely better.

JUNE 5

"When you obey my commandments, you remain in my love, just as I obey my Father's commandments and remain in his love. I have told you these things so that you will be filled with my joy. Yes, your joy will overflow!"
JOHN 15:10–11 NLT

What do you think when you hear the word *obedience?* Unbelievers often react negatively, thinking it implies a restriction of their freedoms. But as Christ followers, we find joy in obeying everything Jesus commanded. Obeying our Lord is an honor.

That's why missionaries get so excited when they talk about ministering to orphans. And that's why Christians who work in prison ministry can exit with a smile. But you don't have to be called to some specific ministry to find such joy. As you share the Word of God with a friend, offer food to a person in need, or simply sit at lunch with a lonely classmate, your spirit will rejoice.

You know what Jesus taught. Look for ways to live out His commands as you go about your day. Joy will overflow as you obey.

MY PRAYER STARTER:
Lord, may obedience never seem like a list of rules
I must follow—help it feel like a crucial ingredient
of a loving and joyful relationship with You.

JUNE 6

You make known to me the path of life; you will fill me with joy in your presence, with eternal pleasures at your right hand.

PSALM 16:11 NIV

Motivational speakers make careers out of helping people find the path they should travel. But here's the question: Is their wisdom sound? Are they directing people toward the right path? Do their audiences ultimately find true joy?

Long before Jesus' birth, the psalmist David had knowledge —under the inspiration of the Holy Spirit—of the Messiah's characteristics, and he penned the words of today's scripture. Centuries later, in Acts 2, Peter referenced this psalm, saying it was indeed about Jesus—the one who makes known the right path and fills people with joy in God's presence.

Don't overlook that last phrase: we find *joy* in the presence of God—the Father, Jesus the Son, and the Holy Spirit. When the troubles of life begin to chip away your joy, the remedy is Jesus. Spend time in His presence.

MY PRAYER STARTER:
Lord Jesus, You are the ultimate motivational speaker.
Your words don't just inspire—they change lives forever.
Grant me the wisdom to follow them always.

*"But now I come to You, Father. I say these
things while I am in the world. In this way,
My followers may have My joy in their hearts."*
JOHN 17:13 NLV

John 17 records a long prayer of Jesus. He prayed for His followers, present and future. (That includes you!) And what did He pray? That they would all have joy in their hearts.

This world will hate and reject us as Christians—Jesus Himself promised that (Mark 13:13, Luke 21:17). But we can still find tremendous joy in everything He's done for us—dying for our sins, conquering death, preparing an eternal home for us, and interceding for us in heaven. It's true—Jesus is still praying for us at God's right hand, whispering our names into the Father's ear (Romans 8:34).

Does that fill you with joy? It should! It's a direct answer to Jesus' prayer in John 17.

MY PRAYER STARTER:

Thank You, Jesus, for praying for me. Even when my own prayers feel like they're hitting the ceiling, I can have peace, knowing You are interceding on my behalf.

JUNE 8

*The jailer brought them into his house and set a meal
before them; he was filled with joy because he had come
to believe in God—he and his whole household.*

ACTS 16:34 NIV

After Paul and Silas shared the gospel with the Philippian jailer,
the man and his family came to faith in Christ. In joy and gratitude, the jailer set a meal before the two missionaries. We can
only imagine their conversation!

Do you recall the day you began your new life in Christ? Did
you feel a joy you had never before experienced? You'd been
washed as white as snow, and you actually felt clean before the
Lord. Even if you were saved as a young child and didn't experience
a major life change, you've certainly had moments in which you
recognized Jesus' mercy and responded with the same joy as the
Philippian jailer.

Whatever your case, may you never lose your sense of joy and
wonder at salvation. Jesus has changed your life forever!

MY PRAYER STARTER:
Father, thank You for the moments of overwhelming peace
and joy that come with knowing You. May these moments
get more frequent as my faith in You grows stronger.

JUNE 9

Rejoice in our confident hope. Be patient
in trouble, and keep on praying.
ROMANS 12:12 NLT

As a human, you hope for many things. Perhaps you hope to have a high-paying job or get accepted into a good college someday. You might hope to make the football team next year. Or maybe you just hope for the well-being of your family. But none of these things is guaranteed.

Today's scripture, however, says we can find joy in our "confident hope"—that is, the good news of Jesus Christ and our assurance of heaven. No matter how difficult or uncertain our current circumstances, we can rejoice in two things: what Jesus has done and what is yet to come as a result.

It's fine to have earthly hopes. But nothing in this world compares to our confident hope in the next. One fades—the other endures. Now that's something to rejoice over.

MY PRAYER STARTER:
Hoping for anything in this life, Lord, can feel like
a sad and futile endeavor sometimes. That's why I
thank You for giving me something I can confidently
hope for: an eternal home with You someday.

JUNE 10

For the kingdom of God is not meat and drink;
but righteousness, and peace, and joy in the Holy Ghost.
ROMANS 14:17 KJV

How often in scripture do we see Jesus partaking in meals? At Simon's home in Bethany, after calling Matthew to be a disciple, at the "last supper," and even after His resurrection, when He ate a piece of broiled fish. Food, while a physical necessity, is also one of life's great joys, given by God Himself.

But there's a much greater blessing for us as believers. . .the righteousness, peace, and joy that come through the Holy Spirit. Yes, Jesus Himself enjoyed sharing food with His friends. . .sometimes as many as five thousand of them (Mark 6:30–44)! But we as His followers don't live on "bread alone," as Jesus told Satan in the wilderness, "but by every word that proceedeth out of the mouth of God" (Matthew 4:4).

Dining with those we love provides an hour or two of pleasure. But we find eternal joy when we read God's Word and get to know our Lord.

MY PRAYER STARTER:
Thank You, Lord, for providing my food—both physical and spiritual. Help me to always place more value on the latter, for that is the only food that satisfies eternally.

JUNE 11

The precepts of the LORD are right, giving joy to the heart.
The commands of the LORD are radiant, giving light to the eyes.
PSALM 19:8 NIV

Turn on the TV, and you'll be told that satisfaction can be found in a nicer phone, a shinier gadget, a fancier car, or a stronger pill. But we know from experience that the shine on these things quickly fades. Culture even has a term for it: buyer's remorse.

But God's Word offers a different sort of satisfaction, one that will never disappoint. Following "the precepts of the LORD" brings joy. Nothing the world has to offer can do that. But once we've accepted the life, work, and teaching of Jesus, we can pursue pleasures that last, happiness that satisfies, and real joy that brings "light to the eyes."

The power that raised Jesus from the dead now enables you to walk in obedience to His commands. And in doing so, your heart finds joy.

MY PRAYER STARTER:
Lord, I'd have a miserable life if I depended on physical things to make me happy. Thank You for offering a better way—for giving me ultimate satisfaction in You.

JUNE 12

May the God of hope fill you with all joy
and peace as you trust in him, so that you may
overflow with hope by the power of the Holy Spirit.
ROMANS 15:13 NIV

Sometimes, pastors pray Numbers 6:24–26 over their congregations: "The LORD bless you and keep you; the LORD make his face shine on you and be gracious to you; the LORD turn his face toward you and give you peace."

In today's verse, the apostle Paul prayed a similar prayer—asking God to fill followers of Jesus with "all joy." Why? Perhaps because we are so prone to getting bogged down in the here and now that we forget all the blessings that Jesus has given us. Or maybe because Paul recognized that once a believer fully realizes the joy of the Lord, he or she can face anything.

Knowing Jesus changes your entire life, and knowing His joy changes your daily experience. If you're struggling to find that joy, don't hesitate to ask. God would love to answer.

MY PRAYER STARTER:
Lord God, help me to find joy in life's mundane moments.
Open my eyes to the splendor of Your mercy, helping me
rise above whatever frustration I may feel at the time.

JUNE 13

In the midst of a very severe trial, their [the Macedonian churches'] overflowing joy and their extreme poverty welled up in rich generosity.

2 CORINTHIANS 8:2 NIV

Having undergone intense persecution, the Macedonian churches were poor. Even so, they gave of themselves and their possessions for the advancement of God's kingdom—and they did so out of an overflowing joy for Jesus' blessings.

Wouldn't it be great to be known as a Christian with overflowing joy? But how do you get to that point? Those Macedonian believers would probably say their own joy overflowed *because of* their trials and poverty. In other words, their hardships gave them an opportunity to show their appreciation for their Savior's gifts, some of which would be known only in eternity. What a poignant representation of their faith.

Nobody seeks hardship. But when it comes—as it surely will— it's the perfect opportunity for us to show the world that we love Jesus. And that may ultimately cause others to follow Him too.

MY PRAYER STARTER:
Lord, help me embrace the hardships I face, not run from them. Help others around me see this unbreakable joy, and may it spark their curiosity to know more about You.

JUNE 14

You followed our way of life and the life of the Lord.
You suffered from others because of listening to us.
But you had the joy that came from the Holy Spirit.

1 THESSALONIANS 1:6 NLV

Christian teens often suffer for following Jesus Christ. Mockery comes to those who take up for the bullied, refuse to attend wild parties, or simply live their lives differently. And sometimes, the persecution only gets worse when they reach adulthood. But in many cases, these Christians are unfazed. They graciously accept such trials as a by-product of following the Lord.

As today's scripture verse indicates, following Jesus often leads to suffering. But it also generates a joy that comes from the Holy Spirit. What's your first response when people criticize your faith? Defensiveness comes from the flesh, but joy is a fruit of the Spirit. This type of joy realizes that trials are temporary, but the love of Jesus Christ is eternal.

Such joy can't be manufactured. But it can be enjoyed by anyone who commits to the Lord Jesus. He will reward you in ways you can't even imagine.

MY PRAYER STARTER:

Father, I know that many people will hate me for following You. Help me never to hate them back; instead, fill me with Your love and joy as I continue shining Your light.

JUNE 15

"Where were you when I laid the earth's
foundation. . .while the morning stars sang
together and all the angels shouted for joy?"

JOB 38:4, 7 NIV

Creation was a time of joy, and it was Jesus Himself who made it happen: "The Son is the image of the invisible God, the firstborn over all creation. For in him all things were created: things in heaven and on earth, visible and invisible, whether thrones or powers or rulers or authorities; all things have been created through him and for him. He is before all things, and in him all things hold together" (Colossians 1:15–17).

The morning stars sang together and the angels were shouting for joy, all in honor of their incredible Creator. Can we do any less? Your vocal quality doesn't matter. . .it's the quality of Jesus that matters supremely. Let's honor Him today with joy.

MY PRAYER STARTER:
Lord, You are holy and far beyond my
comprehension. Let me always find my joy in
You. Fill me with admiration for Your glory.

JUNE 16

*You suffered along with those in prison and joyfully accepted
the confiscation of your property, because you knew that
you yourselves had better and lasting possessions.*

HEBREWS 10:34 NIV

Sometimes, the Bible uses hyperbole to make a point. But today's scripture isn't an exaggeration. The writer wanted to remind early Christians of a time when they actually had joy when their goods were plundered. Why? Because they felt honored to be considered worthy of suffering for Jesus. They knew their heavenly reward would far outweigh anything that could be taken from them on earth.

There are certainly times to stand up for your rights; the apostle Paul did so as a Roman citizen when he was unjustly incarcerated (Acts 16:37). But there are also times to view losses through spiritual eyes, knowing that Jesus gave up so much more for you. . .that losing something for His sake means the world sees you as His true follower.

You can "joyfully accept" any hardship when you suffer for Jesus' sake.

MY PRAYER STARTER:
Lord, help me never to cling to my possessions—money,
health, or even safety—so much that I'm unwilling to give
them up for Your sake. Let each sacrifice be marked with joy.

JUNE 17

*Though you have not seen [Jesus], you love him;
and even though you do not see him now,
you believe in him and are filled with an
inexpressible and glorious joy, for you are receiving
the end result of your faith, the salvation of your souls.*

1 PETER 1:8–9 NIV

First Peter 2:9 calls us Christians "a chosen people, a royal priesthood, a holy nation, God's special possession." We are these things so that we "may declare the praises of him who called [us] out of darkness into his wonderful light." Christians are very different from other people—not better in some boastful sense, but specially chosen to honor the Lord.

You cannot see Jesus, but you can observe His presence in the form of your changed life. If you've trusted Him with your soul, you can trust Him with everything else—even your trials.

Our world is filled with trouble, and we as Christians can't escape it. But as we consider who we are in Christ, we can have an inexpressible joy. In and through Jesus, we are receiving the end result of our faith—the salvation of our souls.

MY PRAYER STARTER:

In a world full of chaos, thank You for being my anchor,
Lord. Since You offer security by remaining unchanged,
help me not be swayed by the world's opinions of me.

JUNE 18

Nehemiah said, "Go and enjoy choice food and
sweet drinks, and send some to those who have
nothing prepared. This day is holy to our Lord. Do not
grieve, for the joy of the LORD is your strength."
NEHEMIAH 8:10 NIV

Pop culture loves to portray Christians as dour, angry, and mean. At times, the overall church—along with some of its members— has probably poured fuel on that fire. We're not perfect yet, just forgiven.

But our default position should be joy—God's own joy that gives us strength. Jesus "endured the cross" (now that's strength!) "for the joy set before him" (Hebrews 12:2). He was "full of joy through the Holy Spirit" (Luke 10:21) and praised His Father. He taught His disciples to obey His commands, "so that my joy may be in you and that your joy may be complete" (John 15:11).

There are three steps to Jesus' joy: look ahead to the reward, praise God, and obey His commands. We serve a Lord of joy who wants us to be joyful too.

MY PRAYER STARTER:

Lord, if my friends misunderstand what being a
Christian truly means, help me not to confirm
their notions. Rather, let my unrelenting joy shatter
their defenses and bring honor to Your name.

JUNE 19

*That which we have seen and heard declare we unto you,
that ye also may have fellowship with us: and truly our
fellowship is with the Father, and with his Son Jesus Christ.
And these things write we unto you, that your joy may be full.*

1 JOHN 1:3–4 KJV

In recent years, health experts have concluded that loneliness is a big risk, with one study claiming it may be as damaging as smoking fifteen cigarettes a day. With more than a quarter of Americans living by themselves, these dangers are more pressing than ever. Researchers identify a simple solution to this problem: friendship.

Scripture also highlights the importance of friendship, and our most vital relationship is the one we have with Jesus Himself. Other aspects of this circle of friendship involve God the Father and our fellow believers.

Jesus is the perfect solution for loneliness—and the only way our joy can be made full.

MY PRAYER STARTER:
Thank You, Lord, for staying by my side and giving me a vast family of fellow Christians for encouragement and fellowship. Help me never to take such gifts for granted.

JUNE 20

Now all glory to God, who is able to keep you from falling away and will bring you with great joy into his glorious presence without a single fault. All glory to him who alone is God, our Savior through Jesus Christ our Lord.

JUDE 24–25 NLT

Have you ever felt smothered by some sin you've committed? Perhaps you've wondered how you could ever be pure enough to enter heaven. If so, today's scripture offers invaluable encouragement.

Jesus Christ, who is your righteousness, will bring you—without a single fault and with great joy—into the presence of His Father. And why wouldn't you rejoice? You will no longer know sorrow, sin, or death.

But you don't have to wait for heaven to experience joy in Jesus' finished work. Romans 5:20 says, "God's law was given so that all people could see how sinful they were. But as people sinned more and more, God's wonderful grace became more abundant." The blood of Jesus has covered your sin, and His grace has set you free. Rejoice!

MY PRAYER STARTER:

Loving God, thank You for turning my life—which, without You, would've been nothing more than a series of mistakes—into a clean slate. Help me embrace Your grace with joy.

JUNE 21

The women ran quickly from the tomb. They were
very frightened but also filled with great joy, and they
rushed to give the disciples the angel's message.

MATTHEW 28:8 NLT

When you attend a committed Christian's funeral, it truly is a celebration. Yes, there is sadness for the loss, but the message of the ceremony is centered on the hope that person had in Jesus Christ. You might leave the service feeling uplifted—joyful, even.

That's what happened in today's passage. The women, who had gone to visit Jesus in His grave, had instead encountered an angel who told them the Lord had risen from the dead. Even better, they would see Him in Galilee! Even in their stunned state, the women were filled with great joy.

Through His resurrection, Jesus conquered death. On the last day, we will rise again, just like Him. We need not fear the grave! Knowing that Jesus has defanged death fills us with joy.

MY PRAYER STARTER:
Lord Jesus, thank You for making something joyful
out of even our worst enemy—death itself. Help
me never lose sight of this awesome truth.

JUNE 22

Blessed are ye, when men shall hate you, and when they shall separate you from their company, and shall reproach you, and cast out your name as evil, for the Son of man's sake. Rejoice ye in that day, and leap for joy: for, behold, your reward is great in heaven.

LUKE 6:22–23 KJV

When is the last time you leaped for joy? Apart from sporting events, perhaps, you don't see a lot of happy leaping. Inhibited by societal norms, you probably don't physically leap in public over a great test score or even an acceptance letter from that college you've been praying about.

If we don't act like that for exciting, happy things, how much less would we leap for joy over trouble and persecution? But that's exactly what Jesus told us to do. If you're hated for His sake, criticized for following Him, or cast out of your friend group for faith in Him, you should "rejoice ye in that day, and leap for joy."

That sounds impossible, and, humanly speaking, it is. But "with God all things are possible" (Matthew 19:26). The key is to put all those troubles into perspective. . .they are absolute trifles compared to your great reward in heaven.

MY PRAYER STARTER:

Jesus, give me a joyful attitude about the good things in life so that rejoicing will be easier whenever things don't go my way. Let joy be my natural response to everything.

JUNE 23

*Hitherto have ye asked nothing in my name: ask,
and ye shall receive, that your joy may be full.*

JOHN 16:24 KJV

A prayerless Christian is a joyless Christian. That's one takeaway of today's scripture. Maybe you've experienced this lack of joy at times. Famed British pastor Charles Spurgeon offers the remedy:

> *Prayer is the natural outgushing of a soul in communion with Jesus. Just as the leaf and the fruit will come out of the vine-branch without any conscious effort on the part of the branch, but simply because of its living union with the stem, so prayer buds, and blossoms, and fruits out of souls abiding in Jesus.*

Plug in to Jesus today. Make your requests known to Him. Worship Him. Confess your sins, knowing He's ready to forgive and cleanse you. Thank Him for what He's already done in your life. Pray for the needs of others and yourself. As you wait expectantly for His answer, your joy will increase.

MY PRAYER STARTER:

Thank You, Lord, for offering the miracle of prayer.
Help me to always take advantage of such a fantastic
privilege, no matter the circumstance.

JUNE 24

Paul and Barnabas shook the dust off from
their feet against them [the Jews in Antioch
who made them leave the city] and went to
the city of Iconium. The missionaries were filled
with joy and with the Holy Spirit.

ACTS 13:51–52 NLV

When you experience opposition to your witness for Jesus, it is cause for joy. Why? Because that opposition means Satan recognizes your work and wants to thwart it in any way he can. Even when the enemy appears to be successful (as in today's scripture), God's kingdom continues to grow steadily. Satan lacks the power to stop it.

When your love for Jesus creates spiritual opposition, "shake the dust off your feet" and move on. To Satan's utter disgust, the message you leave behind may take root long after you're gone.

Believers engaged in kingdom work experience a joy the world cannot understand, regardless of the immediate outcome. Live for Jesus today and get a taste of heaven.

MY PRAYER STARTER:

With You by my side, Jesus, I'm not afraid of Satan's attacks. Instead, I'm actually encouraged when they come, since it lets me know I'm doing the right thing. Thank You for this peace.

JUNE 25

But none of these things move me, neither count I my
life dear unto myself, so that I might finish my course
with joy, and the ministry, which I have received of the
Lord Jesus, to testify the gospel of the grace of God.

ACTS 20:24 KJV

As the apostle Paul neared the end of his ministry—and ulti-mately, his life—his thoughts were focused on finishing well. That meant offering up his life as a "living sacrifice" for the sake of the gospel. By relinquishing his right to himself and his own desires, Paul found joy.

Living that way is countercultural. The world encourages us to chase money, popularity, and pleasure. It tells us to "look out for number one," and it scoffs at anyone who dares to pursue things that will outlast this life.

Jesus told us to lay down our life to find it, to die to ourselves daily, and to pick up our cross (an instrument of death) and follow Him. As we do, we find purpose and joy—not because of what we have accomplished but because of what Jesus does in and through us.

MY PRAYER STARTER:
Lord, just as Paul focused on the finish line, help me focus on my heavenly rewards, even if death seems like a distant thought right now. Life is short, so help me find lasting joy in You.

JUNE 26

But the fruit of the Spirit is love, joy, peace,
forbearance, kindness, goodness,
faithfulness, gentleness and self-control.
GALATIANS 5:22–23 NIV

When you think about the fruit of the Spirit, does joy get its proper due? Many of us focus on love, peace, and self-control. But the entire list is important, the result of God's Spirit working in us.

Joyless Christianity is not contagious. But when people see you living in Jesus' joy—no matter the circumstances—you become the ambassador He's called you to be. You become a magnet who draws others to Him.

If you find yourself lacking in joy, that's a sign you need to spend more time with Jesus. You can't manufacture the fruit of the Spirit on your own, no matter how hard you try. The fruit simply develops on you as branches, as you are grafted into Jesus, the vine. He is the source of all good.

MY PRAYER STARTER:
Lord, whenever my friends see me, help them to see
Your joy inside my soul. May this joy be so contagious
that it causes everyone I meet to want to know You.

JUNE 27

After all, what gives us hope and joy, and what will be our
proud reward and crown as we stand before our Lord Jesus
when he returns? It is you! Yes, you are our pride and joy.
1 THESSALONIANS 2:19–20 NLT

Jesus aligns Himself with His church so closely that when a Pharisee named Saul was persecuting Christians, Christ asked him, "Saul! Saul! Why are you persecuting *me*?" (Acts 9:4, emphasis added).

After his dramatic conversion to faith in Jesus, Saul (later known as the apostle Paul) developed such close bonds with fellow believers that he considered his converts his "pride and joy." God had flipped the script. Paul became so close to his spiritual brothers and sisters that he felt joy when he thought of them standing before Jesus on the final day.

Look for Jesus in your fellow believers. When you seek Him, you will find Him there. . .and all of your joy will increase.

MY PRAYER STARTER:

Lord, help me see You everywhere I look, especially when I speak to fellow Christians. Give me the joy that comes with recognizing Your fingerprints on everything.

JUNE 28

Always be joyful. Never stop praying.
Be thankful in all circumstances, for this is God's
will for you who belong to Christ Jesus.
1 THESSALONIANS 5:16–18 NLT

God's will can seem mysterious at times. But scripture tells us many aspects of His will for every believer, as we see in today's scripture.

The apostle Paul offered a threefold prescription for living within God's will: (1) Always be joyful. (2) Never stop praying. (3) Be thankful in all circumstances. But how do we do these things? And how does joy, our topic for this month, relate to prayer and thankfulness?

Feelings of joy can't be conjured on a whim; real joy overflows from a prayerful heart. John Wesley said it this way: "Unceasing prayer is the fruit of always rejoicing in the Lord, and thankfulness is the fruit of both the former."

When you find your joy tank running low, pray. Thank God, first of all for your salvation in Jesus Christ and then for everything He does for you in good times and bad. Joy will follow.

MY PRAYER STARTER:
Sometimes, Lord, I start running low on joy. That's why
I need Your strength to keep motivating me to stay in
Your will, knowing that the joy will soon return.

JUNE 29

*Consider it pure joy, my brothers and sisters,
whenever you face trials of many kinds, because you
know that the testing of your faith produces
perseverance. Let perseverance finish its work so that you
may be mature and complete, not lacking anything.*

JAMES 1:2–4 NIV

Have you ever known a Christian who handles adversity well—even to the point of being joyful within it? If so, you've probably wondered, *What's that person's secret?*

If you want to impact the world for Jesus, make spiritual maturity your aim. But know that maturity only occurs after you've persevered through many kinds of trials that test your faith. That's why James calls us to consider it "pure joy" when we do indeed face trials.

Are your circumstances starting to test your faith? Is your stress at an all-time high? Do you wish things were different? What you really need is a new perspective. Tough situations are simply an opportunity to learn perseverance, which leads to maturity, which makes you more like Jesus. That makes every trial a potential source of joy!

MY PRAYER STARTER:
Lord God, I'll be honest—I'm facing a lot right now, and I don't know what to do. But I do know that You're using this trial to strengthen my faith—all I need is the patience to endure it.

JUNE 30

Submit to God's royal son, or he will become angry,
and you will be destroyed in the midst of all your
activities—for his anger flares up in an instant.
But what joy for all who take refuge in him!
PSALM 2:12 NLT

Psalm 2 is a messianic psalm, meaning it points to Jesus Christ. Today's scripture was written with kings and leaders in mind, but it also shows the supremacy of Jesus as King of kings and Lord of lords. This verse calls us to submit to Him. When we do, we find joy.

In our modern culture, submission of any form is often viewed as weakness. Most people demand the right to make their own decisions without any interference. As so many of our fellow humans are asserting autonomy from God, we as followers of Jesus know the folly of such a mind-set. We seek refuge in the Lord.

As the world falls apart, you can find joy in the safe, loving arms of Jesus. Remember, He's the one who "existed before anything else, and he holds all creation together" (Colossians 1:17). He can handle anything.

MY PRAYER STARTER:
God, I know some people hate the idea of submitting to You. To me, however, serving You is a priceless honor that gives true joy. Help others to understand this truth as well.

JULY 1

I will walk about in freedom, for I have sought out your precepts.
PSALM 119:45 NIV

Both Christians and nonbelievers claim to walk in freedom. Non-Christians throw off all restraints and live by their own moral code. Sadly, they don't realize that they are enslaved to sin. Christians live by a higher code: God's Word.

However, even believers will struggle against the flesh and never walk in perfect freedom. But Jesus has thrown open our prison doors. He has sent His Holy Spirit to help us walk through them. And He has blessed us with His Word to lead and guide us.

To walk in true freedom, seek the Lord's precepts that are found in the Bible. Spend time and energy on that book and, without fail, you'll hear Jesus speak. Obey what He says, and He will make you free.

MY PRAYER STARTER:

Sometimes, Lord, the allure of sinful "freedom" seems strong in my heart. During these moments, help me recognize that true freedom can only be found in Your Word.

JULY 2

It is for freedom that Christ has set us free.
Stand firm, then, and do not let yourselves be
burdened again by a yoke of slavery.
GALATIANS 5:1 NIV

When Jesus forgave our sins, He set us free—not only from patterns of sin but also from trying to make ourselves right with God through some religious ritual. The earliest Christians were often at odds with the Jewish religious leaders, who wanted believers in Jesus to be holy by adhering to Old Testament ceremonial laws. What they didn't realize was that Jesus had *fulfilled* the ceremonial law. We are made holy in Jesus alone.

Our issue today isn't so much the ceremonial laws as some other form of religious ritual. Most of them aren't inherently bad, but they cannot set us free from sin. They do not make us holy. Jesus does. Today, thank Him for setting you free from the bondage of sin, for enabling you to walk in newness of life.

MY PRAYER STARTER:
Lord Jesus, may I never begin to believe I can save myself
through my own efforts. Help me trust fully in You,
for You are the one who has saved me. Thank You.

JULY 3

*The Spirit of the Sovereign LORD is upon me, for the LORD
has anointed me to bring good news to the poor. He has
sent me to comfort the brokenhearted and to proclaim that
captives will be released and prisoners will be freed.*

ISAIAH 61:1 NLT

Imagine being held captive in a foreign land. You don't speak
the language and have no friends or support team. You've been
bound with ropes and tossed into a dingy cell. With only a minimal
amount of food and water, you've been left to rot. After months,
then years, without rescue, you've lost all hope. You fully expect
to die without ever seeing the light of day again.

Then one day, beyond the prison door, you hear a voice saying
your name. It speaks with authority, demanding that you be set
free. And after years of hopelessness, you are!

This is what Jesus has done for you! Even if you were saved
at an early age, Jesus has still set you free—free from a potential
lifetime of misery that you'll thankfully never experience. You
are free indeed (John 8:36). Now walk every day in the fresh air
and sunshine of His love, and tell everyone you can how to find
freedom too.

MY PRAYER STARTER:

Thank You, Lord, for breaking me out of sin's prison and
relocating me into Your glorious kingdom. Help me to
never be silent about this extraordinarily good news!

JULY 4

Though I am free and belong to no one, I have made myself a slave to everyone, to win as many as possible.

1 CORINTHIANS 9:19 NIV

On the day the United States celebrates its freedom, every Christian can pause to thank God for the liberty He offers through Jesus Christ.

But in today's scripture, the apostle Paul said he was using his freedom to become a slave! Only mature believers can understand this. Paul made himself a slave to others to break down the barriers that might otherwise separate him from them. When he was around people who followed the old covenant law, he followed it too. . .but always with an eye toward sharing the message of salvation through Jesus. And when he was around non-Jews, Paul *didn't* practice the old covenant rites—for the same reason.

In Jesus Christ, you are free! Now use your freedom to become a slave like Paul. . .and break the chains for the people around you.

MY PRAYER STARTER:

It'd be easy for me, God, to use the freedom You've offered as an excuse to "do my own thing." Help me instead to use it to reach out to others who do not know You.

JULY 5

"Now a slave has no permanent place in the family, but a son belongs to it forever. So if the Son sets you free, you will be free indeed."

JOHN 8:35–36 NIV

Adoption is special. It means parents have consciously chosen to bring a child into the family, and the adoptee's place cannot be taken away. No matter how difficult the previous situation, the child is part of its new family forever. The same can be said for you as a Christian.

Before you trusted Jesus for your salvation, your future was dark. In fact, you were bound for eternal separation from God. But after you came to Jesus, eternity became crystal clear. You were adopted into the family of God, sealed by the Holy Spirit, and bound for heaven, where Jesus has gone to prepare a place for you.

You are now a rightful heir of God, a coheir with Jesus, a child of the promise (Romans 8:17). Why not take a moment today to thank God for your freedom in Christ. It's *great* news!

MY PRAYER STARTER:

Father, thank You for adopting me as Your child.
I don't deserve any of this, which makes the freedom
and hope I have all the more wonderful.

JULY 6

*All things are lawful for me, but all things are not
expedient: all things are lawful for me, but all things edify not.*

1 CORINTHIANS 10:23 KJV

One of the key tenets of the Christian faith is that believers are free in Christ. We are bound by the scriptures and our consciences, not by anyone else's rules and regulations.

Of course, some believers seem bound up in rule-keeping. They believe that by pursuing or avoiding certain activities (and often insisting that others must do the same), they'll "earn" God's favor.

In today's scripture, however, the apostle Paul tells us that unless God specifically calls something sin, it is allowable ("lawful") for us as Christians. The other side of the coin, however, is that not every allowable thing builds us up in our life with Jesus. Part of our freedom is knowing which things are "expedient" and which aren't.

Such discernment takes Bible study and prayer. And Jesus will be happy to guide you.

MY PRAYER STARTER:

Lord, before I do any activity—even if I know it's
not plainly forbidden by the Bible—give me the
wisdom to consult You first. I never want to overstep
my bounds and walk away from You.

JULY 7

*Sin is no longer your master, for you no
longer live under the requirements of the law.
Instead, you live under the freedom of God's grace.*

ROMANS 6:14 NLT

The Christian life is full of paradoxes. We gain our lives by losing them (Matthew 10:39). To be first, we must become last (Mark 9:35). We are slaves of God yet free (Romans 6:16).

The apostle Paul taught that our sinful selves must be crucified along with Jesus so that "sin might lose its power in our lives"; then we will be "no longer slaves to sin" (Romans 6:6). If we stay slaves to sin, we find death. If we choose to obey God, we live righteously. We are *His* slaves, which is really the freest way to live.

Are you bound by discontentment, fear, lust, or even addiction? Jesus can break those chains. In Him, you can "live under the freedom of God's grace." Drop the old sin-chains and tie yourself to Jesus with "ropes of kindness and love" (Hosea 11:4).

MY PRAYER STARTER:

Lord, if I have any sin that's controlling me, please break that chain and set me free. Help me live life to the fullest by trusting in Your grace and walking in Your freedom.

JULY 8

Now the Lord is the Spirit, and where the Spirit of the Lord is, there is freedom.
2 CORINTHIANS 3:17 NIV

You've probably known Christians who try to live by "the letter of the law." Their intentions are good, but they've missed an important truth: since Jesus paid the price for our sins, the Holy Spirit lives inside believers and frees us from burdensome regulations.

Of course, you must still obey God's moral laws, the Ten Commandment–type rules against murder, adultery, dishonesty, and such—as well as the rules set forth by your parents or guardians. But you need not worry over other ceremonial or man-made regulations. As the apostle Paul said, "Where the Spirit of the Lord is, there is freedom."

Be grateful for the freedom Jesus won for you—it's a glorious thing. But when the Spirit inside you speaks, listen and obey. Be ready to go where He leads and do what He wants you to do. Christian freedom is much better than a total lack of restrictions. . .it's the ability to do what is right.

MY PRAYER STARTER:

Lord God, grant me the wisdom to discern man-made laws from Your own. However, help me never to use my freedom as an excuse to disobey Your Spirit's leading.

JULY 9

*In [Christ] and through faith in him we may
approach God with freedom and confidence.*
EPHESIANS 3:12 NIV

Adam and Eve's sin had huge ramifications. Not only did they feel a need to hide from God, He separated Himself from them—by ejecting them from the garden of Eden. Later, during the history of His nation Israel, God met only with the high priests, who sacrificed to atone for the people's sin. Common people didn't dare approach God's Holy of Holies.

But the heavy temple curtain that separated God and humanity was torn in two when Jesus died. Suddenly, access to God opened for everyone who would believe in Jesus' sacrificial work.

When we sin, we don't have to hide like Adam and Eve did. We can drag our ugly, embarrassing misbehavior into the light and confess it to God in total confidence. We know He will forgive us based on Jesus' work. *This* is freedom.

MY PRAYER STARTER:
God, thank You for ripping down the barrier between Yourself and me through Jesus' sacrifice. Help me to never feel ashamed or hesitant to confess my sins to You.

JULY 10

*It is God's will that your honorable lives should silence
those ignorant people who make foolish accusations
against you. For you are free, yet you are God's slaves,
so don't use your freedom as an excuse to do evil.*

1 PETER 2:15–16 NLT

Do you ever feel restricted by the rules in your household? Even if your parents or guardians are relatively lax, each of your freedoms probably comes with certain laws—curfews, screen time restrictions, responsibility for chores, and a handful of other dos and don'ts. These regulations are for your own good as well as the good of others.

In today's scripture, the apostle Peter described a similar situation for Christians. In Jesus, we have been set free from our sin, period. But we should not use our freedom as an excuse to do evil. To do so would dishonor our Lord.

Jesus freed us from the ultimate penalty of our sin—eternal separation from God. Now we live for Him as slaves. That's not a popular concept, but remember: God is nothing like a human slaveowner. He always treats His people fairly, and He loves us beyond our ability to comprehend. We are free to voluntarily serve out of love.

MY PRAYER STARTER:

Without Your rules, Lord, I'd be hopelessly lost in a sea of moral relativity, my "freedom" quickly becoming my own demise.
Thank You for the gracious boundaries You've provided.

JULY 11

Jesus said to the people who believed in him, "You are truly
my disciples if you remain faithful to my teachings.
And you will know the truth, and the truth will set you free."

JOHN 8:31–32 NLT

Even non-Christians say, "The truth will set you free." In a sense,
this usage is accurate: anytime truth prevails, it brings a degree
of freedom. But that's not necessarily what Jesus meant in today's
scripture. He was telling His followers that remaining faithful to
Him and His teachings would free them from their own corrupted
motivations and passions.

Hopefully, at some point in our Christian walk, we all experience this truth. Maybe you've stopped to pray for an enemy
when your natural reaction was to fight. Perhaps you've given
generously, beyond what you thought you could, because you
felt it was what Jesus wanted. This freedom from selfish, worldly
behavior develops as you remain faithful to Jesus' teaching. It is
the truth that truly sets you free.

MY PRAYER STARTER:
Lord, I know that Your truth is more than a correct attitude
or statement—it's a life-changing reality that is lived,
not just believed. Help me live in Your truth today.

JULY 12

"I have indeed seen the oppression of my people in Egypt. I have heard their groaning and have come down to set them free."
ACTS 7:34 NIV

God has always been personal with His people. Even under the old covenant—in the days of the Old Testament—He heard the cry of His oppressed people in Egypt, and He arranged for their freedom. Their journey to the land of promise wasn't easy, but God provided for them every step of the way.

At some point, God heard *your* cry for help—a cry begging for His forgiveness. Like the Israelites in Egypt, you were oppressed not by a foreign nation but by the power of sin. God arranged for your freedom by coming to earth in the form of Jesus Christ, who lived a perfect, sinless life before offering Himself as the final sacrifice for sin.

Never forget that God is for you and that Jesus died to save you from sin. Even when you struggle to obey, keep talking to God. He will hear your groaning.

MY PRAYER STARTER:
Father, thank You for hearing my cry for forgiveness, and thank You for setting me free from sin's dark power. May I always devote my very existence to You in return.

JULY 13

"Through [Jesus] everyone who believes is set free from every sin, a justification you were not able to obtain under the law of Moses."

ACTS 13:39 NIV

Some say that any religion or belief system can lead to God. As long as you believe sincerely and are a "good person," you'll enjoy a positive afterlife. But this is far from what the Bible teaches. If all roads lead to heaven, why would Jesus die on a cross to free us from sin?

Jesus' exclusive claim to be the way, the truth, and the life— His assertion that no one comes to the Father apart from Him (John 14:6)—stands in contrast to other religions, which demand that people work their way to heaven. Jesus has already done the work for us.

Jesus stepped into humanity and did what no religion could ever do: He lived a sinless life and died in our place, offering us freedom from the power and consequences of sin. . .forever. Praise God!

MY PRAYER STARTER:
Thank You, Jesus, for offering a unique but easily accessible pathway to heaven. Fill me with the burning passion to tell others that You are the way.

JULY 14

He gives justice to the oppressed and food to the
hungry. The LORD frees the prisoners.
PSALM 146:7 NLT

God hates injustice. When His people endure it, He hears their cries. Sometimes, God delivers them quickly; other times, He calls them to persevere for a while. Either way, His justice will eventually win the day.

In a broken, sinful world, you will face injustices. They might be daily, minor irritations—like the constant and unpunished bullying of a classmate—or massive, life-changing upheavals—like the untimely death of a friend or loved one. But God is always aware, always compassionate, and always on your side. His answer will come, though it will be in His own time and way.

Don't forget that Jesus, the perfect man, faced terrible injustice through His betrayal, arrest, and crucifixion. And though He prayed for His Father to "take this cup of suffering away" (Luke 22:42), God said no. But God said no so that others could be saved—and that Jesus would ultimately be "elevated. . .to the place of highest honor" (Philippians 2:9).

And, as a follower of Jesus, you'll be there with Him forever.

MY PRAYER STARTER:
If anyone knows the sting of injustice, Lord,
it's You. Thank You for enduring such injustice
to promise us a reward that dwarfs any
temporary wrongs we might receive.

JULY 15

Knowing this, that our old man is crucified with him,
that the body of sin might be destroyed, that henceforth we
should not serve sin. For he that is dead is freed from sin.
ROMANS 6:6–7 KJV

The Bible paints a vivid word picture of what happens when you come to Jesus for salvation: your pre-conversion life—described as "the old man"—is crucified with Christ, though you still carry him in the form of your flesh. At times, he weighs you down and trips you up. But you are no longer his slave.

Jesus has given you a new life, one that sets you free from the power of sin. Practically speaking, that means reminding "the old man"—whenever he tries to influence you—that he's *dead*. And it means locking him in his grave by choosing to walk in the Spirit.

Whenever temptation comes, pause, pray, and obey God. You are free to do right because your "old man" was crucified with Jesus.

MY PRAYER STARTER:
Thank You, Lord, for killing off my old self. Help me ensure—through praying and studying Your Word—that he stays dead and that Your Spirit remains alive within me.

JULY 16

*And ye shall hallow the fiftieth year, and proclaim
liberty throughout all the land unto all the
inhabitants thereof: it shall be a jubile unto you;
and ye shall return every man unto his possession,
and ye shall return every man unto his family.*

LEVITICUS 25:10 KJV

Under the old covenant, a trumpet was to be sounded every fifty years on the Day of Atonement. That particular year was set aside as holy. Everyone in servitude was to be set free, and all land that had been purchased was to be returned to its original owner. It was like hitting a reset button: everything and everyone was redeemed and made right.

This practice was a shadow of things to come under the new covenant. The moment Jesus died for our sins, humankind no longer needed a "Day of Atonement." Jesus *was* the atonement, once-for-all-time for all who would believe. He proclaimed liberty throughout the land as His blood covered all our sins.

Now that we've been redeemed, we can carry forward the gospel message and proclaim liberty to anyone who will listen.

MY PRAYER STARTER:

Almighty Lord, thank You for liberating me through Your blood. May I display the same resolve to share the good news of Your sacrifice as You did when You made it.

JULY 17

How can I know all the sins lurking in my heart?
Cleanse me from these hidden faults. Keep your
servant from deliberate sins! Don't let them control me.
Then I will be free of guilt and innocent of great sin.

Though David was a man after God's own heart (1 Samuel 13:14), he was also a great sinner. In a rather bold prayer recorded in Psalm 19, he addressed both his hidden sins—the ones lurking in his heart—and his deliberate sins, asking for cleansing so that he could be free.

We can all relate. We have both hidden and deliberate sins—too many to number—and no chance of eradicating them on our own. But God didn't leave us to fight this battle on our own. Jesus came to set captives free. His blood covers your every sin, even the hidden ones.

His death on the cross doesn't give us a license to sin; rather, it frees us from sin, giving us hearts full of joy that want to worship Him. Let's celebrate everything He's done for us.

MY PRAYER STARTER:

Lord God, only You can help me find and destroy all traces of sin in my life. Please replace these sinful thoughts and memories with joyous reminders of Your freedom.

JULY 18

I prayed to the LORD, and he answered me.
He freed me from all my fears.
PSALM 34:4 NLT

As Christians, we know that fear doesn't come from God (1 John 4:16–18). But as humans, we aren't immune to feeling it. David certainly did. Prior to penning the words of today's scripture, David had been running from King Saul. After ending up in enemy territory, he was found out, so he turned to God in prayer. God then freed David from all his fears.

What frightens you? Plans for your future? Relationship troubles? Problems in your family? Here's the bad news: you often cannot control your circumstances, and that can lead to fear. Now for the good news: Jesus is not only in control of your circumstances, but He can set you free from your fear—even when the Father allows difficulties to continue.

Whatever you fear today, offer it up to Jesus. Then leave it in His very capable hands.

MY PRAYER STARTER:

Thank You, Lord, for making it possible for me to leave all my worries in Your capable hands. May I always remember how far-reaching Your provision is for me. I truly have nothing to fear.

JULY 19

"Come to me, all you who are weary and burdened, and I will give you rest. Take my yoke upon you and learn from me, for I am gentle and humble in heart, and you will find rest for your souls. For my yoke is easy and my burden is light."

MATTHEW 11:28–30 NIV

The Jews of Jesus' day were weighed down by the Mosaic law, and their religious leaders created an even greater burden by adding *more* rules. Jesus wanted people to be free from such stress. He said people could find rest for their souls if they followed His gentle, humble lead.

Human nature hasn't changed much since Jesus' time. Even the best Christians and churches can fall into the trap of those Jewish leaders, creating rules and expectations that go beyond the perfect demands of God's Word. But Jesus would tell us the same thing He told His friends and neighbors—you can be free from all the man-made burdens by simply following Him. He perfectly obeyed every law the Father had issued and then died in your place to pay for the times you fall short.

You are absolutely free in Jesus Christ.

MY PRAYER STARTER:

Father, I'm thankful I don't have to follow a laundry list of arbitrary rules to be right with You. May I never fall into the trap of legalism—help me embrace Your freedom.

*I will walk in freedom, for I have devoted
myself to your commandments.*
PSALM 119:45 NLT

How many of your friends follow the ways of the world and not Jesus' teachings? The Lord's commands are far from their minds, and they insist on doing life their own way. They call it freedom, but they are really bound by the chains of sin.

The writer of Psalm 119 offers a stark contrast to this worldly thinking, connecting his desire to walk in freedom with his commitment to following God's commandments. Placing God first, honoring your parents, loving your enemies, and refraining from lying or jealousy or cheating are all examples of living for something beyond yourself—beyond your own sinful cravings. That is what freedom in Jesus really looks like.

Jesus empowers you to turn your back on sin and pursue Him instead. If some stubborn sin is troubling you, recommit yourself to Jesus and His command to love God and love others. When you do that, you'll be truly free.

MY PRAYER STARTER:

Lord, thank You for saving me from myself. Help those
around me see the freedom that comes with serving You,
and help them desire it as much as You desire them.

JULY 21

*Be sure of this: The wicked will not go
unpunished, but those who are righteous will go free.*
PROVERBS 11:21 NIV

Have you ever seen people who seem to get away with everything? People who steal or lie or cheat but never face consequences? Maybe you've even talked to God about them—especially if they have victimized *you*. You wonder, *Why doesn't God punish wicked people on the spot?*

Of course, we wouldn't want swift justice for our own sins, would we? Thankfully, God is slow to anger and quick to forgive. That's His nature. He gives us far more time and opportunity to repent than we deserve. But today's scripture reminds us that a day will come when the wicked will be punished. . .and the righteous will go free. Their righteousness is perfect because it's based on what Jesus did.

This is a wonderful truth, and it should change the way you view sinful people. Pray for them, and thank God for the freedom Jesus has secured for you.

MY PRAYER STARTER:
God, I know many people who desperately need
Your grace. Please reveal Yourself to them and offer
them a second chance, just as You did for me.

JULY 22

"I have swept away your sins like a cloud. I have scattered your offenses like the morning mist. Oh, return to me, for I have paid the price to set you free."

ISAIAH 44:22 NLT

Revelation 20:12 indicates the dead will be judged according to their actions that are recorded in "the books." Ecclesiastes 12:14 says God will bring every evil deed into judgment, and Jesus added that people will give an account for every idle (empty) word they have spoken (Matthew 12:36).

Imagine how many evil deeds you've committed and the empty words you've spoken. They would be too many to count, but each of them is recorded and waiting for you on the day of judgment—or at least they *were*. Jesus' death prompted God to sweep away your sins, scattering them like the wind disperses a mist. The moment you called on Jesus' name for salvation, you were freed. God no longer remembers your sins or holds them against you.

A breathtaking reality, wouldn't you say? It should move you to praise Jesus right now!

MY PRAYER STARTER:
Lord, I know that I don't deserve Your grace. That's why I praise You—not because I think I can earn Your favor but because You've given it to me anyway.

*"But as for me, I know that the One Who bought me
and made me free from sin lives, and that He will
stand upon the earth in the end. Even after my skin
is destroyed, yet in my flesh I will see God."*
JOB 19:25–26 NLV

It's hard to imagine how much pain Job must have felt after losing so much. It's even worse when you consider the trials came through no fault of his own. In a single day, Job lost his livestock, his servants, and worst of all, his ten children. And in the midst of such unbearable grief, he experienced little human support. Job's own wife wanted him to "curse God and die" (Job 2:9), and the three friends who came to console him eventually accused him of secret sin. But Job knew he had been redeemed. . .and that knowledge got him through an awful situation.

Whatever has troubled, is troubling, or will trouble you is covered by your own Redeemer. Unlike Job, you know His name: Jesus, who has freed you from the power of sin. One day, you will see Him in person, and you will worship.

MY PRAYER STARTER:
Thank You, God, for giving the story of Job as encouragement
for whenever life turns sour. And thank You for giving me
the hope that I, just like Job, will see my Redeemer.

JULY 24

Jesus realized that power had gone out from him. He turned around in the crowd and asked, "Who touched my clothes?" ... The woman, knowing what had happened to her, came and fell at his feet and, trembling with fear, told him the whole truth. He said to her, "Daughter, your faith has healed you. Go in peace and be freed from your suffering."

MARK 5:30, 33–34 NIV

There's a big, overarching aspect to Christian freedom—namely, the breaking of sin's bonds. When you believe and receive Jesus, you are no longer enslaved and bound for hell. That freedom is worth more than anything else in this life.

But Jesus provides smaller, day-to-day freedoms as well. In the story of a woman who had suffered from bleeding for twelve years, the Lord honored her desperate, unspoken prayer (a simple touch) by saying, "Be freed from your suffering." What was the key? "Daughter, your *faith* has healed you."

Faith is what pleases God (Hebrews 11:6) and unlocks our salvation (Romans 3:22). Faith is the precursor to freedom.

MY PRAYER STARTER:

Lord Jesus, strengthen my faith, for I know that it's only by faith that I can unlock Your blessings on my life and experience the full satisfaction of the freedom You provide.

JULY 25

"The Son of Man came not to be cared for. He came to care for others. He came to give His life so that many could be bought by His blood and made free from the punishment of sin."

MATTHEW 20:28 NLV

Do you know someone who cares for you when nobody else does? Maybe it's your mother or grandmother. Looking back, you're probably starting to realize how that person has sacrificed their own hopes and dreams to make sure you have everything you need—and probably many things you want.

Mothers and grandmothers live for their offspring. They'll do anything for them, to the point of giving up their own lives if necessary. But as inspiring as that is, no other person can do what Jesus did. The second Person of the Trinity, God Himself took on flesh for the purpose of dying on the cross, paying the price for sin so that we could be freed from the prospect of hell.

"Because of this, those who belong to Christ will not suffer the punishment of sin" (Romans 8:1). How can you express your gratitude to Jesus today?

MY PRAYER STARTER:
Lord Jesus, just as I express my thankfulness to those who have gone the extra mile to care for me, help me express my gratitude to You for going all the way.

JULY 26

"Then they will see the Son of Man coming in the clouds with power and much greatness. When these things begin to happen, lift up your heads because you have been bought by the blood of Christ and will soon be free."

LUKE 21:27–28 NLV

Do you ever wonder if Jesus will return in your lifetime? Have you considered how you might react? Today's scripture indicates that if we are indeed the generation to see Jesus' return, we will have a brief moment to lift our heads and see that our ultimate freedom is upon us.

If Jesus were to return today, we would never again have to worry about the devastating effects of sin—ours or anybody else's. Our battles would be over. Our countenances would change from that of weary travelers to joyful victors as we realize we are about to be whisked away to a place free of pain or sorrow or injustice.

That day is coming, and it may be sooner than you think. Jesus is near!

MY PRAYER STARTER:

Lord, help me look past the disappointments of this life and focus on the promise of Your coming. I know that when You return, all wrongs will be made right. I can hardly wait!

JULY 27

"God raised [Jesus] from the dead,
freeing him from the agony of death, because it was
impossible for death to keep its hold on him."

ACTS 2:24 NIV

Unbelievers have a difficult time understanding why Christians focus so much on Jesus' death, burial, and resurrection. But the Bible teaches that Jesus' death on the cross made it possible for us to be forgiven of our sin. It also says that our faith would be in vain if Jesus hadn't come back from death, because then we'd be without hope of resurrection ourselves (1 Corinthians 15:17).

It was impossible for death to keep its hold on Jesus. He was destined to die in our place and then conquer death, giving those of us who follow Him the ultimate hope: everlasting life. No matter what troubles you face today, He has freed you from the fear of death. You get to live with Him forever! You will either meet Jesus in the air or He will call you forth from the grave. Either way, you can't go wrong.

MY PRAYER STARTER:

God, I know death seems very far away right now—and hopefully, it is. But because of You, I can have peace even as that day approaches. Thank You for this freedom.

JULY 28

"The Spirit of the Lord is on me, because he has anointed me to proclaim good news to the poor. He has sent me to proclaim freedom for the prisoners."

LUKE 4:18 NIV

In one form or fashion, everyone is a prisoner. Some people languish in actual jail cells. Others are imprisoned by anger or lust or fear or greed. And even if none of these descriptions apply to you, you're still living on a broken earth among sinful people in a dying body. Prisoners we are, every one of us.

Until Jesus comes into our lives, that is. Reading from Isaiah's prophecy, Jesus said to His Nazareth neighbors that He'd come "to proclaim freedom for the prisoners."

No shackles can survive Jesus' proclamation. No anger or lust or fear or greed need restrain us any longer. This broken earth and its sinful people and our dying bodies will be dealt with—perfectly, justly, and eternally—by the Lord Himself. The freedom for prisoners that He announced has been partially fulfilled already and will be completely understood soon enough. In the meantime, live like the free person you are!

MY PRAYER STARTER:

Your freedom, Father, is almost too great to comprehend, even while I'm living in this broken world. I can only imagine the joy I'll feel when I'm at home with You! Thank You for giving me this hope.

JULY 29

O Israel, return unto the LORD thy God; for thou hast fallen
by thine iniquity. . . . I will heal their backsliding, I will love
them freely: for mine anger is turned away from him.

HOSEA 14:1, 4 KJV

Israel had a history of backsliding. One generation would walk
with the Lord, then several successive generations would not. It's
almost shocking to read what those wandering generations did
wrong. Yet God stood ready to heal His people, to turn His anger
away from them because He loved them so freely.

Think about your own life. Have there been times when you
played church while your heart was far from Jesus? Sometimes,
we consciously walk away from Him for a season. But because He
loves you so much, Jesus stands at the ready, willing to forgive you
and heal your soul.

Your mistakes (and even your willful disobedience) don't have
the final word in your life. Through Jesus, you can always enjoy
the freedom of returning to God.

MY PRAYER STARTER:
Thank You, God, for Your never-ending willingness to
forgive, even after I purposely tear myself from Your arms.
Without Your mercy, I'd have no hope for redemption.

JULY 30

*My soul is in great suffering. But You, O Lord,
how long? Return, O Lord. Set my soul free.
Save me because of Your loving-kindness.*

PSALM 6:3–4 NLV

Sin causes suffering. Ever since Adam and Eve's failure, every human being has felt the pain of their own bad choices and the failures of others.

The psalm writer David was experiencing that struggle when he penned the words in today's scripture. He longed to be set free, based on the righteousness of God.

As followers of Jesus, we have all known suffering that is, to some extent or another, related to our own sin. We may even call out like David, asking God how long it will be until we're free.

But Jesus has already set you free. Even if you've chosen to walk back into the prison of sin, Jesus has unlocked your cell door once and for all. You're not a criminal anymore, so leave the jail behind and walk in His freedom.

MY PRAYER STARTER:

God, I know it'd be foolish for me to want to return to sin, to trudge back to my cell again after receiving Your pardon. Give me the strength to always choose Your way over my own.

JULY 31

O Lord, in You I have found a safe place.
Let me never be ashamed. Set me free,
because You do what is right and good.
PSALM 31:1 NLV

The world offers many "escapes," and many of them aren't inherently wrong. Movies and music and activities may help you forget our responsibilities for a while. But if you rely too heavily on entertainment, you'll quickly find that it never really sets you free. . .it just distracts you for a time.

In Psalm 31, David declared that the Lord was his escape—not just a temporary distraction from trouble but a truly safe place. There is no shame in wanting to pursue God in that way.

As Christians, we know that we come to God the Father through His Son, Jesus Christ. The one who "was tempted in every way we are tempted, but. . .did not sin" (Hebrews 4:15) is a loving and sympathetic "safe place." He offers freedom and rest.

MY PRAYER STARTER:
Lord, may I never look to a screen or a quick dopamine rush for the ultimate freedom that only You can provide. Keep my focus on what matters the most— only then can I properly enjoy anything else.

AUGUST 1

*"That joy is mine, and it is now complete.
He must become greater; I must become less."*

JOHN 3:29–30 NIV

August has arrived, and with it the "dog days of summer." This is a month for persevering.

To achieve our goal, we must keep focus. We can't charge at every task like an untrained tackle, never reaching the guy with the ball. John the Baptist sure didn't. He was serious—deadly serious—about his goal, and everything we know about him says he focused, persevered, and succeeded.

John's task was to go ahead of Jesus, baptizing followers to receive the "Lamb of God" (John 1:29). He never stopped, refused to waver, and moved ever closer to victory. He began with the end in sight.

Today, let's be like John, finding a thousand different ways to accomplish the one purpose of leading people to Jesus. Let's make sure that whatever we do shows Jesus to someone every single day.

MY PRAYER STARTER:

Lord God, grant me perseverance in my walk with
You. Help me be like John the Baptist, not stopping
until the whole world knows Your name.

AUGUST 2

After this Jesus went out and saw a man who
gathered taxes. His name was Levi (Matthew). Levi was
sitting at his work. Jesus said to him, "Follow Me."
Levi got up, left everything and followed Jesus.
LUKE 5:27–28 NLV

The excitement of new adventures dances in our hearts and gives a kick to our souls. We're eager to rejoice, share, love. That's what Matthew did after Jesus stunned all of Capernaum.

Jesus demonstrated His divinity by healing a crippled man and forgiving his sins. Then He demonstrated His humanity by turning to another man, whom everyone mistrusted, to request his help. When Jesus asked, Matthew responded in faith and then threw a party—"a big supper for Jesus in his house" (Luke 5:29).

Matthew was an eager servant, committed to his Savior and blind to his future. We now know the treacherous road Matthew started on, and we know he never left it. Maybe, when he was hurting, afraid, tired, and discouraged, he remembered those early days with Jesus and found joy and strength to keep going.

You can too. Jesus delights in helping His own.

MY PRAYER STARTER:
Jesus, You never promised this road would be easy; in fact, You stressed how difficult it would be. During these moments, rekindle the fire I first felt when I started down this path.

AUGUST 3

Whatever work you do, do it with all your heart.
Do it for the Lord and not for men.
COLOSSIANS 3:23 NLV

How busy are you? Between the hustle of classes, drama among friends, relationship issues, and family responsibilities, it's easy for a teen to feel defeated, frustrated, and unable to control this ever-growing list of events. But it's not your *what* that's off—it's your *why*.

No one had more to do than Jesus, and we know what framed His every choice. When He had the opportunity to make someone's life better, His answer was always "yes." He didn't look down at a list—He looked through to a heart. He always chose to love, help, forgive, and share.

Everything Jesus did came from the right place for the right reasons. What are your reasons for the things you do. . .or don't do? If your goal is reflecting Jesus to those around you, you'll frame your choices the way He did. You'll find strength to continue the journey. When you know *why* you're carrying on, you'll have the *will* to carry on.

MY PRAYER STARTER:
Lord, I don't need a break from life's struggles—all I need is a firm grasp on the purpose of it all. Never let me forget that only You can give meaning to my decisions.

AUGUST 4

Because Jesus did these things on the Day of Rest,
the Jews made it very hard for Him. Jesus said to them,
"My Father is still working all the time so I am working also."
JOHN 5:16–17 NLV

Jesus walked and taught, helped and healed, always mindful of the needs of others.

A man lame for thirty-eight years craved help, and he happened to meet Jesus on a Sabbath. Jesus not only healed the man's bones but his heart as well, much to the complaint of the Jewish onlookers. Instead of rejoicing, they missed the end by focusing on the means.

Sometimes, our good works will bother people, regardless of our intent or God's resulting blessings. Jesus experienced that, but He didn't care. He continued.

Sometimes, we'll have to explain our motives or methods to unbelievers. But if we're following Jesus—who followed God—we need only God's blessing. So if your work looks unconventional, if it requires boldness and courage, do it anyway. You're in good company.

MY PRAYER STARTER:
Lord Jesus, thank You for not caring what others thought
when You came to earth. Give me the same sense of
determination, especially when I'm following You.

AUGUST 5

*When Jesus reached the spot, he looked
up and said to him, "Zacchaeus, come down
immediately. I must stay at your house today." So he
came down at once and welcomed him gladly.*

LUKE 19:5–6 NIV

The story of Jesus and Zacchaeus is pure and perfect, full of possible loss but rewarded perseverance instead.

As Jesus passed through Jericho, Zacchaeus wanted to see Him. "*But* because he was short he could not see over the crowd. *So* he ran ahead and climbed a sycamore-fig tree to see him" (Luke 19:3–4, emphasis added). And Zacchaeus *did* see Jesus—more importantly, Jesus saw him. Jesus talked to him, stayed with him, saved him.

If we stop at the "but" without getting to the "so," we'll miss Jesus looking at us too. Seeing Jesus and being seen by Him means finding the tree. Jesus will be at that spot because He's already arranged the answer to our obstacle. He's ready to meet us there.

MY PRAYER STARTER:

Thank You, Lord, for noticing me and my often-trivial concerns. I know You can always see me—help me stay in the right spot for me to see You as well.

AUGUST 6

*Do not allow anyone to change your mind. Always do
your work well for the Lord. You know that
whatever you do for Him will not be wasted.*

1 CORINTHIANS 15:58 NLV

Are we tenacious or just stubborn? When we won't quit, is it annoying or admirable? The answers to these questions depend on your reasons for perseverance. If you just want your own way, that's a problem. If you're intent on completing the job God gave you, more power to you!

The apostle Paul wrote to the church in Corinth about Jesus' grace—grace that, besides giving us eternal life, helps us through our work here and now. When our work is God's work, we can't let anything or anyone change our minds.

Yes, obstacles will come, and they'll be challenging. But in Christ we can walk over them, knock them down, or plow through them to reach our destination. Every bit of work we do is clearing the path God's chosen for us—the path that ultimately leads us and others into Jesus' presence.

MY PRAYER STARTER:

Father, let me be determined but not stubborn—resilient but not unreasonable. Help me ground my actions, beliefs, and attitudes firmly in Your Word so that they can never be moved.

Then Jesus said to Simon, "Don't be afraid; from now on you will fish for people."
LUKE 5:10 NIV

Staring at his empty nets after fishing all night, Simon Peter was tired, frustrated, and ready to quit. Just like all of us when we feel fatigue and doubt, he had choices. He chose wisely.

You don't have to know where the fish are. But you can always believe that your best move is to do exactly what Jesus says—don't give up! Peter chose belief over doubt, taking fishing advice from a carpenter: "Master, we've worked hard all night and haven't caught anything. But because you say so, I will let down the nets" (Luke 5:5).

If you let down your nets because Jesus says so, even if the timing seems strange and the odds are against you, Jesus will fill them. If you keep fishing because of your belief and trust, Jesus will help you complete that work and then lead you to amazing work you can't even imagine. If Jesus says so, it's because He'll have more to say to you as you go. Fish are everywhere.

MY PRAYER STARTER:

Lord Jesus, may I never get tired of "fishing" for You, even when the catches grow increasingly scarce. Whether it's with friends, family, or strangers, help me keep sharing Your good news.

AUGUST 8

*For this very reason, make every effort to add to your
faith goodness; and to goodness, knowledge;
and to knowledge, self-control; and to self-control,
perseverance; and to perseverance, godliness; and to
godliness, mutual affection; and to mutual affection, love.*

2 PETER 1:5–7 NIV

Corruption, deceit, unrest, lies, personal attacks—they defined
the apostle Peter's world just as much as they do ours. Peter knew
every follower of Jesus would have to battle long and hard, so he
taught us how to be effective and productive no matter what.

In today's scripture, faith and love bracket all the other factors
that help you fight on. Peter told us all to learn, remember, trust,
push onward. . .keep hold of Jesus.

When we work with Jesus to grow these qualities in our
lives every day, we welcome even the hardships of this world,
because we know we can make a difference in another person's life.
We know the deep joy of becoming a little more like Jesus. . .if we
"make every effort."

MY PRAYER STARTER:
Thank You, Lord, for letting my hardships draw
me closer to You. Help me always keep the faith,
no matter what difficulties I may face.

AUGUST 9

All these many people who have had faith in God are around us like a cloud. Let us put every thing out of our lives that keeps us from doing what we should. Let us keep running in the race that God has planned for us.
HEBREWS 12:1 NLV

When you think about the day ahead, do you see a path lined with budding possibilities, leading to new and exciting heights? Or do you see a landslide of debris that drags you down?

Fear or pain can easily distract, but our work remains. Abraham, Sarah, Isaac, and others of great faith stayed focused regardless of their circumstances. Jesus did too: when He had to suffer shame and die on a cross, He pressed on because He knew of the joy that would later be His (Hebrews 12:2). All that pain was pushed aside to allow for more faith, and that meant going forward.

The same is true for you. You can give up and become a curator of clutter, or you can push that stuff aside and move ahead. It's a daily choice of faith lived out in action.

MY PRAYER STARTER:
Jesus, give me Your perspective. Help me see the obstacles ahead as opportunities for success, not risks of failure. Give me the optimism that comes with trusting You.

AUGUST 10

So do not throw away this confident trust in the Lord.
Remember the great reward it brings you! Patient
endurance is what you need now, so that you will continue to
do God's will. Then you will receive all that he has promised.
HEBREWS 10:35–36 NLT

Keeping your faith in focus when distractions mount is tough. You've got to change your thinking. The foundation of the past— what you've survived, achieved, and enjoyed—supports your future and keeps you going with confidence.

Don't let today's tough work and tomorrow's unknowns cause you to stumble. Give yourself a pep talk, calling on what you know—your history with Jesus—to continue strong and assured. You can keep doing today's work whenever you remember how you did it yesterday.

Every victory with Jesus leads to another. What He's done with you, for you, and through you becomes a part of you. Remembering means repeating every faithful step with assurance. The confidence you have in Jesus now is the same confidence He'll give tomorrow.

MY PRAYER STARTER:
Jesus, thank You for all the trials You've brought me through.
Keep reminding me of them when I face new challenges.
Increase my faith by strengthening my memory.

AUGUST 11

For we are God's handiwork, created in Christ Jesus to do
good works, which God prepared in advance for us to do.
Ephesians 2:10 niv

Do you believe God knows what He's doing? That's not a trick
question. It's a comfort. God finishes what He starts, planning
ahead for every single future event. But He doesn't do it alone. He
could do it all without our limited, flawed, human contribution,
but He never has and He won't start now.

God chooses to do things the hard way, through us, even
though He knows we'll find a way to get scared, make a mess, and
complain. That's okay, He's decided. He declared good work for
us anyway—lots of it—and thought it out long before we would
ever touch it.

We don't see the end yet, but Jesus does. It is our blessing
simply to accept what He's planned. Let's just approach today's
tasks, perform them with love and obedience, and believe they're
part of all the good that is to come.

MY PRAYER STARTER:
God, thank You for always having a perfect plan, even
when life feels chaotic to me. I'm always eager to see
how You're going to work out the next problem.

AUGUST 12

Let us help each other to love others and to do good.
HEBREWS 10:24 NLV

The work God prepared for you is different from that of others, but at its core, it's the same. Fellow believers—whether they're teens or even adults—can be inspired when they see you giving your best for God and the people He loves. It makes them want to join in too.

When we see others power through difficulties and disappointments, we know they must have a good reason. When we see them love and do good even when it's hard—*especially* when it's hard—we know they don't do it for themselves. We know they have Jesus in their hearts.

Watch those around you who treat each day like the gift it is. Watch them overcome anything in their way to be a little more like Jesus. Follow their example. When we act and react in love no matter what, those around us will learn to do the same.

MY PRAYER STARTER:
Thank You, Lord, for giving me a unique mission. As I grow older, reveal to me what You want for my life, and help me embrace each day as a new opportunity to serve You.

AUGUST 13

He said to his disciples, "The harvest is great, but the workers are few. So pray to the Lord who is in charge of the harvest; ask him to send more workers into his fields."

MATTHEW 9:37–38 NLT

We've all behaved like "sheep without a shepherd" (Matthew 9:36). Jesus knows we feel lost, alone, and overwhelmed in many ways— and He knows we're not at our best then. So He sends helpers.

Maybe your helpers have been parents, teachers, good friends, leaders in your church, or even strangers. They came to help you so that you can help others. In life's big, dark pastures, you learn the skills and grace that help you keep going—that comfort you so you can learn today's lesson. And then you can pass it on.

Touching others with Jesus' compassion is a magnificent part of our job. Treasuring the help we've received from others means becoming Jesus' helper when He puts us with those whose pain we understand. We are blessed so that we can be part of the blessing going forward.

MY PRAYER STARTER:

Lord Jesus, thank You for all the people in my life whom You've used to bless me. May this flow never become one-sided—help me use these blessings to bless others in return.

*So let us come boldly to the throne of our gracious
God. There we will receive his mercy, and we will
find grace to help us when we need it most.*

HEBREWS 4:16 NLT

Jesus knows our weaknesses better than we ourselves do. And
He's not ashamed of us. The reality is that Jesus is exceedingly able
and, more important, *willing* to help us. What is our part? Asking.

Jesus is never annoyed with our pleas. We need to believe
that He hears us and sees us and will have an answer for us—a
way for us to keep going when we don't think we can. When
we're weak or hurting or exhausted or embarrassed, His grace
is waiting. He's there when we realize He's our only source, our
only way to carry on.

Whenever all we see is the long road ahead, we need to look
up to the one who's at the beginning, middle, and end. . .the one
who overlooks our stumbles as long as we continue. Our strength
comes from boldly and confidently asking.

MY PRAYER STARTER:
Lord, thank You for offering a way to press on
when life throws me its worst. Whenever I
need help, I know all I have to do is ask.

AUGUST 15

*Blessed is the one who perseveres under trial because,
having stood the test, that person will receive the crown of
life that the Lord has promised to those who love him.*

JAMES 1:12 NIV

Getting through a tough day of school is hard, but since you know the end is coming, you push through to finish your job. Some life struggles, however, seem endless. But it doesn't matter. The same choice applies.

You can quit or you can continue, trusting in God's daily grace to get you through one step at a time. When you complete one day of living for Jesus, it will give way to a new beginning. Today's accomplishment becomes one part of the whole.

As we keep on, we receive a two-fold blessing. We're living and loving Jesus through every hard thing we do *and* showing others what that means. And with every testimony, every victory, every jaw-clenched vow of determination, Jesus becomes rooted ever more deeply in our hearts. We can't share His love without some of it spilling out onto us, growing faith anew. He promises grace, and we receive it to share it.

MY PRAYER STARTER:
Lord, give me the grace to get through today, the determination
to face tomorrow, and the endurance to never give up.
All that I do, may I do it wholeheartedly for You.

Then Jesus stood up again and said to the woman, "Where are your accusers? Didn't even one of them condemn you?" "No, Lord," she said. And Jesus said, "Neither do I. Go and sin no more."
JOHN 8:10–12 NLT

Mistakes derail us. The embarrassing moments of our lives interrupt our work and threaten our growth. Sometimes, we just want to stop—ashamed, defeated, lost. But Jesus has a better response.

When an angry crowd wanted to stone a woman to death for adultery, Jesus didn't join the attack. Nor did He sanction those who ridiculed the woman. He recognized that they were all the same—that *we're* all the same.

Have you ever been caught doing something that made you want to stop, give up, and shrink away? If so, here's the good news: Jesus chooses not to focus on the past or even the present. He's thinking of your future. Nothing you do changes the plans He has for you.

"Keep going, everybody," He says. "Learn from this mistake. Examine your motives. Change your behavior. Just don't stop. Follow Me. Let's go!"

MY PRAYER STARTER:
Lord Jesus, thank You for not letting my mistakes define me. Continue giving me the encouragement and determination to keep pressing forward every time I stumble.

AUGUST 17

"I have put wisdom in the hearts of all who are wise,
so they may make all that I have told you."
EXODUS 31:6 NLV

Ever feel overwhelmed by your responsibilities? Do you feel poorly qualified to do what God says you should? Relax. You are perfectly equipped, just as the Israelites were thousands of years ago.

After escaping their slavery in Egypt—on the long, hard march to their homeland—God told Moses to oversee construction of the tabernacle and its many detailed furnishings. It was a job of massive scope and importance, something that had never been attempted before. Moses had nothing to go by except God's Word. . .but that was plenty.

Today, we have Jesus, who is "the Word" (John 1:1). Through Him, we are equipped and empowered for every task, no matter what challenges line our way. By His power, we can overcome sin, stand firm in battle, and point others to heaven. Let's get to it!

MY PRAYER STARTER:
Sometimes, Lord, I start doubting whether I can perform the tasks You've given me. Whenever pessimism starts creeping into my mind, drive it out with a healthy reminder of just how powerful You are.

*"This is life that lasts forever. It is to know You, the only
true God, and to know Jesus Christ Whom You have sent.
I honored You on earth. I did the work You gave Me to do."*

JOHN 17:3–4 NLV

Before He was arrested for being the Son of God, Jesus prayed. He prayed for those closest to Him, the men who were charged with carrying on His work in a hostile time. He prayed for those of us who would believe in Him for all time. He talked with His Father about His job—to save us and give us "life that lasts forever."

Jesus wasn't there to teach the disciples how to build tents or dig wells. He isn't in your heart to help you write essays or learn how to drive. He came to love you into understanding who God is. He came to offer you the peace and grace you can't manufacture for yourself.

Jesus left no catalog of inventions or body of writings, but He did everything the Father sent Him to do. He didn't stop one moment too soon. Jesus finished His work, and He set ours in motion.

MY PRAYER STARTER:

Thank You, Lord, for giving me everything I need—Your
Word and Your Spirit—to have a saving relationship
with You. Thank You for Your priceless peace.

AUGUST 19

"Let your light shine in front of men.
Then they will see the good things you do and
will honor your Father Who is in heaven."
MATTHEW 5:16 NLV

When Jesus walked this earth, people were drawn to Him. They followed Him, listened to Him teach, and knew that He was different from everyone and everything else in this world. In all that He did, the pure love of God shone through—and those who were lost, ashamed, afraid, or confused accepted that love and experienced new life.

Jesus is not physically walking our streets today, but He's here. He's still reaching out to people, teaching and helping, loving and healing. . .through you and everyone else who follows Him. So how do we carry out this work with His same compassion, mercy, and love?

Let us greet each new day with this thought: *What will I do that shows Jesus to someone else?* That challenge, purpose, and privilege are why we continue to pick up where He left off, why we're still drawn to follow Him. Work that comes from a heart full of Jesus helps others fill their hearts with Him too.

MY PRAYER STARTER:

Lord Jesus, help me find new ways to show You to my friends and everyone around me, just as You showed Your love to others when You walked on the earth.

*"I have prayed that your faith will be strong and that
you will not give up. When you return,
you must help to make your brothers strong."*
LUKE 22:32 NLV

Our failures, our weaknesses, our episodes of abandonment are
no surprise to Jesus. He lived a human life, so He understands
our fears and lapses. And He prays for us. He prayed for Peter,
who He knew would get scared and deny even knowing his Savior.
But Jesus also knew Peter would overcome that horrible misstep,
remember his faith, and get back to work.

That's what we have to remember too. Jesus sees our troubling times, our weakness of faith and dearth of perseverance,
long before we experience them. And He's always ready to help
us return to what we know. What we learn during those failures
will serve us well as we carry on.

When we start again after we've tripped up, backed away, or
lost our confidence, we go with more gratitude, more purpose,
more strength. And we lend our own lives as examples.

Our failures should be commas, not periods. Start again,
keep going.

MY PRAYER STARTER:
Thank You, Jesus, for praying on my behalf, even
when I don't deserve it. Help me always find strength
in the knowledge that You are on my side.

AUGUST 21

*When Jesus heard this, he was amazed. Turning to
those who were following him, he said, "I tell you the
truth, I haven't seen faith like this in all Israel!"*
MATTHEW 8:10 NLT

In the story of a Roman officer's faith and action, even Jesus was amazed. The officer, believing in the Christ who could do all for anyone who believed, claimed Jesus' unlimited power and grace for himself.

The officer traveled to meet Jesus and ask for healing for his young servant. Jesus, in His compassion, agreed. The officer knew he needed no physical proximity for what Jesus was guaranteeing. "Just say the word from where you are, and my servant will be healed," the soldier said (Matthew 8:8). And that's what happened.

The officer knew what to do, and he didn't stop until he did it. He went to Jesus in faith, plainly asked for help, and believed Jesus would listen. His faith guaranteed the Lord would not withhold His willingness and power to finish the work. Let's follow this soldier's bold, confident lead. He did his part and trusted Jesus to do His. That's how God's work gets done.

MY PRAYER STARTER:
God, thank You for always keeping Your end of the
bargain when it comes to salvation. Please grant me
the faith and perseverance to keep my own.

*The night before Herod was to bring him to trial,
Peter was sleeping between two soldiers, bound with two
chains, and sentries stood guard at the entrance.*

ACTS 12:6 NIV

When we've done all we can, sometimes we have to just wait. Waiting is often part of persevering. When we can't do any more, we're tempted to think everything's over, that we've failed, or that God is disappointed in us. No.

In prison for preaching and teaching about Jesus, Peter could do nothing to help himself—nothing but continue in his faith and rest awhile. Jesus knew we'd need that kind of balance too: "Come to Me, all of you who work and have heavy loads. I will give you rest" (Matthew 11:28 NLV).

Rest isn't quitting—it's just a continuation of your work in peace and quiet confidence. To rest like Peter requires faith and trust. It requires reminding yourself that God is still at work, planning your release, even when your part is simply to wait. You're not stopping, just resting.

MY PRAYER STARTER:

God, help me never to jump ahead of You out of
impatience. Rather, whenever the situation is
out of my control, teach me how to wait.

AUGUST 23

Create in me a pure heart, O God,
and renew a steadfast spirit within me.

PSALM 51:10 NIV

We fail others, we fail God, and we fail Jesus. It's just part of being human. While we strive to be more like Jesus every day, our failures hound us like a homing missile.

But God is watching, helping us respond with His Word, fix the broken parts, and get back to work. It's hard to forgive ourselves when we fail, but failure changes nothing. Whatever we began is still there. Whatever is left undone will stay undone until we get back to it. And we do that through confession, renewal, and determination.

When you mess up, ask for forgiveness. Allow Jesus to move all the garbage out of your heart and sweep it clean for a new round of grace and mercy. Then you'll move to the next step with a little more understanding, humility, and wisdom.

None of us likes to fail, fall backward, or lose momentum. But our saving grace is that it's all temporary. Success, completion, and redemption are next.

MY PRAYER STARTER:

Lord, I've made a mess of myself before—it's a terrible, hopeless feeling. Thank You for allowing me to look up each time and take hold of Your extended second chance.

AUGUST 24

I know how to live on almost nothing or with everything.
I have learned the secret of living in every situation, whether
it is with a full stomach or empty, with plenty or little. For I
can do everything through Christ, who gives me strength.

PHILIPPIANS 4:12–13 NLT

Every time we start again, pure and eager, Jesus is there. He's not looking back at our stumbles but forward to our victories—because they're *His* victories too.

Jesus taught us how to continue when we meet with opposition, how to live the truth we know despite what others say, how to have faith regardless of what we see. Our days might be a mess of delays and distractions, our nights restless with worry and fear—but our attitude of "yes, I can" is what counts. We know we don't fight any of these battles alone.

With that belief, attitude, and confidence as our foundation, we do not doubt or quit. We trust that Jesus has provided the solution to every problem well before it's needed. Then we fear nothing and trust that, in the end, we will see a solution.

MY PRAYER STARTER:
No matter how frantic or depressing life gets, Lord,
I know You're still fighting by my side. Victory is just
around the corner, so help me keep fighting today.

AUGUST 25

*Watch yourself how you act and what you
teach. Stay true to what is right.*

1 TIMOTHY 4:16 NLV

We can learn a lot from the advice the apostle Paul wrote to Timothy. Timothy was an eager student, an enthusiastic believer, and a representative of Jesus, just as we should be. Whatever we do today is on display, and others can tell if we're becoming more or less like Jesus each day.

Your private perseverance is public preaching. How you think and what you believe is reflected in how you live.

A heart that keeps faith in Jesus looks like that person who is kind and gentle, even toward bullies and troublemakers. A mind that stays sure of Christ's grace and direction looks like that one guy who carries on despite mistakes and setbacks. Hands that work to show God's love look like someone who forgives the failures of others. Fish are caught even in broken nets.

We're all students learning from each other. Let's be sure that the one thing others learn from us is never-ending love. Grace is received so that it can be given away.

MY PRAYER STARTER:

Lord, my friends at school and church probably have
various opinions about me. No matter what those
opinions may be, help me ensure they all have one thing
in common: that I accurately reflect Your love.

AUGUST 26

*For [God the Father] chose us in [Jesus] before the
creation of the world to be holy and blameless in his sight.*

EPHESIANS 1:4 NIV

When we're being productive and good things are happening, progress feels easy. We're secure, confident, full of purpose. But when our list of recent decisions and outcomes reads like a tragedy, we're ashamed, discouraged, and empty of hope.

But God doesn't see that disappointment. His vision is better. An unproductive field, a lack of tools, or a growth plan that's failed spectacularly are not retreats but a call to trust.

God saw the nation of Israel as worthy of His songs of joy despite the people's obvious weakness: "The LORD your God is with you, the Mighty Warrior who saves. He will take great delight in you; in his love he will no longer rebuke you, but will rejoice over you with singing" (Zephaniah 3:17).

God celebrates us too. He never gives up on us but trusts His Son, Jesus, to supply the strength we don't feel. He sees what we can't. He expects us to keep going until we see it.

MY PRAYER STARTER:

Thank You, Lord, for Your in-depth plan that
always succeeds. Thank You for making treasure
rise from the ashes of my failure.

AUGUST 27

"For sure, I tell you, whoever puts his trust in Me can do the things I am doing. He will do even greater things than these because I am going to the Father."

JOHN 14:12 NLV

As part of God's plan, Jesus recruited His first disciples, and they recruited more and more workers. Now, here you are. Your work today, tomorrow, and always is to continue Jesus' work, and He says you'll be great at it.

Jesus entrusted the whole world to His followers, and He didn't leave us alone or powerless. We have Him in our hearts in the person of the Holy Spirit, who empowers us to continue everything Jesus began.

And when we do, the effect is cumulative. Whatever we do for someone gets passed to the next person—and on and on it goes. Even when we begin with small, seemingly insignificant things, our good deeds accomplish exactly what God intends.

Nothing is wasted and nothing is small as our footsteps start looking like Jesus'. How great is that?

MY PRAYER STARTER:

Lord Jesus, help me follow in Your footsteps, even if my good deeds are small and go unnoticed by everyone else. I know You can do great things with small offerings.

AUGUST 28

*Be full of joy all the time. Never stop
praying. In everything give thanks. This is what
God wants you to do because of Christ Jesus.*

1 THESSALONIANS 5:16–18 NLV

God assigns all of us our tasks. Each of our roles adds to the whole so that nothing will be left incomplete. The way we talk, the attitude with which we give, and the heart of forgiveness we open to people are all tied up in the way we show God to others. It's hard sometimes, but our efforts make everything better, easier, and more effective.

You don't do your work behind a curtain—you're exposed, watched, and even judged. So pray that your relentless habits of joy, prayer, and gratitude blind all who see them with God's grace.

Find joy in the tasks you've been given, joy in doing your small part each day. Stay in constant prayer for strength, wisdom, abilities, and grace to do the parts no one else can. Thank the Lord for today's work and for the bigger, grander work in progress you're already entrusted with for tomorrow.

Jesus plans big. Let's keep up with Him.

MY PRAYER STARTER:

Lord, show me the bigger picture. Remind me
that my faithfulness and good deeds are not in
vain. Give me the strength to never give up.

Now finish the work, so that your eager willingness to do it may be matched by your completion of it, according to your means. For if the willingness is there, the gift is acceptable according to what one has, not according to what one does not have.

2 CORINTHIANS 8:11–12 NIV

Do you know what sometimes gets in the way of the joy we once had in serving Jesus? Comparison. If we start comparing our duties to those of others, we can feel inadequate, unnecessary, and unworthy of God's time. Suddenly, the thrill of salvation degenerates into a petty schoolyard competition.

You should never stack your responsibilities next to another's for comparison or judgment, but rather for advancement and building—for getting the best from yourself and other believers so that all your combined efforts fulfill God's plan.

Your work follows your willingness. When Jesus sees your heart ready, He rejoices in your eagerness and expects you to follow Him through whatever happens. After you finish that job, you'll move on to the next because God is always building. Start with what you have and finish with something better—then start all over again.

MY PRAYER STARTER:

God, may I never feel jealous or judgmental of a fellow Christian's level of responsibility. Help me never forget that as believers, we're all in this race together—and everyone wins.

AUGUST 30

So let's not get tired of doing what is good. At just the right time we will reap a harvest of blessing if we don't give up.
GALATIANS 6:9 NLT

"Once begun, halfway done," the saying goes. Beginning is often the hardest part, but then everything in and out of this world conspires to keep you from finishing. As you grow older, the fight will grow stronger.

Of course, as the apostle Paul said, you must keep away from everything that even looks like sin, aware of all that threatens your faith and work (1 Thessalonians 5:21–22). But you must also beware of other temptations that come in moments of ease or weariness or when nobody's watching. Sometimes, you might question your abilities, your inclination, or even your commitment. Not knowing the end can make the middle harder.

But when you focus on the promise and example of Jesus, you'll find your strength, stamina, enthusiasm, and belief. Don't allow your good progress to become a casualty of fatigue or insecurity. Live by this new mantra: Once begun, with Jesus—done!

MY PRAYER STARTER:

God, thank You for allowing me to start my walk with You. However, I know that starting isn't the end, so help me stay consistent until I reach my destination.

AUGUST 31

"I am with you always, to the very end of the age."
MATTHEW 28:20 NIV

When you've done all you can for as long as you can, overcome the obstacles, endured the waits, rebounded from the setbacks, and leaned on your faith in the Savior who never leaves, you'll know peace today and forever.

Think of the apostle Paul. He came from so far behind but focused only on completion. Sensing his life on earth was almost done, he had peace: "I have fought the good fight, I have finished the race, I have kept the faith" (2 Timothy 4:7).

Jesus has not changed His mind about entrusting you with His work. . .or about your responsibility to it. Every fight is a good fight if you battle the bad along the way. You live in a troubling world that would love to snatch you from your faith before you reach adulthood, but God gives you fierce grace to walk the challenging road, to reach the blessing at the end.

The work Jesus left you is a privilege. Go at it with focus, fearlessness, and faith, knowing you'll never go alone.

MY PRAYER STARTER:

Lord, help me ignore the siren call of weariness,
sin, and disillusionment. Give me the willpower to
push through and reach Your peaceful shore.

SEPTEMBER 1

Jesus spoke to all the people, saying, "I am the Light of the world. Anyone who follows Me will not walk in darkness. He will have the Light of Life."

JOHN 8:12 NLV

This month, as you go back to school, focus on guidance. No teacher, even the very best one, knows everything. But Jesus does. He has absolute knowledge of everything, everywhere, at all times and in all places.

He always knows what to do, and He told us how: "The Father has not left Me alone. I always do what He wants Me to do" (John 8:29).

He does what pleases His Father. *Our* Father.

How do we do what God wants us to do? How do we know if we're doing that today? It's a big question, and our answers might get shaded by our own fear and uncertainty. But Jesus throws holy light on them—revealing direction, guidance, and companionship as we go.

Jesus says *know* Him and *follow* Him. When we learn what that means, we'll know how to do what God wants us to do too. We'll never take a single step blind, unaware or alone.

MY PRAYER STARTER:
Thank You, Jesus, for Your priceless education. Help me use the ultimate textbook—Your holy Word— as a guiding light for each of my actions.

SEPTEMBER 2

Jesus told them, "This is the only work God wants
from you: Believe in the one he has sent."
JOHN 6:29 NLT

Those who lived and walked with the Son of Man saw the miracles and heard the voice of the Son of God. They could ask Jesus anything and He would answer. They could act on what they heard Him physically speak. . .if they chose to believe. They could enjoy instant direction and follow through.

If *you* choose to believe, Jesus will gladly lead you too. Spiritually speaking, you're in His classroom, sitting at His feet, asking questions, learning who He is, and trusting Him to take charge of everything you do. If you commit all you are and all you'll become to His care, you can enjoy an intimate, undoubting knowledge of your Savior.

This belief in Jesus is much more than simply agreeing that He lived. It's knowing that He still lives and that He knows us personally. It's choosing to walk through this life with Him leading the way. His voice is still the same.

MY PRAYER STARTER:

Lord Jesus, this world is a jungle of different ideas and beliefs, and only You know the way through. Lead me with Your wisdom—and give me the wisdom to follow.

SEPTEMBER 3

When he was at the table with them, he took bread,
gave thanks, broke it and began to give it to them.
Then their eyes were opened and they recognized him.
LUKE 24:30–31 NIV

Jesus delights in spending time with us when we're hungry for Him. The two men He met after His resurrection knew their way home to Emmaus, but they needed far more direction for their lives. Jesus began to guide them—and He wanted more time.

As they approached the village to which they were going, Jesus continued on as if He were going farther. "But they urged him strongly, 'Stay with us, for it is nearly evening; the day is almost over.' So he went in to stay with them" (Luke 24:29).

Jesus waits for us to ask for more time at His table, getting to know Him and understanding more. And He always says yes.

Those men from Emmaus recognized Jesus when He broke the bread. And He's still offering Himself to us in that way today. May we "urge Him strongly" to stay with us and fill us with His presence. May His brokenness for us make us wholly His.

MY PRAYER STARTER:

Fill me with an overwhelming hunger for You, Lord,
and help me never to be satisfied until I'm in Your
presence. I want You to be my everything.

*Simon Peter answered him, "Lord, to whom shall we
go? You have the words of eternal life. We have come to
believe and to know that you are the Holy One of God."*

JOHN 6:68–69 NIV

Have you ever thought the road you're walking with Jesus looks
a little too hard and uncomfortable? Have you hoped for a better
way, a more palatable and pleasing path?

Some of Jesus' early followers chose that way, perhaps because
they didn't know their Guide well enough. So Jesus questioned
those closest to them, the Twelve: "You do not want to leave too,
do you?" (John 6:67).

He asks that question of us too when we wobble in our walk.
When we behave as if we're lost, weak, and alone, He wants us
to recognize that we've forgotten who He is. Simon Peter's reply
should stay front and center in all our minds: "You are the Holy
One of God."

No one else even vaguely compares. To whom else would
we ever go?

MY PRAYER STARTER:

Lord, I know You are the only one who gives purpose
and guidance to my life. Help me remember this truth
whenever I feel distracted or disappointed by life's trials.

SEPTEMBER 5

*I have wandered away like a lost sheep; come and
find me, for I have not forgotten your commands.*
PSALM 119:176 NLT

"Come get me, please!" Has this plea ever burst from your lips?
Even with the clear path of obedience stretched out in front of
you, have you ever wandered off—chasing a new trend or trying
to please your friends—with no clue how to find your way back?

Our sense of direction is a constant work in progress, but we
improve a bit with every lost-and-found journey. That's because
our plea for help comes from the right place—from our trust and
belief in the one who *does* know the way.

Lost or confused or just feeling way too far from Jesus, we
admit our weakness. Thankfully, we know where our help is
found—not in forging ahead on our own but in humbly asking
God to bring us back to His pasture. When we finally trade our
own selfish direction for His perfect guidance, we find ourselves
on a path paved with His grace.

MY PRAYER STARTER:
Whenever I fall, God, open my eyes to my need for Your
mercy. And when You help me get up again, help me
remember Your grace and learn from my failure.

SEPTEMBER 6

"Do not let your heart be troubled. You have put
your trust in God, put your trust in Me also."
JOHN 14:1 NLV

Choice is a wonderful thing. We cherish it and claim it as a God-given gift. And it is, so let's make a choice that will make all the ones that follow far less scary.

Jesus prayed for those who trusted their way to Him: "O Father, Lord of heaven and earth, thank you for hiding these things from those who think themselves wise and clever, and for revealing them to the childlike" (Matthew 11:25 NLT).

As a small child, what did you do when you entered unfamiliar territory? Most likely, you asked someone you trusted for directions, believed the answer, and moved forward with confidence. It's a simple choice but one of total faith and surrender. That choice is yours today, and in a thousand ways every day.

The choice comes with a comfort we can't reason or buy. That comfort comes when Jesus is in the lead. He is the one we know and trust, and when we believe the answer He gives, we can move forward with confidence. We are His surrendered children.

MY PRAYER STARTER:

Although I'm no longer a little kid, God, I want to have the same attitude toward You that I used to have toward adults I trusted. Give me a childlike faith so that I can grow more mature.

SEPTEMBER 7

*"Bring them here to me," he said.... Taking the five loaves
and the two fish and looking up to heaven, he gave thanks
and broke the loaves. Then he gave them to the disciples, and the disciples gave them to the people.*

MATTHEW 14:18–19 NIV

Sometimes the problem in front of us is big and overwhelming,
certainly beyond our ability to solve. That's what Jesus' disciples
saw in the thousands of hungry people on the hill. Their instinct
was to send the problem away, but Jesus replied, "They do not
need to go away. You give them something to eat" (Matthew 14:16).

You can imagine the disciples' surprise—and Jesus' delight in
knowing what was about to happen. "We only have a little," they
said. But He said, "It's enough." And that's what He tells us when
we stand in front of big problems: "Run *toward* whatever you
think is too much for you. Just bring whatever you have to Me."

Jesus knew what to do then and He knows what to do with
your offering now. It doesn't matter how small or unimpressive
it might be—give, receive, and share.

MY PRAYER STARTER:
Lord Jesus, I surrender to You what little I have,
knowing You can multiply it if You desire. Help me
never hold anything back—You can have it all.

SEPTEMBER 8

*Every good and perfect gift is from above, coming down
from the Father of the heavenly lights,
who does not change like shifting shadows.*

JAMES 1:17 NIV

Have you ever felt the deafening silence of God? Scared, pressured, and feeling the weight of an unjust world—or worse, the weight of your own guilt and regret—you yearn for even the tiniest comfort. The shards of your trust are buried in a crime scene of choices gone bad, but no sirens sound, no flashing lights signal help is on the way.

That's because the answers to all your questions have already arrived in the person of Jesus Christ. No matter how much it hurts or how abandoned you feel, His help is already here. No new answer doesn't mean no answer at all.

You'll never be so lost that Jesus can't find you. Maybe that's what God is saying in your times of silence: the promise of His grace and guidance remains. He doesn't change. No matter how crazy our world becomes, God's good and perfect gift of Jesus is always with us.

MY PRAYER STARTER:
During times of silence, God, when I can't hear Your voice
or figure out Your will, may I remember that You've already
spoken to me through Your Word. Grant me the ears to listen.

*"When the shepherd walks ahead of them,
they follow him because they know his voice."*
JOHN 10:4 NLV

An angel visited young Mary and told her an unlikely story: she would become mother of the Savior of the world, Jesus Christ. Surprised more than anyone has ever been, she responded out of a faith that knew and trusted God so well that she could recognize His will in her life. Mary's one question was out of genuine practicality, a request to understand what would happen next: "How will this happen?" (Luke 1:34).

Mary's attitude was one of confident acceptance: *If God says so, it must be true and I will act on it.* Joseph made the same choice, trusting God's voice that led him in the same unlikely direction.

Here is an example of the way we should respond when God's direction goes against our common sense. Sheep should never question the shepherd. . .especially when the Shepherd is the Lord of all creation. You know His voice. Just follow.

MY PRAYER STARTER:
Lord, my knowledge is infinitely small when compared to Yours. So please give me the faith to trust You wherever You lead, even if it doesn't make sense at the time.

SEPTEMBER 10

*"Keep on asking, and you will receive what
you ask for. Keep on seeking, and you will find. Keep on
knocking, and the door will be opened to you. For
everyone who asks, receives. Everyone who seeks, finds.
And to everyone who knocks, the door will be opened."*

MATTHEW 7:7–8 NLT

Jesus doesn't play hide-and-seek with us, but He's not the town crier either. He's present, eager, and able but rarely pushy, interruptive, or loud. He knows how we often panic when we're lost or confused. He knows we're desperate for answers, and He understands our pain when the answers seem slow or incomplete. But even in those times, He's teaching us trust.

When we ask for guidance and direction because we believe Jesus will supply it, we're demonstrating trust. When we beg for help from the only one we know can help, He honors that trust.

When we don't know what to do besides turn to Jesus, that's when we know the next step. And one step at a time is all that's required of us. Keep on asking, seeking, and knocking. The door will ultimately open.

MY PRAYER STARTER:

God, thank You for not leaving me alone to figure out the truth for myself, even when I feel alone sometimes. Thank You for Your steady guidance that's always present in my life.

SEPTEMBER 11

Do not keep good from those who should have
it, when it is in your power to do it.
PROVERBS 3:27 NLV

Jesus was never about the audience, always about the affected. He based His actions on His unchanging mission. Unmoved by critics or complaints, He continued to help and heal. When He saw the need of a man in pain, He answered it. But the lovers of the law who watched Him so carefully missed Jesus demonstrating real love right in front of them.

So Jesus said to His critics, "I will ask you one thing. Does the Law say to do good on the Day of Rest or to do bad? To save life or to kill?" (Luke 6:9).

Just as Jesus was Lord of Israel's Sabbath day (and every other), He is Lord of our lives in every particular. As we encounter people we can help, may we follow His lead by keeping our focus on them, regardless of any criticism from others.

The best choice always involves one of mercy, help, love...and whatever else looks like Jesus.

MY PRAYER STARTER:
Lord, help my actions look like You. May all my
friends, my classmates, and everyone else around
me see that You are the Lord of my life.

SEPTEMBER 12

*And this is my prayer: that your love may abound
more and more in knowledge and depth of insight,
so that you may be able to discern what is best and
may be pure and blameless for the day of Christ.*

PHILIPPIANS 1:9–10 NIV

Jesus gives us a lot of credit, trust, and opportunity to exercise the power of our relationship with Him. He believes that if we *know* what is right, we're more likely to *do* what is right. . .that's why He's so interested in making Himself known to us.

The more we know Jesus, the more we'll love Him. We'll see that everything He did for us was and is because He loves us—that's what guides Him. We hear it when He says we're not alone, we rejoice over it in answered prayer, and we see it in the care and help of a friend.

Jesus, Savior of the whole world, is the center of yours—just Him and you, together, navigating your way through this puzzling, temporary home. You grip the steering wheel, but all you need to know is His direction. You'll discover your way *with* Him.

MY PRAYER STARTER:
On the road of life, Lord, I know You're the only
road sign I should follow. Open my eyes to see
Your guidance, and teach me how to obey.

SEPTEMBER 13

"If you take your gift to the altar and remember your brother has something against you, leave your gift on the altar. Go and make right what is wrong between you and him. Then come back and give your gift."

MATTHEW 5:23–24 NLV

We start our day with requests for Jesus to guide us on the right path, to give us answers and direction. We ask Him for the roadmap to the mountaintop. "Of course," He says, "but the way may not be as direct as you think."

Before we know it, He's led us toward the tree line, straight into the undergrowth. "Clear the path," He says, "and then we'll be moving forward again."

We don't always like this part of the journey. But that thick, twisted undergrowth of offenses, grudges, and simple misunderstandings between us and others needs to be addressed. Left unattended, it will get in the way of everywhere we want to go with God. Jesus tells us to go and clear up the mess so that we can just *go*!

MY PRAYER STARTER:

Lord, I know that life can get messy sometimes, and my heart has a way of finding itself in a tangle. Help me cut through the bramble of selfishness and ingratitude with the sword of Your Spirit living within.

SEPTEMBER 14

Be wise in the way you live around those who are not Christians.
Make good use of your time. Speak with them in such a way
they will want to listen to you. Do not let your talk sound
foolish. Know how to give the right answer to anyone.
COLOSSIANS 4:5–6 NLV

Every time you ask Jesus for direction and do what He says, people notice. You go forward on renewed strength and a well-exercised trust that never fails. Your walk becomes your witness, so always be mindful of your words and actions so that Jesus is never misrepresented.

You may know some teens who are in such pain that they can't imagine the Jesus you know. What an opportunity! If you keep stepping out on faith and joy and dependence because of your confidence in the one who knows you, perhaps others will come to know Him too.

Maybe when the lost and hurting see that Jesus guides our steps, the way we walk and talk won't be so hard to understand anymore. Others are always watching, so let's invite them along for the journey.

MY PRAYER STARTER:

Lord, may the kindness I show to others tear down whatever wrong ideas they may have about You. When they look at me, may they see an authentic portrayal of who You really are.

SEPTEMBER 15

*"Do for other people whatever you would
like to have them do for you."*
MATTHEW 7:12 NLV

We can complicate anything with our procedures and protocols, rules and regulations, history and histrionics. We can listen to those who've studied or traveled more than we have—the "experts" who seem to have it all together—and wonder how we'll become the disciples Jesus wants. We see the many times we've gone in the wrong direction and wonder how He'll ever find us useful. Here's the good news: we can stop worrying.

Jesus made things simple. He told us to love, forgive, and share. He told us to be honest, fair, and hospitable. His every reaction was straightforward and uncomplicated.

If you want to follow Him, start today with the simplest of questions: What will my next move mean to those around me? How will my choices affect those I know and love? How will I model Jesus when I cross paths with others?

No need to worry—just ask and answer one simple, useful question each time. You don't need any information you don't already have.

MY PRAYER STARTER:

Lord, help me to worry not just about the effects of
my actions on my own life—help me consider the
feelings and well-being of others as well. May I never
put my own wants over the needs of others.

SEPTEMBER 16

Set my steps in Your Word. Do not let sin rule over me.
PSALM 119:133 NLV

Given long ago but so needed now, the apostle Paul's advice to believers is simple and profound: "Do not act like the sinful people of the world. Let God change your life. First of all, let Him give you a new mind. Then you will know what God wants you to do. And the things you do will be good and pleasing and perfect" (Romans 12:2).

That "new mind" is a daily challenge—and comfort—for us. Each day in our ordinary lives, in all the ordinary things we do, we can renew ourselves in God's extraordinary grace through Jesus Christ. So much is waiting! The new mind is learning new things from God's Word, understanding ever more what we should do.

Your behavior reflects either the world or Jesus. Deciding which way you'll go is a conscious act of either defiance or obedience. Welcoming renewal begins with a small step in His direction.

MY PRAYER STARTER:
Lord Jesus, whether I'm in class, out with my
friends, or simply relaxing at home,
continue renewing my mind each day. Let each
moment be a chance to look more like You.

SEPTEMBER 17

"These things dominate the thoughts of unbeliev-
ers, but your heavenly Father already knows all your
needs. Seek the Kingdom of God above all else, and live
righteously, and he will give you everything you need."
MATTHEW 6:32–33 NLT

Have you ever known a "hoarder"—someone who frantically gathers everything that might be useful in the future? When commonsense preparation devolves into a crazed preoccupation, it becomes easy to forget our whole reason for being on earth.

Life isn't about how much we can hold but about where we are held. It's not about satisfying our needs but about needing only one thing.

When we know, believe, and trust Jesus to be who He says He is, we find peace. We live in a place where we're completely loved, cherished, and directed. We can go about our days in total confidence, not trying to *get* so much as to *give*, not trying to build a kingdom but living in the one God's already designed for us.

When we've learned to follow Jesus' lead, "hoarding" isn't necessary—we have plenty enough already.

MY PRAYER STARTER:
God, help me trust You for everything—even for the
things I don't have but think I should. Only in You can
I find true contentment and freedom from worry.

"I have given you an example to follow. Do as I have done to you."
JOHN 13:15 NLT

You can learn a lot by watching the spiritual lives of those around you. You might not even realize all the examples of grace, patience, discernment, and forgiveness you've seen until you're older and suddenly need to find those qualities in yourself. Then you'll remember, discovering help from others' experience.

Jesus always was and is the picture and pattern of love, no matter the situation. He washed His disciples' feet as a demonstration of love, perfectly showing His humility and service. At other times, He modeled love and grace with His forgiveness, compassion, and wisdom. Whatever question or confusion you face, Jesus demonstrated the best response.

If you watch and learn from Him (and those who love Him), you'll know what to do too.

MY PRAYER STARTER:
When I read about all that You did for other people,
Jesus, may I be inspired to do the same. Teach me how to
follow Your example and love others wholeheartedly.

SEPTEMBER 19

"But go and learn what this means: 'I desire mercy, not sac-rifice.' For I have not come to call the righteous, but sinners."
MATTHEW 9:13 NIV

Jesus was never afraid to visit untidy places, to talk with unschooled people, to bet on unproven hearts. He did these things because He could do nothing else.

At a public dinner, facing criticism over His choice of friends, Jesus drew on the Old Testament prophet Hosea, who spoke of God's love and how we should love Him in return by loving others.

God's not interested in showy but empty declarations of our devotion—He wants to see mercy and loving-kindness toward others. At some time or another, we've all been the one who looks undesirable, unworthy, and unlikely to share the Lord's company. . .but He came to us anyway. Following Him is about showing up for dinner but not showing off. It's about letting compassion be our guide.

Jesus is looking for true hearts, the ones that wade in their own humility and seek ways to see others, not to be seen.

MY PRAYER STARTER:
Lord Jesus, help me show Your love and kindness toward those who need it most—the outcasts, the poor, and the unloved. Help them see You in me.

SEPTEMBER 20

"Go and do likewise."
LUKE 10:37 NIV

Jesus' stories hit His followers where they lived. When the Good Samaritan helped a wounded traveler, Jesus provided guidance for us all. When the unmerciful landowner, blessed and forgiven of his debts, offered no such treatment for the one who owed him, Jesus intended conviction.

We've been the selfish, uncaring character in the story too many times. But Jesus never lets the vast distance between us and His perfection interfere with His mercy. He doesn't plan our path based on the number of mistakes in our rearview mirror. . . but He certainly uses our every experience to direct us.

The right choice is always mercy. The requirement is always faith, not fanfare. Jesus is not looking for your grand abilities, but your anchoring to forgiveness, love, and grace you've already received. You never know who will help you. . .or who will need you.

Be the conduit for Jesus' love. Fellow travelers are waiting.

MY PRAYER STARTER:
Lord, may Your love overcome my selfishness and banish
it from my life. Work through me in everything I do.

*But whoever obeys His Word has the love of God made
perfect in him. This is the way to know if you belong to Christ.*
1 JOHN 2:5 NLV

With profound regret, we remember the times we ignored God's
guidance. The guilt is heavy. But His mercy says, "Follow Me now.
Let's make the best of all that remains."

Released from captivity, the Israelites went home to rebuild
their ruined temple. They started working on their own houses,
though, and the results weren't good. Through the prophet Haggai's
guidance, they repented with sincere remorse for the wrong way
they'd gone. God forgave them and focused on going forward, on
filling their life to the full: "Is the seed still in the store-house?
The vine, the fig tree, the pomegranate and the olive tree have
not given any fruit. Yet from this day on I will bring good to you"
(Haggai 2:19).

Peter's fragile faith led to his momentary betrayal of Jesus,
but the Lord didn't let that change His plan for the great apostle.
Jesus knows what great temples obedient believers can build.
Looking back at irrelevant ruins won't change your past, but
looking toward Jesus will utterly transform your future.

MY PRAYER STARTER:
God, I'm sorry for the times I've slipped and disobeyed Your
guidance. I know You've already forgiven me, so help me
learn from those mistakes instead of wallowing in guilt.

"It is bad for him who says to a piece of wood, 'Wake up!' or to a stone that cannot speak, 'Get up!' Can this teach you? See, it is covered with gold and silver. There is no breath in it."

HABAKKUK 2:19 NLV

Moses understood the principle of never looking back, of overcoming his past to get to his future: "Because Moses had faith, he left Egypt. He was not afraid of the king's anger. Moses did not turn from the right way but kept seeing God in front of him" (Hebrews 11:27).

Jesus leads us forward, through anything in the way. He won't get so far ahead that we can't see Him, but He stays in front, awaiting our commitment to follow. We certainly can't lead ourselves out of any kind of captivity, but God can.

Maybe you're held back by guilt, depression, anxiety, or peer pressure—it doesn't matter. Looking toward Jesus is the only thing that can break your captivity. Going forward in your faith is what guides you away from sin and toward the good work you'll do for Him.

MY PRAYER STARTER:
Thank You, Lord, for freeing me from the bondage of sin and self-loathing. Be my guide as I walk toward Your perfect Light.

SEPTEMBER 23

For God is not a God of disorder but of peace.
1 CORINTHIANS 14:33 NIV

Jesus always gave one simple, forward-moving direction: "Follow Me." In His encounters with the sick or hurt or lost, His words were straightforward and without confusion. He told the lame man to pick up his mat and walk. He told the guilty to go and sin no more.

Jesus always focused on the immediate task, and that led to the eternal triumph. That's order and control, not worry and disarray. As we think about the obstacles in front of us, we see a tangled, scary mess. . .but Jesus sees a box of choices. He points out the most obvious one, the one that will lead us where He wants us to go. It's up to us to believe and follow.

Yes, there's another box, full of the choice to worry and grumble. But first, do this one thing today: simplify the confusing. Listen, understand, obey. . .and move.

MY PRAYER STARTER:

Lord Jesus, out of all life's confusing choices, guide me into the path that pleases You. Help me make all my decisions by first looking for Your footprints.

SEPTEMBER 24

Make it your goal to live a quiet life,
minding your own business and working with your
hands, just as we instructed you before.
1 THESSALONIANS 4:11 NLT

Are you a no-nonsense, gimme-a-plan type of guy? If so, you probably find great comfort in the apostle Paul's three-point directive above. The answers you need usually fall somewhere within.

It's hard to find a "quiet life" in our cymbal-clanging, attention-demanding world, but Jesus modeled that life for us. His singular focus—following only God's direction—maintained peace in His life.

When drama grips your social life and chaos flashes on the news, grab hold of the quiet voice of God, which drowns out all the other voices saying they know better.

Quiet means focused, confident, committed, and unafraid to trust Jesus' lead. What is He saying to *you*?

MY PRAYER STARTER:

Thank You, Lord, for showing me how to live a
peaceful life. Amid the chaos around me, help me
discern Your voice—and follow it closely.

SEPTEMBER 25

His mother said to the helpers, "Do whatever He says."
JOHN 2:5 NLV

No matter how smart we think we are, we can get lost trying to take someone else's road. Many of those around Jesus wanted Him to be the warrior king that would save them in worldly battles with stunning heads-on-sticks victories. He said no.

It was Jesus' business to save His people from this world and teach us how to help save others. *That's* the plan Jesus followed to the end. He never wavered or tried to do anything other than what He began. His practical focus says, "Tend to your work where you are." That was John's approach—he baptized where there was "much water" (John 3:23). With no worries about what wasn't there, he used what was and carried on.

God's guidance always fits *you*, not another person. And when you put it on, then you can really go places with Jesus, minding the business He says is yours.

MY PRAYER STARTER:

Lord, I realize that I'm simply incapable of some of the deeds I see other Christians doing for You. But that's okay. Thank You for giving me my own purpose—and giving me the resources to fulfill it.

SEPTEMBER 26

*Do not merely listen to the word, and so
deceive yourselves. Do what it says.*
JAMES 1:22 NIV

Do you crave a big purpose—a world-changing mission that only you can do? Do you want your actions to matter? If so, here's some great news: you don't have to wait. Jesus' mission *did* change the world, but it also changes one person at a time.

Sometimes, the most important thing Jesus could do was a very small thing He did willingly. He paid attention and didn't overlook the chance to help, to be in the flesh what He was in the Spirit. You can too.

Your big purpose has just begun, but you've got to approach it one day at a time—just like Jesus. Ask yourself, *What can I do right now in my family, my school, my church, and my community?* Pay attention, as you consider the whole big world, to the one person you see in front of you.

MY PRAYER STARTER:
Even the biggest forests, Lord, are made of individual
trees. So whenever I'm searching for Your master
plan for my life, help me also notice the tiny
opportunities that present themselves each day.

SEPTEMBER 27

"You have done well. You are a good and faithful servant. You have been faithful over a few things. I will put many things in your care. Come and share my joy."
MATTHEW 25:21 NLV

Jesus told the story of a man who gave three servants bags of gold. He was pleased with the two who were unafraid to go forward and used what they had been given to make more. That's our story every day: our trust must match our bag of gold.

Let us receive what Jesus gives us and hide nothing. Let us remember that every divine touch is meant to be used in the most human ways. When He gives us boldness, wisdom, compassion, and talent—and He will, regularly—let us ask who needs the blessing of those gifts passed on. Let us listen and follow Him.

Others will see when God elevates the most ordinary and humble to "good and faithful." We become effective representatives for Jesus when we're grateful for all we've been given and let Him direct us to use it all well.

MY PRAYER STARTER:
Lord, help me be thankful for all Your blessings—
so thankful that I burn with the passion to share them
with others. May I find new ways to do so every day.

SEPTEMBER 28

"We have no power to face this vast army that is attacking us. We do not know what to do, but our eyes are on you."

2 CHRONICLES 20:12 NIV

"What now?" we ask when our enemies—in whatever form—approach, and we see no good way to go.

When Judah's King Jehoshaphat was outnumbered and about to be attacked, he chose to completely depend on God. His was a confident, expectant faith.

What a comfort that leadership must have been to the warriors! In his transparency, Jehoshaphat showed everyone that prayer and surrender to God's control are the first moves to make, not the last. The king couldn't see himself doing anything on his own, but he believed that God would show him the way.

Sometimes, you're the warrior who needs to see a mature Christian live out that faith in a frightful time. And sometimes, it's up to you to lead others into the battle encouraged and unafraid. When the first step is always in Jesus' direction, perfect direction will follow.

MY PRAYER STARTER:
Lord, help me know when to follow and when to lead. Give me the humility to accept instruction and the wisdom to guide others to You.

SEPTEMBER 29

In everything set them an example by doing what is good. In your teaching show integrity, seriousness and soundness of speech that cannot be condemned.

TITUS 2:7–8 NIV

Maybe you've tutored a fellow student or helped a friend resolve an important issue. If so, you know that we often learn the most when we teach someone else. Similarly, knowing what Jesus wants us to do isn't a formula or a spreadsheet, but it is something we learn even better by teaching.

When your life splits into different roads, you must choose. Sometimes, those roads are major highways with lifelong implications. They matter greatly. But far more often, the choice is a tiny little trail that reveals far more about who (and whose) you are.

The "least of these" (Matthew 25:40) moments are everywhere, and others see when we act with love, courage, humility, and compassion. Jesus walks among us, giving us the opportunity to walk with Him and bring others along too. What an awesome privilege! As we travel this world in His footsteps, we teach those around us how to follow Him too.

MY PRAYER STARTER:

God, may all my relationships be two-way streets of learning. Teach me how to encourage—and be encouraged by—other members of Your church.

SEPTEMBER 30

For this God is our God for ever and ever;
he will be our guide even to the end.

PSALM 48:14 NIV

Jesus once exclaimed, "I have come into the world as a light, so that no one who believes in me should stay in darkness" (John 12:46).

That's a promise that will never fail—and it brings us right back where we started this month. When we know and believe in the most faithful Guide ever, we leave the darkness, never to return. We can let go of fear and confusion and worry and doubt and never be lost again.

We know how to put trust in the Savior who came to anchor Himself in our hearts. And we hold tight to the opportunities to obey and follow Him, even through the dimly lit times, with great courage and confidence so that others may see their journey lighted as well.

Your life will cause others to ask in awe, "How do you know what to do?"

Stand in the light of Jesus, the one you know and love, the one who knows and loves you. Say in pure devotion, "I go where You lead."

MY PRAYER STARTER:

Savior, may my life be a lighthouse, guiding others toward
the truth. When other people look at me and wonder
what I live for, help me point them to Your grace.

OCTOBER 1

His divine power has given us everything we need
for a godly life through our knowledge of him who
called us by his own glory and goodness.

2 PETER 1:3 NIV

Autumn is upon us, and change is in the air.

As a teenager, you know how stressful change can be, even when you know it's for the best. But you have an advantage. Many times, people who live apart from God (and sometimes even Christians) try to dig down deep and muscle through difficult times of change on their own. Then they crash.

But Jesus' relentless call is "Come to Me. . . ." He wants to supply you with everything you need, including the power and endurance to do what He has called you to.

Each moment is a moment of change, so welcome Jesus into every detail. Talk with Him, listen for His voice, and request His supernatural strength to help you. Then watch in amazement at what He does.

He is the unchanging, everlasting God. As you head into a season of change, remember that Jesus is steady, safe, and secure.

MY PRAYER STARTER:

Thank You, Jesus, for giving me an anchor point in the midst of change. No matter what aspects of life dissolve and morph around me, I know You will stay the same.

OCTOBER 2

"I, even I, am the Lord. There is no one who saves
except Me.... I am God and always will be.
No one is able to take anything out of My hand.
I do something, and who can change it?"

ISAIAH 43:11,13 NLV

We live in a world of falsity. Fake smiles. Fake news. Fake people. Both teens and adults are addicted to screens, finding it hard to relate to the real world. Surrounded by so much unreality, it's hard to know what is true and good. But God wants you to know and live in *His* truth—that He is the unchanging, everlasting God.

And, to keep the theme of this book, so is Jesus. The writer of Hebrews reminded us that "Jesus Christ is the same yesterday and today and forever" (13:8). We know Jesus was loving and compassionate to the people He met two thousand years ago. He's still that way today. We know He was wise and powerful when He formed the universe. He's just as wise and powerful today. And, young Christian, He is on your side.

MY PRAYER STARTER:
Lord Jesus, may Your truth cut through the blurry fog
of fake news and manufactured outrage. May Your
Word be the only source of information I trust.

OCTOBER 3

*So all of us who have had that veil removed can see
and reflect the glory of the Lord. And the Lord—
who is the Spirit—makes us more and more like him
as we are changed into his glorious image.*

2 CORINTHIANS 3:18 NLT

God's Word reminds us, over and over, that we are to be light in a world darkened by sin. Where do we get that light? It comes from God Himself, from spending time in His presence. Think of those solar lights people put along their sidewalks: the longer they're in the light of a sunny day, the brighter and warmer they glow.

When you spend time with Jesus, He lights up everything about you. Psalm 34:5 says, "Those who look to him for help will be radiant with joy; no shadow of shame will darken their faces." You can emanate His light, love, and peace—even during times of change—because you've been soaking in it. Ask Jesus to give you a deep desire for His Presence. He'll answer, and you'll begin to light up your world.

MY PRAYER STARTER:

Lord, I know You're the only true light that can brighten my soul. May it grow ever brighter until I reach heaven's shore.

OCTOBER 4

"Do not be afraid. For I have bought you and made you free. I have called you by name. You are Mine! . . . You are of great worth in My eyes. You are honored and I love you."

ISAIAH 43:1, 4 NLV

During times of change, it's important to remember who you are. Take another look at today's scripture: Can you picture Jesus saying these words directly to *you*? Do you really believe that God loves you this much?

When God Himself tells you who you are, it changes everything! Let Him speak to your heart every day and remind you of your worth—how much you matter to Him. Before you get out of bed every morning, thank God for a new day and ask Him to remind you of His truth.

You are God's child because you accepted Jesus' work on the cross. You have nothing to fear. God is always with you and calls you by name. You are of great value to Him.

MY PRAYER STARTER:

God, thank You for allowing me to rest in Your love, even in the midst of change. May Your grace be on my mind each morning as I open my eyes and begin my day.

OCTOBER 5

The LORD is my strength and shield. I trust him with all
my heart. He helps me, and my heart is filled with joy.
I burst out in songs of thanksgiving. . . . Lead them like
a shepherd, and carry them in your arms forever.

PSALM 28:7, 9 NLT

In times of change, Jesus is right there with you, ready to help in any way you need. God values you, and He is committed to caring for you in every way.

The Lord leads you like a shepherd leads his sheep. He even carries you in His arms! Jesus knows exactly what you need, and He knows how to get you from one place to the next. When you allow Him to help you work through your challenges and fears and complex emotions, miraculous things happen. Things you once thought impossible begin to take place before your eyes.

Picture yourself as a little lamb carried in the arms of Jesus. Nothing in the world can disrupt the peace and security He provides.

MY PRAYER STARTER:
God, thank You for holding me when I can't walk—
for leading me in Your path when I can't find my way.
Thank You for being the Good Shepherd in my life.

OCTOBER 6

*"For the Holy Spirit will teach you at that
time what you should say."*
LUKE 12:12 NIV

Some people thrive in high-pressure environments. Others run from them. Whether you thrive, run, or land somewhere in the middle, Jesus wants to help.

Next time you find yourself in an intimidating situation—a difficult test, a new summer job, or maybe even a complex issue that threatens a friendship—just take a deep breath and relax. *That sounds great*, you may be thinking. *But how?*

Here's the thing: if Jesus Christ is alive in you, then He is at work. If He wants you to do or say something in a particular situation, then you can trust Him to give you the guidance you need. And you don't even have to worry about it ahead of time.

This is a faith thing, and it might take some practice, so whenever you know you're headed into a stressful situation, be sure to take Jesus with you. Invite Him to speak to you. Tell Him how you're feeling. Then let it rest in His hands.

MY PRAYER STARTER:
Lord, I know life isn't always stress-free—sometimes, it seems like what I'm facing is too much to bear. During these moments of tension, may I find peace in Your presence.

OCTOBER 7

Don't worry about anything; instead, pray about everything. Tell God what you need, and thank him for all he has done. Then you will experience God's peace, which exceeds anything we can understand. His peace will guard your hearts and minds as you live in Christ Jesus.

PHILIPPIANS 4:6–7 NLT

Teens face more anxiety now than ever before, and both science and common sense show that holding these worrying thoughts inside can cause harm to our bodies. It's actually dangerous to carry such heavy burdens, but during times of change, they're inevitable.

God wants you to always take your fears and worries to Him. He wants you thankful rather than stressed—and He alone can help you get there. When you turn to Him in grateful prayer, He gives you His peace. It's a peace that won't make sense to anyone but you and God. . .a peace that floods your heart no matter what you're facing.

Just sit down with Jesus and say, "Lord, it's too much. I don't know what to do." Release everything into His hands, and allow Him to carry your burdens.

MY PRAYER STARTER:

Lord, I'm sick of constantly worrying about my past, present, and future—I'm ready to make a change. Flood my mind with Your peace, driving out all the anxiety and fear.

OCTOBER 8

*A cheerful heart is good medicine, but a
broken spirit saps a person's strength.*
PROVERBS 17:22 NLT

Change and stress go hand in hand. And we know that stress is hard on us both physically and mentally. That's one reason God doesn't want us to carry everything on our shoulders.

Life can be hard. Traumatic things do happen. Does God want you to just sweep them under the rug and paste on a fake happy face? Of course not. Jesus invites you to go to Him with all your struggles. He knows how hard life can be (He lived a pretty challenging human life Himself), and He wants you to know that He is with you. He will stay with you through anything you face, everything that could possibly sap your spirit's strength.

As you linger in Jesus' presence, give Him permission to comfort you and give you a cheerful heart. In times of stress and change, He will fill you with true joy, cheering your heart and mind. That's the best medicine you could ever take.

MY PRAYER STARTER:

Thank You, Jesus, for staying with me through the midst of heartbreak, chaos, and trauma. I know that no matter what happens in the future, You will always be by my side.

OCTOBER 9

Let the peace of Christ rule in your hearts, since as members of one body you were called to peace. And be thankful.
COLOSSIANS 3:15 NIV

Letting the peace of Christ rule in your heart means you have an inner calm that can only come from trusting Jesus. As problems arise (and they will), you are pacified by the Lord's power over them all. Letting the peace of Christ rule in your heart means you'll begin to see life as an adventure of overcoming. Along with Jesus, you'll anticipate challenges and changes instead of fearing them, knowing that God will bring good out of everything that you submit to Him.

Get in the daily habit of praying, taking all of your problems, worries, and concerns to Jesus—then enjoy the peace He offers. And thank Him for His peace working in your heart as you make your way through life's changes. He's walking through them with you.

MY PRAYER STARTER:
Lord, thank You for reassuring me that I'll never face
life's obstacles alone. Thank You for the help Your
Spirit provides each day. Thank You for Your peace.

OCTOBER 10

When I am afraid, I put my trust in you.
PSALM 56:3 NIV

Have you ever wasted time and energy worrying about something that ended up working itself out? Life's uncertainties can put us in a place of almost overwhelming fear, and fear of the unknown brings sleeplessness and stress.

Ever since Adam and Eve's disobedience brought sin into the world, humans have struggled with fear of the future. But Jesus has said, "Who of you by worrying can add a single hour to your life? Since you cannot do this very little thing, why do you worry about the rest?" (Luke 12:25–26).

Jesus calls you to come to Him for rest. You can unload your biggest worries and fears and trust Him with all of them. Remember, He has promised to always be with you. So place your questions, your concerns, and your unsettled fears in His capable hands. He will calm your anxious heart.

MY PRAYER STARTER:
God, thank You for taking the fear out of the unknown.
Help me embrace life's uncertainties,
knowing that You're working them out for the best.

OCTOBER 11

*"I have told you these things, so that in me you may
have peace. In this world you will have
trouble. But take heart! I have overcome the world."*

JOHN 16:33 NIV

C. S. Lewis has written, "Life with God is not immunity from difficulties but peace within difficulties." These words reflect Jesus' warning that we *will* have trouble in this world. This world isn't heaven, after all, so we can't expect our lives to be perfect. But Jesus offers something amazing in the midst of our troubles: His presence, which in turn brings perfect peace.

The world God created is a beautiful place. But because of sin, it's also a messed-up place—a constantly shifting labyrinth of fear and worry. Because we live in a fallen world, things will never be wholly right until Jesus returns. In the meantime, He promises to be with us, helping us overcome this world and the heartburn it causes us.

Don't expect an ideal life on this earth. Just embrace the reality of God's peace and presence in your life.

MY PRAYER STARTER:
Lord God, may this fallen world never drag my spirits
down so much that I lose sight of Your master plan.
Give me peace in the face of troubling mysteries.

OCTOBER 12

"Anyone who listens to my teaching and follows it is wise,
like a person who builds a house on solid rock.
Though the rain comes in torrents and the
floodwaters rise and the winds beat against that house,
it won't collapse because it is built on bedrock."

MATTHEW 7:24–25 NLT

The Leaning Tower of Pisa is famous for its poor foundation. It leans precariously, and vast amounts of time and money have been expended trying to correct the problem. All this because the tower was built on soft land, with a foundation only about ten feet deep.

Without doubt, foundations are important—for construction projects as well as for life. That's especially true when the earth below us starts to shift and change.

Is your foundation built on the solid rock of Jesus Christ? Aligning your heart and mind with God's truth—especially when you are still young—will keep you firm and steady as you grow older, no matter what's happening around you. When the earth below is shifting, you can hang on to the truth of Jesus' great love for you. If your hope is built on Him, you will not fall (Psalm 121:3–5).

MY PRAYER STARTER:
Lord Jesus, be the foundation for my life—as I
mature into adulthood, as I find my way in the
world, and as I close my eyes in death.

OCTOBER 13

Cast all your anxiety on him because he cares for you.
1 PETER 5:7 NIV

In the *Amplified Bible,* today's scripture reads like this: "casting all your cares [all your anxieties, all your worries, and all your concerns, once and for all] on Him, for He cares about you [with deepest affection, and watches over you very carefully]."

Have you ever cast a specific care on Jesus, only to reel it back in later? This amplification of this famous verse implores us to cast all of our cares, anxieties, worries, and concerns onto Jesus—and then leave them with Him once and for all. But how can we do that?

It's a test of your faith. Do you truly believe that Jesus cares about you with the deepest affection and concern? Do you really believe that He constantly and carefully watches over you today and every day? If you answer "yes" to those questions, you will trust the Lord's faithfulness to care for you. You'll allow Him to handle every one of your worries today and every day.

MY PRAYER STARTER:

Lord Jesus, only You can relieve me of the worries and fears that keep me up at night. Give me the faith to cast all these cares on You—and leave them in Your hands.

OCTOBER 14

Give your burdens to the LORD, and he will take care of
you. He will not permit the godly to slip and fall.
PSALM 55:22 NLT

"Lord, I don't know what to do right now!" That's a valid prayer. When you feel helpless, Jesus wants you to come with that kind of humility. Not every challenge has an obvious solution. You can't fix everything, even when you want to. Some things were never yours to fix in the first place. When you're in over your head, Jesus is there.

A modern paraphrase of today's scripture verse says, "Pile your troubles on GOD's shoulders—he'll carry your load, he'll help you out. He'll never let good people topple into ruin" (The Message).

When you're going through times of change, ask Jesus to help you discern His voice. Ask Him to make Himself clear. Then simply rest and trust, knowing that He is faithful and that He has good plans for you.

MY PRAYER STARTER:
Lord, may my lowest point be the beginning of my
upward climb toward You. Please turn my times of
fear and uncertainty into opportunities for faith.

OCTOBER 15

When anxiety was great within me, your
consolation brought me joy.

PSALM 94:19 NIV

You probably already know that Psalm 119:11 urges us to hide God's Word in our hearts. And that Jesus said, "The Advocate, the Holy Spirit, whom the Father will send in my name, will teach you all things and will remind you of everything I have said to you" (John 14:26).

Hide the following scriptures in your heart and ask the Holy Spirit to remind you of them when you need them most:

- "Peace I leave with you; my peace I give you. I do not give to you as the world gives. Do not let your hearts be troubled and do not be afraid" (John 14:27).

- "I keep my eyes always on the LORD. With him at my right hand, I will not be shaken" (Psalm 16:8).

- "God has said, 'Never will I leave you; never will I forsake you.' So we say with confidence, 'The Lord is my helper; I will not be afraid. What can mere mortals do to me?'" (Hebrews 13:5–6).

MY PRAYER STARTER:

Lord God, help me hide Your Word in my heart. That way, when my friends and others around me ask me what gives me peace—and even when I myself wonder the same—I will have a sure and perfect reply.

OCTOBER 16

"I have loved you just as My Father has loved Me.
Stay in My love. If you obey My teaching, you will live
in My love. In this way, I have obeyed My Father's
teaching and live in His love. I have told you these things
so My joy may be in you and your joy may be full."

JOHN 15:9–11 NLV

Jesus very plainly told us how we can show God that we love Him: by obeying His commands. What are those commands? To love Him and to love others. Everything in God's law, Jesus said, depends on those two things (Matthew 22:36–40).

The Bible warns us never to forget our first love, Jesus. Here's what He Himself told the church in first-century Ephesus: "You do not love Me as you did at first. Remember how you once loved Me. Be sorry for your sin and love Me again as you did at first" (Revelation 2:4–5).

This world is ever changing, but our love for Jesus must remain firm. And He has given us clear direction for staying in His love and returning to it when necessary. What an amazing Lord we serve!

MY PRAYER STARTER:

Lord Jesus, may my love for You stay strong, no matter the situation. But if it does begin to dim or flicker, please rekindle it by reminding me of Your own love toward me.

There is no one like You among the gods, O Lord.
And there are no works like Yours. All the nations You
have made will come and worship before You, O Lord.
And they will bring honor to Your name. For You are
great and do great things. You alone are God.
PSALM 86:8–10 NLV

Time spent with Jesus will accomplish more than anything else you could ever do. Worry and stress cause harm, but taking everything to Jesus in prayer shifts the burden onto His capable shoulders.

Make Jeremiah 32:17 your sincere prayer today: "O Lord God! See, You have made the heavens and the earth by Your great power and by Your long arm! Nothing is too hard for You!"

Over the course of the day—when your alarm goes off, in between classes, on your free time, and as you get ready for bed—repeat that verse again and again. Ask God to help you, believing that *He can do anything!* No problem is too hard, too big, or too small for His help. Remember, Jesus said His Father cares when sparrows fall to the ground. . .and that He cares for *you* in much greater measure (Matthew 10:29–31).

MY PRAYER STARTER:
Almighty God, thank You for providing a way to
spend time with You throughout each day.
Help me never to take this privilege for granted.

OCTOBER 18

Trust in the LORD with all your heart and lean not
on your own understanding. In all your ways submit
to him, and he will make your paths straight.

PROVERBS 3:5–6 NIV

Good decision-making is a vital life skill—especially when we face the stressful uncertainties of this world. But we often make things harder than they need to be. Why? Because we forget that Jesus wants to help us make our decisions. When we leave Him out of the process, it causes us unnecessary trouble. But it doesn't have to be that way.

Go to Jesus in prayer. Talk to Him about the decisions you're facing. Ask Him to forgive you for the times you've left Him out of the equation. Ask Him to transform your thinking. Then listen for His voice as you go through your day, trusting that He will be with you. Jesus, your good shepherd, will always lead you in the right way.

MY PRAYER STARTER:
Lord, You know everything, and I don't. Every time
I'm faced with a decision that seems out of my league,
help me rely on Your wisdom, not my own.

OCTOBER 19

Now may the Lord of peace himself give you peace at all times and in every way. The Lord be with all of you.

2 THESSALONIANS 3:16 NIV

Imagine being taught by someone who really knows the answer to everything. Here's the amazing news: you are! Centuries before Jesus' birth, the prophet Isaiah wrote, "All your children will be taught by the LORD, and great will be their peace" (54:13). If you've committed your life to Jesus Christ, His Spirit is within you to teach you all things—and that results in peace.

Jesus has authority and power over *all things.* It's important to remember that truth in every moment, every challenge, and every circumstance, because it means you can go to Him with every question. He is bigger than all of your problems, failures, and fears—bigger than the changes, uncertainties, and disappointments of your life.

You have access to this divine power at every moment!

MY PRAYER STARTER:

Lord, let me be taught by Your truth—not the so-called "truth" of the world. Life is full of hard decisions, so I need Your Spirit to direct my thoughts at every point.

He reached down from heaven and rescued me; he drew me out of deep waters. He rescued me from my powerful enemies, from those who hated me and were too strong for me. They attacked me at a moment when I was in distress, but the LORD supported me. He led me to a place of safety; he rescued me because he delights in me.

PSALM 18:16–19 NLT

Ever been in big trouble—or, as today's scripture puts it, "deep waters"? At some time or another, we all face situations that just seem too big to handle, times we feel we have nothing firm to stand on. And we're not sure we can tread water long enough for anything to change.

But you know what? The Lord supports you. Jesus cares about everything that has, is, and will happen to you. . .and He wants to reach down from heaven to help. He will lead you to a place of safety, and He can use any means He chooses to meet any need you have.

Just talk to Jesus about your struggles. He loves to change things for the better.

MY PRAYER STARTER:

Thank You, Jesus, for pulling me out from the deep waters of my sin, doubt, and insecurity. Thank You for the love and safety You offer as I walk with You.

OCTOBER 21

The LORD gives his people strength.
The LORD blesses them with peace.
PSALM 29:11 NLT

On your own, you'll never find lasting peace. But when you obey God, He gives you true peace. That's good news! Though there is a bit of a catch. . .obedience isn't a once-for-all thing.

Here's what the psalm writer David told us to do: "Turn away from evil and do good. Search for peace, and *work to maintain it.* The eyes of the LORD watch over those who do right; his ears are open to their cries for help" (Psalm 34:14–15, emphasis added). This means you have the privilege of giving your worries to Jesus and replacing them with obedience. . .every single day.

Turn away from evil and toward God to find peace. You can't assume that trouble won't find you. . .the enemy is constantly looking for ways to destroy your peace by getting you to turn away from God (1 Peter 5:8). Ask Jesus to keep you facing in the right direction.

MY PRAYER STARTER:
Lord, let my obedience flow naturally from
my love for You. May it be as constant as the
blessings You pour down on me each day.

OCTOBER 22

You will lead me by telling me what I should do.
And after this, You will bring me into shining-greatness.
PSALM 73:24 NLV

Moment by moment, Jesus is with you, ready to guide you through any and every situation. He wants to speak to you. He wants to share in your joy during times of blessing and comfort you in pain and sadness. And He wants to give you wisdom for times of change and choices.

The prophet Isaiah wrote, "Whether you turn to the right or to the left, your ears will hear a voice behind you, saying, 'This is the way; walk in it' " (Isaiah 30:21 NIV). For Christians, that means you don't have to figure things out by yourself.

The Holy Spirit is inside you, always speaking wisdom. He will guide you as you listen for Him. He will make the Lord's expectations clear. If Jesus wants you to know something, you'll start hearing it everywhere—in His Word, in a song, in the advice of a faithful friend, and in the deepest voices of your heart. The ways God speaks are limitless. Be listening!

MY PRAYER STARTER:

Lord God, whenever Your Spirit urges me in a certain direction, open my heart to His leading and give me the strength to obey.

OCTOBER 23

When they saw the courage of Peter and John
and realized that they were unschooled,
ordinary men, they were astonished and they took
note that these men had been with Jesus.

ACTS 4:13 NIV

Peter and John obeyed Jesus' command to go tell the world about Him. These apostles weren't educated men; they were simply fishermen. But they spoke and acted courageously because they knew Jesus personally. Jesus had given Peter and John authority, and that made all the difference.

You too, no matter how young you might be in your age or faith, have received authority from Jesus. Are you walking in it? Are you living and speaking with the courage you receive from knowing Him? Can people around you tell that you've been with Jesus?

Through Him, supernatural power is available to you. Jesus is ready to help you in whatever challenges you face. Spend more time with Him. Like Peter and John, you'll become the courageous believer He wants you to be.

MY PRAYER STARTER:

Thank You, Jesus, for giving me the authority to face whatever life throws at me. Whenever I get overwhelmed, I take comfort in the fact that You've already won the fight.

OCTOBER 24

Rejoice always, pray continually, give thanks in all circumstances; for this is God's will for you in Christ Jesus.
1 THESSALONIANS 5:16–18 NIV

If you've ever wondered what God's will is, you can start right here. Sometimes, God spells things out so clearly that you simply can't miss it: "Rejoice always, pray continually, give thanks in all circumstances."

This is a clear directive. But you might read the apostle Paul's words and think, *How can I possibly rejoice all the time? How do I pray continually? How can I be thankful in every situation? How can I do those things during times of challenge and change?*

Well, the Bible answers those questions too. You *can't* do these things on your own. You can only succeed through the power of Jesus' Spirit, which is alive and working in you (Romans 8:26–27). As always, God has you covered!

MY PRAYER STARTER:
Lord God, help me apply today's scripture to every aspect of my life. May I be thankful during trials, prayerful in times of uncertainty, and joyful in the face of tragedy.

OCTOBER 25

For You have set my soul free from death. You have kept my feet from falling, so I may walk with God in the light of life.
PSALM 56:13 NLV

Jesus wants you to take a long walk with Him. . .a walk that truly never ends.

Walking with Jesus means having a relationship with your Creator and Savior. It is knowing Him, loving Him, trusting Him, and worshiping Him in each moment. What does that look like in everyday life? It's more than just reading a Bible passage and checking God off your to-do list for the day. It's knowing that Jesus is with you in every moment and inviting Him to be part of your daily experience. It's allowing Him to be involved in all your conversations, your activities with friends, your private thoughts. It's starting each day with gratitude, seeing your life from an eternal perspective.

As you pray, invite Jesus to take your hand on this walk. Where will He lead you today?

MY PRAYER STARTER:
Lord Jesus, I can hardly wait until I'm finally home with You forever. Until then, help me stay steady in my walk with You.

*I know how to get along with little and how to live when
I have much. I have learned the secret of being happy
at all times. If I am full of food and have all I need,
I am happy. If I am hungry and need more, I am happy.
I can do all things because Christ gives me the strength.*

PHILIPPIANS 4:12–13 NLV

Happiness may not seem like a choice, especially when circumstances have you down. But the book of Philippians suggests otherwise. The apostle Paul said he had figured out "the secret."

Spoiler alert: The secret is contentment, a conscious decision to rely on Jesus Christ as your source of strength and happiness no matter what.

Are you content? Take an honest inventory. If you often find yourself wishing for some "better" thing, ask Jesus to fill you with contentment instead. You will need supernatural power to choose happiness each day, but notice the end of today's scripture: "I can do all things because Christ gives me the strength."

You get to make this choice, every single day. Jesus will help.

MY PRAYER STARTER:
Lord Jesus, help me never think the grass is somehow
greener on the other side. Rather, help me find contentment
in the pastures You're leading me through right now.

OCTOBER 27

Christ was before all things.
All things are held together by Him.
Colossians 1:17 NLV

Jesus holds the whole world together—and He holds you too. He is more powerful than anything you can imagine, yet He loves you and cares for you, deeply and personally. He knows everything about you, including the hard things you might be enduring right now. And He will show up and be very real in your life if you let Him.

Jesus wants you to talk with Him every day about everything. Whether your problem feels too small (or too big?) for God, tell Jesus what you're thinking and how you really feel. Ask Him to help you believe how much He cares.

The closer you get to Jesus, the more you'll walk with Him every day and the more your thoughts will begin to match His thoughts. Your problems will seem to shrink as you experience the greatness of Christ, who holds the whole world together.

MY PRAYER STARTER:
Lord, if You can hold the universe together,
I know You can keep my life from falling apart
as well. Help me put my petty questions and
problems in their proper perspective.

Jesus said, "Come!" Peter got out of the boat and walked on the water to Jesus. But when he saw the strong wind, he was afraid. He began to go down in the water. He cried out, "Lord, save me!"
MATTHEW 14:29–30 NLV

It seems Jesus loves a good adventure. Today's scripture tells of the time He welcomed His friend Peter to step out of his boat and walk atop the water. You already know how the story goes: Peter jumped out of the boat and walked on the wind-whipped waters like Jesus. But then, noticing the swirling seas and realizing he was doing something impossible, he took his eyes off the Lord, became frightened, and sank like a stone.

It's easy to be afraid when we lose sight of Jesus.

But you don't have to live in fear. Here's what Jesus says to you: "Take hope. It is I. Do not be afraid!" (Matthew 14:27). Keep your eyes on Jesus, and no storm can touch you.

MY PRAYER STARTER:
Lord Jesus, when it feels like I'm drowning in stress, depression, uncertainty, and emotional pain, give me the faith to take Your hand and rise above the waves.

OCTOBER 29

*You, God, are awesome in your
sanctuary; the God of Israel gives power and
strength to his people. Praise be to God!*

PSALM 68:35 NIV

Hardship and change are inevitable. But something powerful happens when you take your gaze off your situation and turn it to Jesus. Today, let worship be your focus and see how it changes things.

Making music, memorizing scripture, telling a friend what God's doing in your life—they're all forms of worship. Thank God, through Jesus Christ, for all the blessings He's given you. Thank Him for pulling you up out of darkness and placing you into His light. Thank Him for His daily provision—for you, for your family and loved ones, and for the entire world.

Ask Jesus to strengthen you through your worship of Him. He is the awesome God of all creation. He is worthy of all your praise.

MY PRAYER STARTER:
God, I praise You for the countless blessings and privileges I enjoy each day. Fill me with the desire to tell others about the good things You've done for me.

OCTOBER 30

"See, God has come to save me. I will trust in him
and not be afraid. The Lord God is my strength
and my song; he has given me victory."

ISAIAH 12:2 NLT

It's a leap of faith to sing and praise God during times of trouble, change, and stress. But there is great power in our praise. We tone our faith muscles when we thank God in difficult times.

When you feel like running away from your problems, hide out in Jesus instead. He's the one who longed for sinful Jerusalem, saying, "How often I have wanted to gather your children together as a hen protects her chicks beneath her wings" (Matthew 23:37). He feels the same way about you. . .so thank Him, honor Him, and praise Him.

Praise will keep you healthy in so many ways. Worry only holds you back. Which will you choose today?

MY PRAYER STARTER:

Lord, remind me to pray at all times—not just when
things seem to be going well or when I need an
answer right away. Help me pray through the stress,
disappointments, and mundaneness of everyday life.

*"For the LORD your God is going with you!
He will fight for you against your
enemies, and he will give you victory!"*

DEUTERONOMY 20:4 NLT

Spiritual warfare is real. There is a major battle ongoing in the unseen world (Ephesians 6:12). The Word tells us to be alert because our enemy, the devil, prowls around looking to devour us (1 Peter 5:8). One of his main weapons against us is fear.

In unsettled times, fear is natural. That's why we need supernatural help. Through Jesus, we have been given everything we need to overcome. We don't fight these spiritual battles in our own human strength! Jesus has told us not to worry, since He has overcome for us (John 16:33). And Jesus' lead disciple, Peter, elaborated on that theme: "By his divine power, God has given us everything we need for a godly life. We have received all of this by coming to know him, the one who called us to himself by means of his marvelous glory and excellence" (2 Peter 1:3).

Stand firm in God's truth, always remembering, "the Spirit who lives in you is greater than the spirit who lives in the world" (1 John 4:4).

MY PRAYER STARTER:
God, thank You for allowing me to overcome
fear. With Your strength, I can face Satan's most
powerful weapon and come out victorious.

NOVEMBER 1

*Now all glory to God, who is able, through his mighty power
at work within us, to accomplish infinitely more than we
might ask or think. Glory to him in the church and in Christ
Jesus through all generations forever and ever! Amen.*

EPHESIANS 3:20–21 NLT

We all have a choice to make every morning—we can be thankful for the new day, knowing that Jesus is with us and for us in whatever challenges come our way. . .or we can try taking matters into our own hands. The latter choice usually brings stress and worry; the former brings peace. And why wouldn't it? We serve a God who, through Jesus Christ, does "infinitely more than we might ask or think."

Kingdom life is not natural—it's supernatural. It is a daily choice to invite the Spirit of Jesus to come and fill you with goodness, peace, and joy (Romans 14:17). It's thanking your Savior for all that He is and does, minute by minute, hour by hour, day by day. He's infinitely more worthy than you can even think!

MY PRAYER STARTER:
Lord, I know that whatever I touch tends to fall apart when
I try to do things on my own.
Please fill me with an attitude of reliance—
a pure, childlike trust in Your power.

NOVEMBER 2

Let my soul be at rest again, for the LORD has been
good to me. He has saved me from death, my eyes
from tears, my feet from stumbling. And so I walk
in the LORD's presence as I live here on earth!

PSALM 116:7–9 NLT

Have you ever taken time to count your blessings? Really. . .as in stopping to think about each one, even writing them down on paper? Literally counting your blessings can transform your outlook. When life feels overwhelming and out of control, your grateful reflection on God's past goodness will encourage your soul with His goodness now and in the future.

Take a few minutes today to jot down all the ways Jesus has been good to you—your home, your family, your friends, your church family, your relationship with God, and anything else you can think of. Then, when you're tempted to stress over the difficulties of life (and those days are sure to come), look at your list and remember His goodness. Jesus Christ is the same yesterday, today, and forever (Hebrews 13:8). What He's done for you in the past, He'll do for you today, and He'll continue to do for all eternity. Now that's reason for gratitude.

MY PRAYER STARTER:
Thank You, Jesus, for giving me plenty of reasons to be
thankful. Help me be mindful of these blessings and
intentional in my efforts to praise You for them.

NOVEMBER 3

Jesus said to them, "I am the Bread of Life.
He who comes to Me will never be hungry. He who
puts his trust in Me will never be thirsty."

JOHN 6:35 NLV

Don't you love the smell of homemade bread? As your mom or grandma takes out the loaf, that combination of flour, yeast, and other ingredients fills the kitchen with a mouth-watering aroma. It's really one of life's simple pleasures. . .and then there's the joy of actually *eating* it.

Our Lord Jesus Christ likened Himself to this essential and enjoyable foodstuff: "I am the Bread of Life." Each and every day, let's enjoy the aroma of His presence, then take Him in for the spiritual nourishment we need. Only He can satisfy the hunger in our souls.

And that's a perfect reason to stop and say, "Thank You." Jesus provides everything we need for life, on this earth and throughout eternity.

MY PRAYER STARTER:
Lord Jesus, give me a hunger for You and nothing else.
Help the joy of my salvation be the bread on which
I feast each day. Only You can satisfy my soul.

NOVEMBER 4

*Let all that I am praise the LORD; with my whole heart,
I will praise his holy name. Let all that I am praise the
LORD; may I never forget the good things he does for me.*

PSALM 103:1–2 NLT

Pastor and author John Piper has said, "Genuine thankfulness is an act of the heart's affections, not an act of the lips' muscles." Put another way, true gratitude begins in the heart before it comes out of your mouth.

Look at all God has done for you through Jesus Christ and say, "Thank You! Thank You! Thank You!" Then go out and actively live your life in a spirit of genuine gratitude. Show your friends at school, the people at your church, and the stranger on the street just how thankful you are! Notice the psalm writer's commitment to praise the Lord with "all that I am" and "my whole heart."

A heart of gratitude can transform you—how you think, how you talk, and how you live your daily life. If you need help in this area, Jesus stands ready. Ask Him to change your heart so that you too can live a life marked by deep gratitude.

MY PRAYER STARTER:

Thank You, Jesus, for this beautiful life
You've given me. Help me use each day
I have to praise You for all You've done.

The faithful love of the LORD never ends!
His mercies never cease. Great is his
faithfulness; his mercies begin afresh each morning.
LAMENTATIONS 3:22–23 NLT

In the classic novel *Anne of Green Gables*, heroine Anne Shirley says, "Tomorrow is always fresh with no mistakes in it." That line is reminiscent of today's scripture, which celebrates the faithful love of God. It never ends. His mercies begin afresh each morning.

When you feel the need for God's mercy—and we all will, regularly!—bring your failures to Jesus. Because of what He did on the cross, God won't punish you. Our sins deserve punishment, but because of Jesus, the Father now showers us with mercy.

When you've failed God, lift your head and thank Him for mercy and forgiveness. God the Father sees you through the lens of Jesus. . .you can move forward confidently, knowing that Christ has made your way.

Tomorrow is always fresh with no mistakes in it. Let tomorrow begin right now.

MY PRAYER STARTER:

Lord, thank You for Your infinite mercy. Even though
I don't deserve to be forgiven, You still offer forgiveness
every day. May I never become too proud to accept.

NOVEMBER 6

*The blessing of the LORD makes a person
rich, and he adds no sorrow with it.*
PROVERBS 10:22 NLT

God's blessings—both large and small—do indeed make life rich.
So instead of just asking, "What's next, God?" take time to thank
Him for what He's already done for you. When God blesses people
around you, don't ask, "Why not me, God?" Gratefully celebrate
His goodness in their lives!

God has placed joy and beauty and blessing all throughout His
creation. Take pleasure in nature and the beauty of each season.
Smile at the children you see and learn from their simple trust in
Jesus. Build relationships with the trustworthy friends and godly
adults He's placed on your path, experiencing the joy of loving
and being loved. These simple blessings are truly gifts from our
generous Lord. Don't take any of them for granted!

MY PRAYER STARTER:

God, I'm reminded of Your presence everywhere
I look—from the sprawling Milky Way above me
to the faintest smile on the lips of one of Your
children. Thank You for these undeserved gifts.

NOVEMBER 7

*"Those the Father has given me will come to
me, and I will never reject them."*

JOHN 6:37 NLT

When you turn to Jesus, you can be sure that His arms are open.
He will never turn you away—even if you've messed up badly. The
apostle Paul told us something amazing about God: "Don't you
see how wonderfully kind, tolerant, and patient God is with you?
Does this mean nothing to you? Can't you see that his kindness is
intended to turn you from your sin?" (Romans 2:4).

It's God's kindness that leads us away from our sin and to
Jesus! Is that your perception of God? If not, ask Him to lead you
to a full understanding of this breathtaking truth.

When you sin, the best thing you can do is go straight to Jesus.
Don't run away. Don't try to hide. Jesus has promised that He will
never reject you. He'll simply assure you of His love and forgiveness
then grant you power to change. Thank You, Lord!

MY PRAYER STARTER:

Thank You, God, for Your patience. Help me never to
see You as waiting to punish me; rather, let me see the
full extent of the love You have for Your children.

NOVEMBER 8

*"The robber comes only to steal and to kill and to destroy.
I came so they might have life, a great full life."*
JOHN 10:10 NLV

Solomon wrote Ecclesiastes to remind people that life on earth
is meaningless—unless we follow God and obey His commandments (Ecclesiastes 12:13–14). Ecclesiastes is a bit of a dreary book,
apparently written as the king looked back on his own life. He
had wealth and power and everything he wanted but confessed
it meant nothing when he chose to ignore God for many years.

Solomon wrote: "I know that there is nothing better for men
than to be happy and to do good as long as they live. And I know
that every man who eats and drinks sees good in all his work. It
is the gift of God" (Ecclesiastes 3:12–13). This is a reminder that
God wants us to enjoy life—but *with* Him, not apart from Him.

Jesus is the one who brings us to God, giving true joy and meaning to our lives. How can we not express our gratitude every day?

MY PRAYER STARTER:
God, open my eyes to how meaningless life is without
You—and how meaningful it becomes when I serve
You. Thank You for the hope and purpose You offer.

NOVEMBER 9

The commandments of the LORD are right,
bringing joy to the heart. The commands of the
LORD are clear, giving insight for living.

PSALM 19:8 NLT

God's Word can generate a sense of freedom and gratitude. . .if we allow it to. Where Jesus tells His followers to "obey my commandments" (John 14:15), some people see that as constrictive and joy-killing. Nothing could be further from the truth. In fact, today's scripture says God's commands give joy to our hearts.

God didn't create rules just to spoil our fun. Jesus didn't reemphasize God's laws to make us feel unfulfilled, like we're missing out on something. Just as your parents have set wise rules and boundaries for you, God has given precepts to keep us from trouble and help us enjoy life. This truth should bring gratitude to our hearts.

MY PRAYER STARTER:
Lord, I am grateful for Your commandments, even
when I sometimes can't see their purpose. Thank
You for always knowing what's best for me.

NOVEMBER 10

*How abundant are the good things that you have
stored up for those who fear you, that you bestow in
the sight of all, on those who take refuge in you.*

PSALM 31:19 NIV

When we trust God, He becomes our "ever-present help in trouble"
(Psalm 46:1). Think about that: God is *ever* present. . .meaning He
is with you this very moment, even as you read these words. His
power and comfort are constantly available. He is good, and He
wants to show His goodness to you on a daily basis.

When we focus on problems and worry about things that
haven't even happened, we're taking our eyes off of God. But when
we focus on the Father and His gracious provision of Jesus Christ,
He will show Himself to us in each moment. He will make ways
for us when we didn't believe there could be one.

Jesus, our refuge, is a perfect reason to thank God every day.

MY PRAYER STARTER:
Thank You, God, for Your Son, who provides constant
comfort and peace each day in my heart. Whenever life starts
getting me down, help me lift my eyes back up to Him.

NOVEMBER 11

I will give thanks to you, LORD, with all my heart;
I will tell of all your wonderful deeds. I will
be glad and rejoice in you; I will sing the
praises of your name, O Most High.

PSALM 9:1–2 NIV

If you praise Jesus daily with a heart full of love, others can't help but notice. "Praise and worship" isn't just about songs at church on Sunday—it's about living your life with daily thankfulness to God and allowing that gratitude to motivate everything you do.

A life of praise and worship means there's an ongoing song of contentment in your heart. As you trust Jesus to guide you and meet your needs, your faith grows. Are you experiencing that growth right now? If not, talk to Jesus, asking Him to do any necessary "heart surgery." Ask Him to place a song of gratitude inside and fill you to overflowing with His joy.

MY PRAYER STARTER:

Lord Jesus, help my life be a continuous song of praise to You.
Tune my heart to the rhythm of your goodness and mercy.

NOVEMBER 12

The Word became flesh and made his dwelling among us.
We have seen his glory, the glory of the one and only Son,
who came from the Father, full of grace and truth.

JOHN 1:14 NIV

When God made a way for us to be saved, He showed us the true meaning of love. Jesus—who is the Way—told His followers, "Greater love has no one than this: to lay down one's life for one's friends" (John 15:13). Giving up your life for someone else is true, unselfish love, and that's exactly what Jesus did for us.

God the Father chose to send His Son into the world to live a life like ours and then to eventually lay down that life for us. Jesus knew the physical—and emotional—pain He would suffer when He was betrayed by Judas, deserted by His other disciples, and sentenced to an excruciating death on the cross. But He faced it all so that we could be made right with God.

Be thankful for the "Word made flesh"—there is no greater love.

MY PRAYER STARTER:

Lord Jesus, thank You for giving Your life so that I can share in eternal life with You. Thank You for Your indescribable love.

NOVEMBER 13

"I call heaven and earth to speak against you today. I have
put in front of you life and death, the good and the curse.
So choose life so you and your children after you may live.
Love the Lord your God and obey His voice. Hold on to Him.
For He is your life, and by Him your days will be long."

DEUTERONOMY 30:19–20 NLV

Life with Jesus is the most wonderful thing a human being can experience. The Bible says eternal life is knowing God through His Son (John 17:3) and that Jesus came to give us abundant life (John 10:10)—not only in eternity but right now on this earth. You don't have to wait for heaven to experience a great full life. It starts now!

We all have a choice to make every day of our lives on this earth: to follow Jesus and stay close to Him. . .or not. Following Jesus isn't always easy. Some days, it will be very difficult. But it is always worth it. If your friends ridicule you, if the world shuns you, or even if you are someday martyred for Jesus' name, you are blessed (Luke 6:22). And the apostle Paul says any trouble on earth can't even compare with the glory to be revealed in you (Romans 8:18). No matter what, you have a reason for gratitude.

MY PRAYER STARTER:

Lord, I want to follow You, even when it isn't easy. Let the joy of eternal life with You start in me today, motivating me to press on until Your full glory is revealed.

NOVEMBER 14

"Have I not told you? Be strong and have strength of heart! Do not be afraid or lose faith. For the Lord your God is with you anywhere you go."

JOSHUA 1:9 NLV

The Bible teaches that God's Spirit is working inside believers at all times. What an astounding miracle! Along with the apostle Paul, we can shout in gratitude: "Let us honor and thank the God and Father of our Lord Jesus Christ. He has already given us a taste of what heaven is like. Even before the world was made, God chose us for Himself because of His love. He planned that we should be holy and without blame as He sees us" (Ephesians 1:3–4).

Even when we feel like we're alone, God is with us. We have the Father's love, the Spirit's presence, and Jesus' prayers. The blessed Trinity will never leave or forsake us. Let's always thank Him for working everything out for our good and His glory.

MY PRAYER STARTER:

I praise You, God, for Your Spirit that is working within me each day. Thank You for never leaving my side and for giving me a hope that will last forever.

NOVEMBER 15

Since, then, you have been raised with Christ, set your hearts on things above, where Christ is, seated at the right hand of God. Set your minds on things above, not on earthly things.

COLOSSIANS 3:1–2 NIV

Is life bombarding you with trouble? Are family tensions, problems at school, relationship problems, or other daily trials breaking your spirit? Jesus beckons you to focus on Him instead of your worries. Don't be like Peter, who miraculously walked on water until he took his eyes off Jesus! May we never miss out on life's blessings because we let our gaze wander from Jesus to our troubles.

God wants to bless you, right now, in the midst of the mess of life. But that will take action on your part: you'll need to set your heart on "things above." Look up, "where Christ is, seated at the right hand of God." Consciously leave the "earthly things" behind. When you do, you'll be filled with gratitude for the overcoming power God provides.

MY PRAYER STARTER:

Lord, please help me fix my gaze on You. Let all worldly distractions fade away into oblivion when I compare them to Your eternal grace.

NOVEMBER 16

Trust in the LORD and do good; dwell in the land
and enjoy safe pasture. Take delight in the LORD,
and he will give you the desires of your heart.
PSALM 37:3–4 NIV

It's easy to read today's verse and think, *Hey, if I "delight" myself*
in God, He will give me everything I want! But what this verse
means is that our true submission to Jesus will change our hearts
so completely that we'll want what *He* wants. When we commit
everything we do to the Lord, we'll begin to see the desires of our
hearts matching God's own desires.

Practically speaking, how can you take delight in the Lord?
Start your day with gratitude. Go to Jesus first, before school and
other distractions get in the way, and thank Him for His love.
Ask Him to bless your day and give you opportunities to bless
others. Talk to Him about every opportunity and problem you
face. Commit your entire self to Him. . .and thank Him in advance
for the blessings that will come your way.

MY PRAYER STARTER:
Lord, please let my own desires match up with Yours. That
way, not only will I never be disappointed but I will always
know that my actions and attitudes are pleasing to You.

NOVEMBER 17

Yes, even if I walk through the valley of the shadow of death, I will not be afraid of anything, because You are with me. You have a walking stick with which to guide and one with which to help. These comfort me.

PSALM 23:4 NLV

Jesus has promised to be with us through everything. He has the tools we need for every job and the map we need for every journey. If He asks us to go somewhere or do something, He promises to be with us, providing exactly what we need, when we need it. And we can count on Him to keep His promises.

Look at what Psalm 139:7–10 says: "Where can I go from Your Spirit? Or where can I run away from where You are? If I go up to heaven, You are there! If I make my bed in the place of the dead, You are there! If I take the wings of the morning or live in the farthest part of the sea, even there Your hand will lead me and Your right hand will hold me."

No matter where you go, He is always right there with you. Thank You, Jesus!

MY PRAYER STARTER:

Lord Jesus, thank You for being impossible to run from. Even when I disobey You and try to step out of Your will, You gently draw me back with Your love.

NOVEMBER 18

He giveth power to the faint; and to them that have no might he increaseth strength. Even the youths shall faint and be weary, and the young men shall utterly fall: but they that wait upon the LORD shall renew their strength; they shall mount up with wings as eagles; they shall run, and not be weary; and they shall walk, and not faint.

ISAIAH 40:29–31 KJV

Could you use a big helping of Jesus' power in your life? Who couldn't? The Bible says that those who wait for the Lord—the people who pray and depend on Him for everything—will gain new strength.

God gives strength and power to those who know they don't have any. . .if they simply "wait upon the LORD." That means praying in the full expectation that He will show up and keep His promises, no matter how long it takes. It means looking for Him, longing for Him, and putting your full hope in Him.

In this cruel and tiresome world, how appreciative we are for a Savior who gives us strength to soar like eagles! Don't miss this blessing by rushing out of His presence.

MY PRAYER STARTER:
Thank You, Jesus, for the power and encouragement
of Your Spirit. Help me always to stand firm
in the comfort of Your presence.

NOVEMBER 19

It is for freedom that Christ has set us free.
Stand firm, then, and do not let yourselves be
burdened again by a yoke of slavery.
GALATIANS 5:1 NIV

"Freedom in Christ" means we know that our eternal life is secure. But how grateful we should be to know that freedom in Christ also means we can be free *here and now*—free from our tendency to sin, free to live a life of purpose, free from the worry of what other people think or say about us.

Freedom in Christ gives us confidence to be all that God has made us to be. Fear no longer holds us captive because Jesus' perfect love casts out all fear (1 John 4:18), giving us true peace. We can enjoy a peace that transcends all understanding while we live our daily lives here on earth.

When we live in the freedom Jesus provides, our insecurities fade, our fears diminish, and love takes over. Praise and thank Him for such a gift.

MY PRAYER STARTER:
Thank You for Your amazing love, God, that's able to annihilate whatever traces of fear that linger in my heart. May my life constantly reflect what You've done for me.

NOVEMBER 20

"The God who made the world and everything in it is the Lord of heaven and earth and does not live in temples built by human hands. And he is not served by human hands, as if he needed anything. Rather, he himself gives everyone life and breath and everything else."

ACTS 17:24–25 NIV

Isn't it amazing that the God who established the earth is the same Lord who knows you intimately and wants a deeply personal relationship with you? His Word says He knows when you sit down and stand up, and even your words before you speak them (Psalm 139)! Long before you were born, God had already determined where and when you should live. Ponder these things, and let them inspire thankfulness for everything the Lord has done for you.

What a comfort it is to know Jesus is in control of your life. He knows everything that has happened and everything that will happen to you. Everything that comes your way has passed through His hands first. You are safe and secure in the strong arms of Jesus.

MY PRAYER STARTER:

Lord, I'm amazed by the fact that You knew me long before I was even born. I surrender all illusions of pride and control—You're the only one who knows what's best for me.

NOVEMBER 21

There is no fear in love. Perfect love puts fear out of our hearts.
People have fear when they are afraid of being
punished. The man who is afraid does not have
perfect love. We love Him because He loved us first.

1 JOHN 4:18–19 NLV

Sadly, many followers of Jesus waste time believing God is angry with them. He's not. God sees you through the love and sacrifice of His Son, Jesus. That means you can always approach Him without fear.

Saved people who worry about punishment don't understand who they are in Jesus. We don't have to work harder or be "better Christians" to somehow earn God's love. Nothing we do would make Him love us any more or less than He does right now.

Truly understanding who you are in Christ changes everything. You leave fear behind. You embrace perfect love. You live a life of thanksgiving.

NOVEMBER 22

I remain confident of this: I will see the goodness of
the LORD in the land of the living. Wait for the LORD;
be strong and take heart and wait for the LORD.

PSALM 27:13–14 NIV

We can all take great comfort today knowing that when we wait on the Lord, trusting in His purpose and timing, we will see His goodness *in this life*. He promises that if we cast our burdens on Him, He will sustain us. He won't let us fall (Psalm 55:22).

Jesus sees your circumstances. He knows your struggles. He loves you and cares deeply about what you experience, and that will never change. He will make every event in your life work together for your good (Romans 8:28).

Trust that the Lord is working in your life, often behind the scenes, orchestrating a grand finale that you can't yet recognize. Ask for His guidance, wait on Him, and be grateful for every miracle and blessing—big or small—that He sends your way.

MY PRAYER STARTER:

All-knowing God, thank You for giving me the assurance that You've got everything under control. I don't know what direction life will go, but that's okay because I know You do.

NOVEMBER 23

Keep your minds thinking about whatever is true, whatever is respected, whatever is right, whatever is pure, whatever can be loved, and whatever is well thought of. If there is anything good and worth giving thanks for, think about these things.
PHILIPPIANS 4:8 NLV

If we don't take control of our thoughts, they can get us in trouble. It's easy for many teens to get off track, thinking about things they shouldn't. . .even when they're praying! They start off with good thoughts but soon get distracted. The result is never good.

Next time you find your mind wading into unsavory waters, ask Jesus to step into your thoughts and change them. Speak His name and call out for rescue. He can guide the direction of your thoughts, making them like His own—pure and true and lovely.

The name of Jesus has all power in heaven and earth (Philippians 2:10). Call on Him to turn your thoughts to love, praise, and thanksgiving.

MY PRAYER STARTER:

Lord, rescue me from my thoughts. Destroy each selfish
or sinful thought and replace it with Your purity,
transforming my mind and aligning with Your will.

NOVEMBER 24

*I will praise you, L*ORD, *with all my heart; before the "gods" I will sing your praise. I will bow down toward your holy temple and will praise your name for your unfailing love and your faithfulness.*

PSALM 138:1–2 NIV

Make it a habit to thank God for each new day, knowing that His mercies and compassion are new every morning. Keep a song of praise in your heart, expressing gratitude for His many blessings. Praise Him for the simple pleasures of life: family, friends, food, a home, and a million other things.

During your day, thank Jesus out loud. Tell Him how much you appreciate His love and His gift of life, now and for eternity.

And as you lay your head on your pillow at night, thank Him for the day, for all the blessings He sent your way, and for His presence through it all. Rest knowing He'll be with you through the night, the next day, and all eternity.

MY PRAYER STARTER:

Lord God, I don't deserve all the blessings scattered throughout my life. Fill me with an attitude of praise and thanksgiving whenever I think of all You've given me.

NOVEMBER 25

All praise to God, the Father of our Lord Jesus Christ.
God is our merciful Father and the source of all comfort. He
comforts us in all our troubles so that we can comfort others.
When they are troubled, we will be able to give them the same
comfort God has given us. For the more we suffer for Christ,
the more God will shower us with his comfort through Christ.

2 CORINTHIANS 1:3–5 NLT

This is a season of thanksgiving. Why not take a moment to count and record your blessings? Write them in a journal, make notes in your Bible, store them on your phone—whatever works best for you. Keep the list handy for those moments of stress or discouragement.

Remember that hard times will come your way. That's a guarantee in this life. But you'll find encouragement in the midst of your trials when you pull out your chronicle of God's blessings in your life—headlined by the salvation that comes through Jesus Christ. Not only will that take your mind off your troubles, it will generate thanks to God, who is absolutely worthy of your praise.

MY PRAYER STARTER:

Lord, remind me of the good times whenever life gets hard. Help me see that You are still good and faithful no matter what.

NOVEMBER 26

Let the message of Christ dwell among you richly as
you teach and admonish one another with all wisdom
through psalms, hymns, and songs from the Spirit,
singing to God with gratitude in your hearts.

COLOSSIANS 3:16 NIV

What does "the message of Christ" do for us? It saves us from sin and the punishment our sin deserves. It helps us to understand who God is. It gives us purpose in an otherwise meaningless world. And, as today's scripture indicates, it develops gratitude in our hearts.

Even non-believers recognize the value of gratitude. Good parents teach their kids to say "thank you" since that will help them throughout life. Thankfulness smooths off the rough edges of human interactions, making the world just a little bit kinder each time it's expressed.

How much more thankful should we Christians be. The message of Jesus Christ has changed everything for the better. Let's "teach and admonish one another" to be more thankful. . .first to God and then to each other.

MY PRAYER STARTER:
Lord Jesus, let my every word and action display
the thankfulness inside me, brightening the lives
of those I meet and pointing them to You.

NOVEMBER 27

Give thanks to the Lord for He is good!
His loving-kindness lasts forever!

No one will be faithful to you all the time—no one except Jesus, that is.

Here are some wonderful truths to bank your life on: Jesus will never leave you. He'll never give up on you. He'll never speak anything but truth to you. He'll never stop loving you. Nothing you do will ever change His mind about how much He loves you. Jesus is the embodiment of God's love—and that will never change because God never changes.

The Father looks at you with loving-kindness because He sees Jesus in you. You don't have to be afraid to approach Him or tell Him honestly what's going on in your life. He already knows. . . He just wants to hear from you.

Be thankful for God's goodness and love, purchased for you by the blood of Jesus.

MY PRAYER STARTER:

Whenever I think of Your mercy, God, I'm
overwhelmed by feelings of appreciation. Out of this
sea of billions of souls, You've singled me out to love
and care for me in unique ways. Thank You!

NOVEMBER 28

*I have seen you in your sanctuary and gazed upon your
power and glory. Your unfailing love is better than life
itself; how I praise you! I will praise you as long as I live,
lifting up my hands to you in prayer. You satisfy me more
than the richest feast. I will praise you with songs of joy.*

PSALM 63:2–5 NLT

During this season of thanksgiving, focus your mind on grateful-
ness to Jesus. Ruminate on these scriptures:

- "Since we are receiving a Kingdom that is unshakable, let
  us be thankful and please God by worshiping him with
  holy fear and awe" (Hebrews 12:28).

- "All who are victorious will inherit all these blessings,
  and I will be their God, and they will be my children"
  (Revelation 21:7).

- "From his abundance we have all received one gracious
  blessing after another. For the law was given through
  Moses, but God's unfailing love and faithfulness came
  through Jesus Christ" (John 1:16–17).

Every blessing comes to us through Jesus. He is worthy of
our thanksgiving.

MY PRAYER STARTER:
I'm continuously amazed, God, when I think of the
magnitude of the hope that awaits me in heaven.
Thank You for Your unimaginable grace.

NOVEMBER 29

*"These people honor me with their lips, but their
hearts are far from me. They worship me in vain;
their teachings are merely human rules."*

MATTHEW 15:8–9 NIV

The Pharisees were high-ranking religious leaders in Jesus' day.
They knew a lot about the Old Testament laws and prided themselves on looking good on the outside. They thought they were
pleasing God, but by rejecting Jesus, they only distanced themselves from Him.

As Christians, we welcome Jesus, and He reconciles us with
God the Father. We have a real friendship with our Lord, who kindly
teaches us every day. Unlike the Pharisees, Jesus doesn't pile up
weighty rules and duties. He takes us by the hand and helps us
along. His yoke is easy and His burden is light (Matthew 11:28–30).

As our relationship with Jesus grows, we sense His love for us
more and more. How can we be anything but thankful?

MY PRAYER STARTER:

God, teach me how to follow You—not by obeying a
lengthy list of arbitrary rules but by loving You and
following the gentle leading of Your Word and Spirit.

NOVEMBER 30

I will sing of the LORD's great love forever; with my mouth I will make your faithfulness known through all generations. I will declare that your love stands firm forever, that you have established your faithfulness in heaven itself.

PSALM 89:1–2 NIV

God shows love for us in so many ways. One of the simplest ways to actually see God's love in action is to go outside and enjoy His creation.

You can see the Lord's handiwork in the flowers and trees in spring and summer and in the bright leaves changing in the fall and the blankets of snow He sends in the winter. The skies proclaim His wonders in every season. Animals and creatures great and small know their Creator. The birds God created compose songs of praise as they go about their daily tasks. . .and you can too.

God gave you your voice to talk to Him, to tell others of the great love He demonstrated when He sent Jesus to save them from their sin, and to sing His praises every day of your life.

So spend some time with Jesus in creation every day. Allow His handiwork to spur thankfulness in your heart.

MY PRAYER STARTER:

As I look around Your creation, God, I'm struck by its overwhelming beauty and grandeur. You alone are all-powerful and worthy of my praise. Help me use my gifts for You.

DECEMBER 1

The Lord is near to all who call on him,
to all who call on him in truth.

PSALM 145:18 NIV

December has arrived! Christmas is coming! In just twenty-four more days, we'll celebrate the birth of Jesus, that point in which God Himself broke into our time and space to save us.

Who would have guessed that the almighty Creator of the universe would arrive on the scene as a baby? Nobody would expect salvation to begin in the womb of a godly young girl who'd never yet been with a man. What kind of Messiah is this?

Well, it's Immanuel, "God with us" (Matthew 1:23). It's Jesus Christ, the Son of God, second member of the Trinity, the focus of all history, before whom "every knee should bow, in heaven and on earth and under the earth" (Philippians 2:10). On that first Christmas, He came near physically to draw us near spiritually. Let's be sure to "call on him," the first time for salvation and then unceasingly for daily mercy, grace, and love.

MY PRAYER STARTER:

Lord Jesus, thank You for leaving Your perfect home in heaven to come to this imperfect world to die for my sin. You gave it all to be near to us—help me give my all to draw near to You.

DECEMBER 2

One who has unreliable friends soon comes to ruin,
but there is a friend who sticks closer than a brother.
Proverbs 18:24 niv

Relationships are vital. Whether it's sharing good news with someone as you pass them in the hall or longing for a friend to walk with you through adversity, you need someone to journey with you through life—and so does everyone else. We were not made to travel alone.

Every Christian has that person, "a friend who sticks closer than a brother." Jesus Christ is always with us, supporting, protecting, helping, and guiding. He's always interested in our joys and trials. He's always ready and able to carry us through the rough places of life. He's like the perfect brother, only better—wiser, stronger, more loving, and closer.

You'll never find a better friend. You'll never be nearer to another person. Jesus made you, keeps you, loves you. . .and will continue to love you for all eternity.

MY PRAYER STARTER:
Thank You, Lord, for taking interest in my life and leading me through each tough decision. Thank You for being not just my Master but also my friend.

DECEMBER 3

Come near to God and he will come near to you.

JAMES 4:8 NIV

After Adam and Eve chose to sin in the garden of Eden, they tried to hide themselves from God. Imagine separating yourself from the one you walk with daily. . .the one who knows you intimately. . .the one who created you! That's how crazy sin is.

Of course, God knew exactly where Adam and Eve were, and He pursued them—just as He pursues every sinful person born into their line. From the very beginning, God the Father had prepared a plan to restore human beings to a right relationship with Himself: He would send His Son, Jesus Christ, to die as a sacrifice for sin.

Jesus' obedience to His Father closed the gap that human disobedience had created. Jesus came near to us. In Him, we come near to God. The divine-humanity fellowship has been restored.

MY PRAYER STARTER:

Thank You, Lord, for tearing down the wall between me and the Father by dying on a cross. I don't deserve such love, yet You offer it anyway because of who You are.

DECEMBER 4

Look for the Lord and His strength. Look for His face all the time.
PSALM 105:4 NLV

Some days are not so great. Others are wonderful. The latter are those days when everything goes right. You wake up well rested. Getting ready for the day goes smoothly, and you get out the door early to catch the bus. The weather is perfect, and classes speed by with ease. No one—at school or at home—seems angry or irritated, you have a fabulous dinner and maybe even a movie night with family or friends, and you fall right to sleep when you climb into bed.

On days like that, do you feel nearest to Jesus? If so, great! If not, there's a reason: we're often quicker to call on Him in times of trouble than we are when everything goes swimmingly.

But the fact is that we need Jesus at all times. Good days give way to dreary days that roll into atrocious days. But Jesus is always near. Let's look for His face at all times.

MY PRAYER STARTER:

Lord, life can be difficult sometimes, so I thank You for the great days that break the tension. On these days, help me still remember Your goodness and praise You for Your blessings.

DECEMBER 5

*Then you will experience God's peace, which exceeds
anything we can understand. His peace will guard
your hearts and minds as you live in Christ Jesus.*

PHILIPPIANS 4:7 NLT

A *guard*, as a noun, can be found in prisons, on basketball courts, or (when attached to the word *rail*) along the sides of roads. Guards protect other things, defending against harm. As a verb, *guard* indicates the action of protecting and defending.

When you are near Jesus—according to today's scripture, actually living "in" Him—your heart and mind are protected and defended from the crazy world around you. You get a peace that goes far beyond your human comprehension. You'll weather the storms of life in ways that baffle your unbelieving friends, neighbors, and classmates. But it's not because of your own strength. . .it's all thanks to the incredible nearness of Jesus.

May we always stay as close to Him as He is to us.

MY PRAYER STARTER:

Thank You, Jesus, for Your unending nearness to me.
May I never resist Your presence or feel as if I could live
without You—I need You every second of my life.

DECEMBER 6

The LORD is close to the brokenhearted;
he rescues those whose spirits are crushed.

PSALM 34:18 NLT

Brokenhearted and crushed are discouraging words. But they often accurately reflect our feelings. This world can crush our dreams or break our hearts in an instant. At times, the pain seems impossible to bear.

There is good news, though. In these moments, Jesus comes near—just like a good friend who steps in to help when you can't make it alone. He experienced the same emotional turmoil when He walked the earth, so He's sympathetic. Even better, He's also able to heal our wounds.

As God Himself, Jesus is completely capable of carrying us through trials. What we learn on the way can deepen our faith—lessons that we can then share with others.

MY PRAYER STARTER:
Thank You, Jesus, for Your nearness. Thank You for letting me know You'll always be by my side, even when life falls apart.

DECEMBER 7

He answered and said, Lo, I see four men loose, walking in the midst of the fire, and they have no hurt; and the form of the fourth is like the Son of God. Then Nebuchadnezzar came near to the mouth of the burning fiery furnace, and spake, and said, Shadrach, Meshach, and Abednego, ye servants of the most high God, come forth.

DANIEL 3:25–26 KJV

Nebuchadnezzar had ordered everyone to bow and honor him as a god. But three young Hebrews refused—they wouldn't bow to anyone but the one true God.

So the Babylonian king had the three thrown into a blazing furnace, only to be astonished at what he saw inside: the young men were completely unharmed. . .and joined by a fourth person! According to the venerable King James Version, the fourth was like "the Son of God."

Even today, Jesus—"the Son of God"—goes with us through all fires of adversity. We are never alone; He promises to always be with us.

MY PRAYER STARTER:
Lord Jesus, I know that the fires of this life—stress, depression, tragedy, or whatever else—could never separate me from Your presence. Thank You for Your faithfulness.

DECEMBER 8

"For God so loved the world that He gave His only Son. Whoever puts his trust in God's Son will not be lost but will have life that lasts forever."

JOHN 3:16 NLV

The perfect creation was tainted. People became selfish, disrespectful, rebellious. Yet God still loved them.

Our human tendency is to associate with people who treat us well—to form cliques and friend groups and exclude everyone else. Devoting ourselves to the worst of the worst, to those who intentionally misuse others, seems like madness. But our all-loving God initiated a plan to forgive humanity and restore the relationship they had ruined. That plan was to send Jesus to earth as a man.

While He was here, Jesus invested tirelessly in people. In return, they intentionally mistreated Him. . .to the point of killing Him on a cross. But that was part of God's plan too. Jesus came near only to be pushed away. But He doesn't stop. He keeps pursuing people, keeps reconciling them to God. That's what love does.

MY PRAYER STARTER:
Thank You, Jesus, for Your unrelenting love. Help me reflect that kind of love in my own interactions with friends, strangers, and even enemies.

DECEMBER 9

*"Who can hide in secret places so that I cannot
see them?" declares the LORD. "Do not I fill
heaven and earth?" declares the LORD.*

JEREMIAH 23:24 NIV

Has anyone not played-hide-and-seek? In big groups or small, daytime or night, indoors or out, the game is the same: the seekers pursue the hiders, who stay as quiet and still as possible. The hiders' goal is not to be found.

That's the way sinful people respond to God—they try to stay out of His sight. That's not possible, of course, since God knows and sees all. But even Jesus plays the game: "The Son of Man came to seek and to save the lost" (Luke 19:10). Be thankful He got close enough to "find" you. When Jesus tagged you, *you* won. . .eternal life, with pleasures at His right hand (Psalm 16:11).

MY PRAYER STARTER:

Lord, I know playing hide-and-seek with You would be pointless because You already know where I am. Thank You for giving me the freedom to give myself up to You.

DECEMBER 10

*And ye shall seek me, and find me, when ye
shall search for me with all your heart.*
JEREMIAH 29:13 KJV

Moving toward Jesus is not some kind of guessing game. The Bible gives us clear guidelines for coming to Him, for both salvation and daily renewal. And He has promised that He will be found when we search for Him with our whole heart.

"Search the scriptures. . .they are they which testify of me" (John 5:39). "Whosoever shall call on the name of the Lord shall be saved" (Acts 2:21, Romans 10:13). "Come unto me, all ye that labour and are heavy laden, and I will give you rest" (Matthew 11:28). "Abide in me, and I in you. As the branch cannot bear fruit of itself, except it abide in the vine; no more can ye, except ye abide in me" (John 15:4).

Seek Jesus, and He'll be found. Draw near to Him, and He'll draw near to you.

MY PRAYER STARTER:
Thank You, God, for making the path to You
obvious and easy to understand. Let each moment
of my life bring me closer and closer to You.

DECEMBER 11

See what great love the Father has lavished on us, that we should be called children of God! And that is what we are!

1 JOHN 3:1 NIV

What joy when an orphaned child is chosen as a member of a new family! With much anticipation and preparation, a family readies for adoption. But the process is not finalized until the child is physically united with and welcomed into his or her new family.

When you came to Jesus, you were adopted into God's family. You had heard that God loves you, that He offers forgiveness through His Son, and that He will accept anyone who comes to Him. . .and you'd heard right.

Our spiritual adoption is finalized by our confession, "I want to belong to You." We can be no closer to God than when we become members of His family through faith in Jesus. May we never lose our thrill of that moment.

MY PRAYER STARTER:
I don't deserve to be a member of Your family,
God, yet You still adopted me. Thank You for
this magnificent, undeserved favor.

DECEMBER 12

*Pray in the Spirit on all occasions with all kinds of
prayers and requests. With this in mind, be alert and
always keep on praying for all the Lord's people.*
EPHESIANS 6:18 NIV

Jesus performed countless miracles during His time on earth. He made the blind to see, the lame to walk, the deaf to hear, and the mute to talk. He even raised the dead, multiplied food, and calmed stormy weather. Most of His miracles took place when a person was in the presence of Jesus, but He wasn't limited by their physical proximity (Matthew 8:5–13). Even from a distance, He could speak a word and heal the afflicted.

Jesus is not physically present with us, but He actually lives within us through His Spirit. His power is just as strong today as it was two thousand years ago. Whether you pray for healing, peace, safety, or guidance, He is just as willing to work in your life as He was with the blind, lame, deaf, and mute.

Jesus is near! Boldly ask Him for His touch today.

MY PRAYER STARTER:
Lord Jesus, I know You did many miracles
when You walked the earth, and I know that
You can still do the same for me today.
Thank You for these wonderful promises.

DECEMBER 13

Taste and see that the LORD is good.
PSALM 34:8 NLT

So what does it mean to "taste" the Lord's goodness?

Think of it this way: tasting is a necessary step in enjoying food. A chef could explain exactly what he's put into a dish, even describing its flavors in detail. . .but until you actually taste the food, you can't really appreciate its goodness.

It is the same with Jesus. We can read all about Him in the pages of scripture. But until we actually "taste" Him, we cannot fully comprehend all that He is.

If you're a believer, you've tasted and seen that Jesus is good. (If you're not, why not choose Jesus now?) But even after that first delicious taste of salvation, there will always be deeper and more satisfying tastes to come. Draw near to Him in Bible study, prayer, and service. . .Jesus will become more flavorful with every passing day.

MY PRAYER STARTER:
Lord God, thank You for giving me the breathtaking
privilege to experience Your love and grace firsthand.
May I never cease to revel in these delights.

For we are to God the pleasing aroma of Christ among
those who are being saved and those who are perishing.
2 CORINTHIANS 2:15 NIV

A rose. Warm chocolate chip cookies. Ocean breezes. The interior of a new car. There are many aromas that please.

How about adding "Christ follower" to that list?

The apostle Paul said God likes our smell when we walk in Jesus' triumphal procession. And our Jesus aroma, so pleasing to the Father, brings life to other people.

To smell the cookies, you lean over the oven. To enjoy the ocean breeze, you need to be on the beach. And to enjoy the smell of a new car, you need to get inside. In other words, getting close gives you the best experience of the aroma.

How close are you to Jesus today?

MY PRAYER STARTER:
God, I don't want my relationship with You to be
founded on just knowledge and facts—
I want to know You, to experience Your love in
my life. Help me get closer to You each day.

DECEMBER 15

Then a great and powerful wind tore the mountains apart. . .but the LORD was not in the wind. After the wind there was an earthquake, but the LORD was not in the earthquake. After the earthquake came a fire, but the LORD was not in the fire. And after the fire came a gentle whisper.

1 KINGS 19:11–12 NIV

At times in biblical history, God thundered. Sometimes, He blasted trumpets. And at other times, He spoke with an audible voice clearly heard by many.

But when God told the prophet Elijah that He was going to "pass by," a mighty wind blew outside the cave, an earthquake rumbled, and a fire roared by, but God wasn't in any of them. Rather, He came to Elijah in a "gentle whisper."

Our world is full of noise, and it always threatens to draw our attention away from Jesus. But even though He is the actual voice of truth, He doesn't scream to get our attention. Let's be listening closely for Him, waiting for that gentle whisper that says He is near.

MY PRAYER STARTER:

Thank You, God, for the still, small voice of Your Spirit that guides me in every decision I make. Each time You speak, may I always be listening.

DECEMBER 16

For now we see only a reflection as in a mirror;
then we shall see face to face. Now I know in part;
then I shall know fully, even as I am fully known.
1 CORINTHIANS 13:12 NIV

If you use social media, you know how easy it is today to maintain long-distance relationships, even when your friend is oceans away. However, you also probably agree that friendships are still best in person. Being in the same room with someone, in that person's physical presence, brings the deepest levels of joy.

Our relationship with Jesus looks different from that. We can't see Him, so it may feel more like a long-distance relationship sometimes. But scripture assures us that He is present with each of His children at all times, wherever they are: "Surely I am with you always, to the very end of the age" (Matthew 28:20).

Our "sight" for now is faith, but when we reach our heavenly home, we will see Him face to face.

MY PRAYER STARTER:

Thank You, Jesus, for maintaining close contact with me. I'm glad I don't have to use a phone or computer to talk with You. You speak directly to my heart.

DECEMBER 17

A woman who had suffered for twelve years with constant bleeding came up behind him. She touched the fringe of his robe, for she thought, "If I can just touch his robe, I will be healed." Jesus turned around, and when he saw her he said, "Daughter, be encouraged! Your faith has made you well." And the woman was healed at that moment.

MATTHEW 9:20–22 NLT

You can't get much closer to Jesus than this woman did. . .but you can enjoy the same blessing.

Weighed down by twelve years of sickness, she believed that Jesus could provide healing. And so she crept up behind Him, hoping to simply touch the edge of His robe. She did, He knew it. . .and that was all it took for her to be healed. Jesus commended the woman's faith, and her decade-plus of wearying illness was history.

Those of us who follow Jesus—who know Him personally and who house His own Holy Spirit—never have to sneak up on Him. We can draw near in confident assurance that He will gladly welcome us and hear our requests. As that hopeful woman realized, faith is the key.

MY PRAYER STARTER:

Lord, I'm grateful that Your blessings and love are so easily accessible. Thank You for opening Your heart and healing me from sin whenever I reach out in faith.

DECEMBER 18

*But as [Jesus] came closer to Jerusalem and
saw the city ahead, he began to weep.*

LUKE 19:41 NLT

As Christians, we celebrate Jesus' nearness in the Christmas season. Just as He came to earth, He comes to us, knocking on the door of our heart (Revelation 3:20). But not everyone responds.

As He neared His death on the cross, Jesus drew near to Jerusalem—the city of His ancestor David, the favored place of God on earth. But Jerusalem largely dismissed Jesus. "How I wish today," Jesus tearfully lamented, "that you of all people would understand the way to peace. . . . Before long your enemies. . .will crush you into the ground, and your children with you. Your enemies will not leave a single stone in place, because you did not recognize it when God visited you" (Luke 19:42–44).

Having recognized the visitation of God ourselves, may we always stay close to our Lord Jesus Christ. And may we constantly encourage others to draw near as well.

MY PRAYER STARTER:

Lord, thank You for visiting earth to take away my sins.
Thank You for opening my heart to understand and
receive Your sacrifice. And thank You for staying near.

DECEMBER 19

And the Word was made flesh, and dwelt among us,
(and we beheld his glory, the glory as of the only
begotten of the Father,) full of grace and truth.

JOHN 1:14 KJV

"A king is coming! A king is coming!" The Jewish people were ready for the pageantry of a king's arrival. What would He look like? When would He ride into town? Surely, there would be robes and jewels, evidence of the royalty they were expecting. But a baby? From Nazareth? Nothing good comes from Nazareth, they concluded. This couldn't be the Messiah. Their expectations did not match reality.

Maybe you have a solid vision for where you want to be in five, ten, or fifteen years. And that's okay, but remember: the outcome won't always match your anticipation, yet God still has a plan. Whatever might flummox your expectations could be something even more beautiful than you ever imagined.

The Messiah came near, looking much different than the people expected. But what perfection arrived in that little baby, the focal point of God's plan to save us all!

MY PRAYER STARTER:

Lord, I'll admit that I don't know what my future holds. I make plans and try to peer ahead, but I know that only You have control. Thank You for the perfect blueprints You've made for my life.

DECEMBER 20

The angel said to him, "My name is Gabriel. I stand near God.
He sent me to talk to you and bring to you this good news."
LUKE 1:19 NLV

Angels are messengers of God. In Bible times, He sent them to many different people. The angel Gabriel, mentioned in today's verse, appeared by name three times in scripture: to the prophet Daniel, to the virgin Mary, and to the priest Zacharias, who would become father of John the Baptist. To Zacharias, Gabriel introduced himself by saying, "I stand near God" (Luke 1:19). Imagine not just serving in the presence of God but actually standing near Him.

Jesus takes that a step further. He didn't simply stand near God; He is God in the mysterious reality of the Trinity. God the Father sent Jesus from heaven to earth to be born as a baby in Bethlehem. Unlike the angels, Jesus didn't come with just a message. He was the once-for-all sacrifice for sin. His nearness was an intentional, eternal gift offered to every person.

MY PRAYER STARTER:
Lord, thank You for opening the door so that I can be near to You. Help me take every chance I get to draw closer to You.

The angel said to her, "Mary, do not be afraid.
You have found favor with God."

LUKE 1:30 NLV

Who could be nearer to Jesus than Mary, His own mother?

An angel had carried the incredible news to the young virgin: she would give birth to Jesus, the Messiah—God's Son! Some quality of her heart had brought her to God's attention: she had "found favor" with the Lord. Mary's humble response was simply, "I am willing to be used of the Lord" (Luke 1:38).

We may feel as if our own calling is insignificant compared with Mary's. Yet as followers of Jesus, all of us can fulfill God's purpose for our lives. And we can be just as near to Jesus as Mary was. "Who is My mother? And who are My brothers?" Jesus would ask many years later. "Whoever does what My father in heaven wants him to do is My brother and My sister and My mother" (Matthew 12:48, 50).

MY PRAYER STARTER:

Thank You, God, for ensuring that my life has a purpose—
that no matter how small I may feel in the grand scheme
of things, You are working something glorious.

DECEMBER 22

The angel said, "Joseph, son of David, do not be afraid to take Mary as your wife. She is to become a mother by the Holy Spirit."
MATTHEW 1:20 NLV

Joseph was planning to wed Mary. But after he learned she was pregnant, he made the agonizing decision to break off their engagement. The news that she was expecting a child that wasn't his was just too much to take.

But then, in one of the most distressing moments of his life, Joseph was visited by "an angel of the Lord." He explained that Mary's child had been conceived by the Holy Spirit. "A Son will be born to her," the angel said. "You will give Him the name Jesus because He will save His people from the punishment of their sins" (Matthew 1:21).

God came near to Joseph and stayed close to Mary. Mary then bore Jesus Christ, who brings all who believe into God's presence. No wonder Christmas is a time of celebration!

MY PRAYER STARTER:
Thank You, Lord, for giving us a reason to celebrate this time of year. Because You stay near to Your people, we can have an eternal, indestructible hope.

DECEMBER 23

When Joseph woke up, he did what the angel of the Lord had commanded him and took Mary home as his wife.

MATTHEW 1:24 NIV

We love the story of the first Christmas—with its picturesque characters like Mary, Joseph, and the shepherds—and its drama—featuring a very pregnant young woman's awkward journey to Bethlehem. But there are other lessons here too, less obvious but equally important.

Notice in today's scripture that Joseph immediately obeyed the angel's instruction to make Mary his wife. And after Jesus' birth, when the angel told Joseph to escape the wrath of King Herod by taking his little family to Egypt, the humble carpenter awoke from his visionary dream and left in the night (Matthew 2:14).

This kind of obedience draws us nearer to God. As Jesus Himself told us, "Whoever has my commands and keeps them is the one who loves me. The one who loves me will be loved by my Father, and I too will love them and show myself to them" (John 14:21).

MY PRAYER STARTER:

God, I know that as I mature in both my age and my faith, the decisions I face will get bigger and more important. Teach me how to always stay obedient to You.

DECEMBER 24

Joseph. . .had to go to Bethlehem in Judea, David's ancient home. He traveled there from the village of Nazareth in Galilee. . . . And while they were there, the time came for her baby to be born. She gave birth to her firstborn son.

LUKE 2:4, 6–7 NLT

After learning that they had been chosen to parent God's Son, Jesus, Mary and Joseph set out on a journey to Bethlehem so that they could be counted in a Roman census.

It must have been a challenging journey for Mary, so near to her due date. But the situation got even worse when she and Joseph learned there was no lodging available at their destination. Most likely, Jesus' birth was not at all what Mary had envisioned. . .but it was God's plan.

Think of the hardships Jesus experienced in coming near to us that first Christmas. Simply leaving the splendor of heaven is inconceivable, but then to be born in a stable? And yet, out of love, He was willing. This is the God we serve!

MY PRAYER STARTER:

Thank You, Jesus, for giving up unimaginable glory in order to suffer unthinkable agony so that I can draw near to Your Father. I don't deserve such love, and all I can offer in return is my devotion.

DECEMBER 25

Behold, a virgin shall be with child, and shall bring
forth a son, and they shall call his name Emmanuel,
which being interpreted is, God with us.

MATTHEW 1:23 KJV

For thousands of years, the Israelites had read about their promised Messiah. Many people knew those scriptures well and could recite them from memory. Yet when Jesus arrived, nearly everyone missed out. They were expecting a lavish kingdom to come with royal fanfare. Instead, the Messiah arrived as a baby, wrapped in swaddling clothes and placed in a feeding trough.

How often does God perform an amazing work in our lives today, yet we somehow overlook it? We want fireworks when our prayers are answered. But the God who sent His Son in humility two thousand years ago is the same God today. He still works for our good.

God's provision may come quietly and in unexpected ways. But because of Jesus, we experience all the blessings reserved for children of God. God is with us! What a gift!

MY PRAYER STARTER:

Lord God, help me never to forget the true meaning
of Christmas. May I never focus on the gifts alone;
instead, remind me of the infinitely valuable gift
You've given us all—the gift of Your Son.

DECEMBER 26

*When the angels had returned to heaven, the shepherds
said to each other, "Let's go to Bethlehem! Let's see this
thing that has happened, which the Lord has told us
about." They hurried to the village and found Mary and
Joseph. And there was the baby, lying in the manger.*

LUKE 2:15–16 NLT

Only God knows exactly how many shepherds were out in the
nearby fields the night Jesus was born. Whether it was two or
twenty-two, they found themselves participating in the most
dramatic event in history.

You might think Jesus' birth would be announced to kings
and senators, the educated and influential. But no. . .God chose
some of the humblest people of all to be first to learn that He had
come near, that in Immanuel—a prophetic name for Jesus—God
was indeed "with us" (Matthew 1:23).

While the rich and famous are certainly welcome to come to
Jesus, the good news of salvation is for everyone. As the apostle
Paul said, "Few of you were wise in the world's eyes or powerful
or wealthy when God called you" (1 Corinthians 1:26). Praise Him
for His kindness!

MY PRAYER STARTER:
Thank You, God, for choosing to reveal Yourself to
everyone—not just those whom society deems worthy.
Because of Your love, I am richer than the wealthiest king.

DECEMBER 27

*"For my eyes have seen your salvation, which you
have prepared in the sight of all nations."*

LUKE 2:30–31 NIV

The "righteous and devout" Simeon spent his life waiting for the Messiah—and the Holy Spirit revealed that he would not die until he saw the promised one. Anna, an elderly prophetess in the temple, had devoted her life to worship.

Eight days after Jesus was born, Mary and Joseph took Him into the temple to "present him to the Lord" (Luke 2:22). . .and the faithful old-timers were blessed by His presence. Simeon recognized the Messiah, took the baby in his arms, praised God, and spoke a blessing over Mary and Joseph. Anna also gave thanks to God, witnessing to all nearby that the Messiah had come.

Our experience of Jesus is purely through faith. But, by His Spirit, He is just as near to us as He was, an eight-day-old baby, to Simeon and Anna. One day soon enough, we'll be in His presence forever.

MY PRAYER STARTER:

Lord, even when my senses can't detect Your presence,
I know You're still there, leading me gently with Your
Holy Spirit. Thank You for never leaving us.

DECEMBER 28

"But very truly I tell you, it is for your good that I am going away. Unless I go away, the Advocate will not come to you; but if I go, I will send him to you."

JOHN 16:7 NIV

We all need help at times. A big stack of books might be too much for one person to carry. Modern technology is way too complicated for the average person to repair. And God bless the adults who worry about taxes and bills so that their kids don't have to!

Two thousand years ago, Jesus lived thirty years on earth. He lived a perfect life and accomplished amazing things, which are recorded for us in the pages of scripture. He was crucified and resurrected and then He returned to heaven. But the story, of course, didn't end there.

Just as promised, Jesus sent His Holy Spirit—the Advocate, the Comforter, the Helper—to be with His children. Jesus' presence through His Spirit is a tremendous blessing in itself, but He's more than just near us. . .He lives inside us. There is no greater nearness than that!

MY PRAYER STARTER:

Thank You, Jesus, for taking on the job that I could never do. When I'm faced with a challenge, help me never assume I can go it alone—rather, show me how much I need You.

DECEMBER 29

*Then Jesus told him, "Because you have seen
me, you have believed; blessed are those who
have not seen and yet have believed."*

JOHN 20:29 NIV

Following His death and resurrection, Jesus appeared to many
people. They saw Him and spread the news that He was alive. But
one disciple, Thomas, was absent at the time and missed Jesus'
first appearance. Thomas had heard the talk, but he wanted proof.
"Doubting Thomas," as he is now known, said he wouldn't believe
unless he saw the Lord in person.

In His compassion, Jesus went straight to Thomas. Entering
the house through a locked door, Jesus invited this oh-so-practical
disciple to touch His hands and side. And then came the directive:
"Stop doubting and believe" (John 20:27).

Jesus drew near to Thomas and dispensed with his doubt. Then
the Lord pronounced a blessing on us, we who have believed in
Him without seeing. That is the essence of our faith (Hebrews 11:1).

MY PRAYER STARTER:

Lord, keep my doubts from growing. Just as You appeared
to Thomas, I sometimes need You to appear in my heart and
remind me that You're still here, even when I can't see You.

DECEMBER 30

Search for the LORD and for his
strength; continually seek him.

1 CHRONICLES 16:11 NLT

As this calendar year draws to a close, we recognize the nearness of the new year. For some, this is a welcome and joyous thought. For others, the realization brings hesitation, sorrow, or fear. We have no guarantee of what the new year will hold.Will it be good or bad? Happy or sad? Of course, God knows. Nothing that happens over the course of the next year will surprise Him.

So let's walk through the coming months in faith. There will be moments of delight. There will be seasons of adversity. But Jesus, our Savior, cares deeply about His children. . .and He will walk with us through every experience.

As you approach the new year, know that your Lord is already aware of what you'll need, as well as what He, in His love, will provide for you. He's here right now, and He'll be there tomorrow—and the day after that, and the day after that, and all throughout all eternity.

MY PRAYER STARTER:

God of new beginnings, I don't know what next year will hold—but I know You hold the next year, and that's all that matters to me. May each uncertainty teach me how to trust You more and more.

DECEMBER 31

He Who tells these things says, "Yes, I am coming soon!" Let it be so. Come, Lord Jesus.
REVELATION 22:20 NLV

It is said that "all good things must come to an end." A good movie. A delicious meal. A perfect vacation. But sometimes, an end—of a good year. . .of a relationship. . .of childhood—can be painful.

However, when our days on earth come to an end, God has provided something so much better. We see the Bible's description of heaven with our limited human understanding, but know this for sure: it will be far better than we could ever imagine.

The promise of an eternal home with Jesus will be reality sooner than you know. Each painful end in this life brings you one day closer to seeing Him face to face.

"Yes, I am coming soon!" Jesus said. And when He does, you will enjoy eternal nearness with your Creator, Redeemer, and Friend.

MY PRAYER STARTER:

Lord, as the bells signal the death of this year and welcome the birth of a new one, may I dwell on how wonderful it will be when the final trumpets sound—when this world gives way to glories unseen. I can hardly wait!

AUTHOR CREDITS

Writers for the *Jesus Each Day
for Teen Guys* devotional include
Glenn Hascall
Jennifer Hahn
Josh Mosey
Karon Phillips
Lee Warren
MariLee Parrish

Editorial assistance by Elijah Adkins.

SCRIPTURE INDEX

REVELATION

MORE DEVOTIONS FOR GUYS

Guys, you've got a free minute now and then. You can always use a boost. So why not read *Power Minutes for Men*? Here are 365 brief daily devotions for guys of all ages, promising challenge and encouragement. Each entry focuses on who God is and what that means to you today.

Paperback / 978-1-63609-261-4

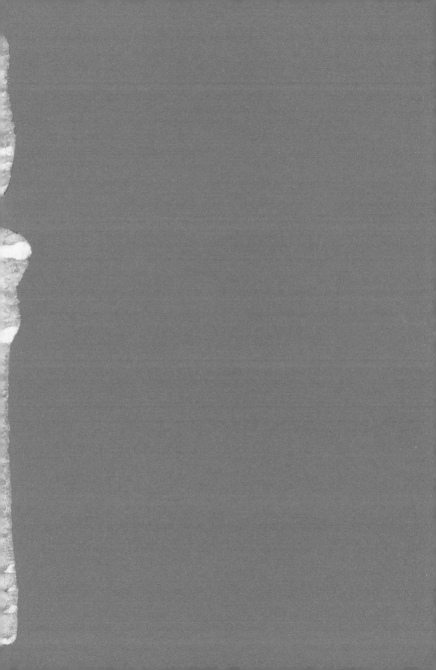